DEDICATION

This Millennium Book, a History of Orangeism in County Armagh
is dedicated to the memory of the 59 brethren of the County
who were murdered by terrorists in the recent 'Troubles'.

Their individual details can be found
within the pages of the district lodges.

Published by: G.O.L.I. Publications, 368 Cregagh Road, Belfast BT6 9EY

ISBN: 0-95014-449-5

Printed by: T. H. Jordan Ltd., 1a Millar Street, Belfast BT6 8JZ

Front Cover picture: The County Bannerette

Back Cover picture: The Banner of L.O.L. No.118

LIST OF CONTENTS

Bicentenary Parade, Loughgall, September 1995

FOREWORDS

It is a great honour to be asked to write a foreword to this impressive publication.

County Armagh holds an important (some would say pivotal) place in the history and development of the Orange Institution.

This book, as it deals with the major topics of the last century, accurately records for future generations the dedication and foresight of the Order in County Armagh.

As we move forward into a new Millennium let us take heart from the courage and conviction of those who have gone before and rededicate ourselves to the cause they served so well.

Robert S. Saulters
GRAND MASTER
GRAND ORANGE LODGE OF IRELAND

This excellent book is a welcome and valuable addition to the list of publications, which provide a comprehensive insight into the Orange Order.

There literally is something for everyone in the book. Whether you are a historian, involved in Orange research or simply someone who wants to know more about Orangeism, this is for you.

The style is such that it can be read from cover to cover as you become absorbed in it.

Equally it is a book which you can return to again and again "dipping into" and gleaning little gems of information and interest.

The inclusion of notes on the Private Lodges is particularly commendable. These clearly show that Orangeism is community based and the important part it has played and continues to play in the lives of so many.

George Patton
EXECUTIVE OFFICER
GRAND ORANGE LODGE OF IRELAND

It is fitting at the beginning of a new century and a new millennium to reflect on the history of Orangeism in the County of the Diamond where our Order was founded in 1795. Since then the Order has been involved in every major event in Irish History and this Millennium Book records the story in our own words of the Lodges in the County at all levels- County, District and Private Lodges. The section on the Parades Controversy sets out our view of the right to free assembly and free expression of our culture and religion.

I would express the thanks of the County Grand Lodge to Wor. Bro. R. Whitten, who consented to act as Editor, and to all the County, District and Private Lodge secretaries who contributed to the production of this book.

We must never lose sight of our goodly heritage but we cannot wallow in past glories. Our faith is still under threat, as never before, not only from those alien to the Protestant ethos but more seriously from ourselves.

In a world of ever shifting values there are standards that remain and we must continue to re-affirm our humble and sincere faith in Jesus Christ, as our personal Saviour and Mediator.

We remember with gratitude, our predecessors, many of whom paid the supreme sacrifice for their faith, to ensure that our liberty and freedom of conscience is maintained.

We must build on their gallant efforts as we accept the challenge and enter into the new Millennium as we maintain the Brotherhood, Honour the King, and keep the flag of civil and religious liberty flying.

Our cause, which is just, requires an ever present witness which must be maintained by upholding and supporting our faith as we celebrate the anniversary of the Birth of the True King.

Denis J. Watson, J.P., P.A.G.M.I.,
COUNTY ARMAGH GRAND MASTER

Frank Orr, The May Day Champion, 1998

EDITOR'S INTRODUCTION

The idea of a book to mark the start of a new Millennium and a new Century was first mentioned in 1998 at the County Grand Lodge of Armagh. By then eight of the eleven Districts had published booklets to coincide with the Twelfth Demonstration in each of their Districts, giving brief histories of the District and their private Lodges. Rather than losing this information over time, it was decided to combine these Twelfth booklets and up-date the information they contained, into a County Book. In addition the Editor undertook to read the minute books of the County Lodge and prepare a history of the County from 1892, covering the second century of Orangeism in the County.

It soon became clear that all this information would produce a rather large book. The decision was therefore made to confine the history of the County Lodge to the 20th century. The first full century of Orangeism in this county (period 1795 to 1895) had been adequately covered by many articles, books, and publications, and anyone interested in that period should consult "Orangeism in Portadown District by W. H. Woolsey", published in 1935, and an article by Canon S. E. Long entitled "The Orange Institution – the Early Years" in the book "A Celebration 1690-1990" published by G.O.L.I. in 1990. In addition the booklet "The Diamond in its Historical Setting" by Cecil Kilpatrick and the book "The Formation of the Orange Order" both published by G.O.L.I. and still in print, can provide valuable information for the early period.

All books and publications by G.O.L.I., which are still in print, can be purchased at Grand Lodge Headquarters, and also locally at Dan Winter's Cottage, the Diamond, Loughgall.

My personal thanks are due to the following for their help and advice: Denis Watson, County Grand Master, Cecil Kilpatrick, Orange Historian, and archivist to the Grand Lodge of Ireland. Stephen McLoughlin, County Grand Secretary, George Patton, Executive Officer. All the District Masters and District Secretaries and the private Lodge secretaries, Trevor Geary for allowing me to read his collection of newspaper cuttings on past Twelfths,

Miss Claire Thompson for typing large parts of the text, Arthur Clarke and Albert Nicholl for supplying photographs.

I hope that this millennium book will be of value to the members of our Institution in this County as a record of the Lodges at all levels – County, District and Private Lodges. It should also be of interest to anyone concerned with local history and the momentous events in the history of Ulster and Ireland in which the Order has had a part. As it says in the Bible, Genesis 6, 4:-

"And there were Giants in the Earth in those days"

We should also remember the observation of King William as he travelled between Hillsborough and Scarva in 1690:-

"This is a country worth fighting for".

J. R. Whitten, W.D.M. District No.4
Editor
April 2000

COUNTY ARMAGH GRAND MASTERS

DATE	NAME	DISTRICT	PRIVATE LODGE
1797-1821	Colonel William Blacker	Lurgan	12
1821-1836	Colonel Sir William Verner	Loughgall	162
1836-1846	Colonel William Blacker	Lurgan	12
1846-1885	Colonel Sir William Verner	Loughall	162
1885-1901	Parker George Synnot	N'hamilton	670
1901-1928	Sir James Stronge	Killylea	775
1928-1948	Sir William Allen	Lurgan	204
1948-1949	John A Peel	Armagh	184
1949-1950	VACANT		
1950-1968	Robert J. Magowan	Portadown	322
1969-1972	Joseph Twyble	Lurgan	44
1972-1984	J. A. (Sandy) Anderson	Armagh	94
1984-1994	Norman Hood	Lurgan	278
1995-1996	Norman Allen	Loughgall	85
1996-	Denis Watson	Lurgan	278

Dan Winter's Cottage

THE GRAND LODGE OF COUNTY ARMAGH 1892-1981

PART I 1892-1914

The minute books of the County Grand Lodge of Armagh provide a continuous record of the meetings of the County Lodge from November 5th 1892. For convenience this section is divided into three parts.

A special meeting on March 11th 1893 indicates that politically some things have not changed very much in the last 100 years.

" There was a very large attendance. On the motion of Bro. Peel, seconded by Bro. Edgar, the following resolution was unanimously adopted: - Resolved – That the County Grand Orange Lodge of Armagh, having seriously and thoroughly considered the proposals in the 'Bill to Amend the Government of Ireland' and their future influence on the political, social, financial, moral, and religious condition of Ireland, hereby declare that it is the duty of every loyal man and well-wisher of his country to oppose as far as he is able the passing of the proposed measure; and, should it unfortunately become law, to resist to the death the enforcement of its provisions, and with this view it becomes every loyal man to be prepared for the worst. This County Grand Lodge also declares it to be the duty of every loyal man to stand upon the defensive only, and neither by word or deed give the enemy of our religion and our race a cause of offence – in defence of all they hold dear, and when need be to fall into line, stand together as one man, and do and dare as our fathers did and dared".

This was the considered response of the representatives of the Orange Order in the County to Prime Minister William Gladstones 2nd Home Rule Bill. We should note that one of the resolutions in 1893 presages the wording of the Ulster Covenant of 1912.

On the motion of Bro. Campbell, seconded by Bro. Fallerton, the following resolution was also adopted: - "That the masters of all Lodges in the County Armagh be, and are now called upon to enrol all Protestants between the ages of sixteen and sixty years who are willing and ready to pledge themselves to resist by all lawful means the setting up of a Parliament in Dublin, and if such a Parliament should unfortunately be set up, to refuse to acknowledge its authority, and be ready for any emergency that may arise out of such circumstances." The following petition to Parliament against the Home Rule Bill was unanimously adopted:-

TO THE HONOURABLE THE COMMONS OF THE UNITED KINGDOM OF GREAT BRITAIN AND IRELAND, IN PARLIAMENT ASSEMBLED.

The humble petition of the members of the County of Armagh Grand Lodge, representing over ten thousand members of that Order, staunch Loyalists,

Sheweth –

That petitioners respectfully but earnestly approach your Honourable House to submit their views in regard to the proposed measure, entitled "A Bill to Amend the Provisions for the Government of Ireland," which your petitioners view with very great alarm and dread.

That petitioners are the descendants of English and Scotch settlers, who, in carrying out the policy of the English Government, during the 16th and 17th centuries, were Brought over to and "planted" in Ireland, and that petitioners consequently find themselves located and settled in that part of the United Kingdom called Ireland.

That petitioners and those whom they represent have always endeavoured to be upon good terms with "all men," and they have successfully devoted themselves to the cultivation of the soil, the promotion of manufactories, the extension of trade, the pursuit of the highest professions and the arts, the result being that they converted a wilderness into fruitful fields; and this inland county in Ulster is one of the most orderly, most peaceable, and most prosperous in Ireland.

Those petitioners are anxious to continue to live in this way, and, in conjunction with every other Irish-man, to enjoy the very many great privileges, which each loyal man under the paternal Government of the United Kingdom enjoys.

These resolutions were followed up by an Address presented to Lord Salisbury the leader of the Conservative opposition to the Liberal Government when he visited Ulster. The phrase "folly and ambition of an aged politician" is of course a reference to Gladstone.

TO THE MOST NOBLE THE MARQUIS OF SALISBURY, K.G.

My Lord Marquis – We, the members of the Grand Orange Lodge of the County of Armagh, desire, on behalf of over 10,000 men whom we represent, to tender to your Lordship our most sincere thanks for your opportune visit to our country while she is passing through the grave crisis in her fate, Brought upon her by the folly and ambition of an aged politician and the blindness of the party which still follow him. We look back with regret to the days so lately gone by when the firm and even-handed administration of the day by the Government of which you were the chief was allaying strife, and rendering it possible for men of all parties to devote themselves to the development of the resources of our common country. While we make no undue claim to religious, political, or social ascendancy over our Roman Catholic fellow-subjects, we are firmly resolved never to submit to any infringement of our civil and religious liberties. The precious birthright bought by the blood of our ancestors we are determined to bequeath unimpaired to our children. We are convinced that the new-fangled constitution now proposed for this country would, if established, be fatal to religious liberty, and, though we have many other serious objections to its provisions, it is chiefly upon this account that it excites our abhorrence. Under these circumstances we venture to accept your Lordship's visit as a token of the sympathy, which is felt for our cause by the great Unionist party in Great Britain. We beg that you will convey to our loyal kinsmen on the other side of the Channel our sincere thanks for the efforts which they are making on our behalf; and we hope that you will feel able to report upon your return that the men of their race and religion in this country deserve a better fate than the slavery to which Mr. Gladstone desires to consign us. We feel that to your Lordship personally we owe a deep debt of gratitude for your present visit and for your untiring exertions in the cause of the Union, and we hope that before long we may again find you at the head of a Government under which Ireland may look for law, order, peace, and prosperity. – Signed by order,

Parker G. Synnot, Grand Master, Co Armagh.
James H. Stronge, Deputy Grand Master.
Jos. Atkinson, jun., Deputy Grand Secretary.
Wm. J. Griffiths, Grand Treasurer.

Armagh, May 25th, 1893.

In 1897 the County Lodge decided to mark the 60th anniversary of Queen Victoria's reign by sending her an illuminated address:-

ADDRESS FROM THE COUNTY ARMAGH GRAND ORANGE LODGE.

At the special meetings of the County Armagh Grand Orange Lodge it was decided to present a congratulatory address to her Majesty. The following address was prepared and illuminated on a parchment scroll by Mr. M. Watters, and forwarded to her Majesty. The illumination of the address was handsomely executed:

Address to her Most Gracious Majesty Queen Victoria, of the United Kingdom of Great Britain and Ireland, Defender of the Faith, Empress of India, and so forth.

MAY IT PLEASE YOUR MAJESTY,

We, the members of the Grand Orange Lodge of the County of Armagh, respectfully and humbly desire – on behalf of over ten thousand of your Majesty's subjects, members of the Orange Institution, whom we represent – to lay our hearty congratulations before your Most Gracious Majesty upon the attainment of such a remarkable event in your glorious reign.

In the past, as in the present, Orangeism has always been noted for its unflinching loyalty to Throne and Constitution, even from its very foundation by one of your illustrious predecessors.

We beg respectfully to assure your Majesty of our devotion and loyalty to the Crown of the United Kingdom of Great Britain and Ireland; and we pray that the King of kings may still further abundantly bless and prosper you and all the members of your illustrious house; and that your Majesty may be long spared to rule over a people by whom you are beloved and reverenced, and over dominions on which the sun never sets. (Signed on behalf of the Grand Lodge)

Parker G. Synnot, County Grand Master.
James H. Stronge, County Grand Deputy Master.
Wm. Jas, Griffiths, County Grand Treasurer.
Thomas G. Peel, County Grand Secretary.
Geo. Crozier, Assistant Grand Secretary.

Armagh, 22nd June, 1897.

In 1901 Queen Victoria died and Irish Nationalists questioned the Protestant nature of the succession and coronation oath.

The minutes for May 4th 1901 record:-

Resolved, that at this our 1st meeting since the lamented death of our late Queen we beg to express our deep sense of the benefits conferred on the country by her great example and our devoted loyalty to her successor His Majesty King Edward the Seventh, and our respectful sympathy with him in his heavy bereavement.

It was proposed by Bro. Rev. R. J. Whan, seconded by Bro. Wm. Locke, and unanimously resolved: 'that we strongly object to the weakening of the security for the Protestant Succession by any alteration of the oath of the sovereign but we suggest that those to whom the oath and declaration are offensive should be excused from attendance'.

In 1900 the following officers headed The County Grand Lodge of Armagh:

County Grand Master	Parker G. Synnot J.P. of Lurgana, Whitecross
Deputy County Grand Master	Sir James H. Stronge of Tynan Abbey
Grand Chaplain	The Archdeacon of Armagh
Grand Secretary	Thomas G. Peel, Oulart Villa, Armagh
Grand Treasurer	William I. Griffiths, Clifton Villa, Armagh.

(Parker Synnot died in 1900 and in 1901 Sir James Stronge was elected County Grand Master).

The 10,000 Orangemen of the County were divided into 205 Lodges organised as follows:-

Portadown District No.1 –34 Lodges	W.M. Bro. W. J. Locke, Portadown D.M. Bro. W. H. Wright, High St, Portadown
Richhill District No.2 –8 Lodges	W.M. Bro. John Troughton, Mullalelish D.M. Bro. Robert Compston, Hamiltonsbawn
Loughgall District No.3 –24 Lodges	W.M. Rev. F. M. Moeran, Loughgall D.M. James Gilpin, Derrycorry
Tandragee District No.4 –25 Lodges	W.M. Rev. W. F. Johnston, Acton Rectory, D.M. Robert Whitten, Clare
Armagh District No. 5 –15 Lodges	W.M. James Irwin, Scotch Street, D.M. Thomas G. Peel, Oulart Villa
Lurgan District No. 6 –32 Lodges	W.M. Rev. R. S. O'Laughlin, Lurgan Rectory D.M. James Malcolm, Florence Villa, Lurgan
Killylea District No. 7 –19 Lodges	W.M. Sir James Stronge, Tynan Abbey D.M. William Anderson, Bracknagh Killylea
Keady District No. 8 –9 Lodges	W.M. Andrew Gordon, Tassagh D.M. George Fleming, Tassagh
Newtownhamilton District No.9 –17 Lodges	W.M. James McKee, Tullyvallen D.M. James Rainey, Darkley
Markethill District No. 10 –17 Lodges	W.M. David Spence, Loughgilly D.M. William Sinton, Markethill
Bessbrook District No. 11 – 5 Lodges	W.M. Samuel McKnight, Bessbrook D.M. Robert Morrow, Bessbrook

For the Twelfth celebrations in 1900 the Districts of County Armagh were divided over three separate demonstrations.

The principal meeting was at the Primatial City for Armagh, Portadown, Richhill, Killylea, Keady and Newtownhamilton Districts in the Palace Demesne.

Markethill, Tandragee, Bessbrook, and Lurgan Districts met in Markethill in a field lent by Mr. Singleton on the Hamiltonsbawn Road about a mile from the town. The Armagh Guardian newspaper estimated that these Districts took 45 minutes to pass in procession.

Loughgall district joined with Districts from County Tyrone and met in a field at Tamnamore belonging to Mr. Averell Lloyd.

The minute books show the emphasis placed at the end of the 19th Century and beginning of 20th Century on Orange funerals, on assisting orphans, and on paying-off debts of deceased members which of course reflects in part on the absence of any welfare state at that time.

Of course political crisis was ever present. In tandem with the Home Rule controversy, a land war was raging in many parts of Ireland as the tenant farmers demanded ownership of the farms from the Landlord class (mostly Anglo-Irish Ascendancy). In Ulster the antipathy between tenant farmers and landlord was never as bitter because (a) most tenants and landlords in Ulster were Protestant and (b) The Ulster Tenant Right custom had given tenants in Ulster better conditions of tenure.

The trouble in the other 3 Provinces often seemed to be an anti-Protestant war. It became hard to distinguish, especially with the introduction of Boycotts, between a war over land ownership and a political campaign to drive Protestants and Unionists out of Ireland.

An example from the County minutes of 1908 gives a flavour of those times:-

ARMAGH, 21st December, 1908.

Dear Brethren,

At the recent Meeting of the Grand Orange Lodge of Ireland attention was called to the cruel tyranny to which Loyalists are now exposed in many districts of Ireland, and our Brethren representing those districts having stated that the help of the Orange Institution would be welcomed, and had been long looked for, the Grand Lodge then on considering the matter decided to re-appoint an Emergency Committee, as follows:-

The Earl of Erne, K.P.
Lord Farnham, D.L.
Colonel The Hon. H. E. Maxwell.
Major Sir James H. Stronge, Bart.
Colonel R. H. Wallace, C.B.
Mr. E. M. Archdale, D.L.
Mr. W. H. H. Lyons, D.L.
Mr. C. W. Dunbar-Buller, D.L.
Mr. David W. Foy.
Mr. Frank Donaldson.
Captain Somerset Saunderson, D.L.
Mr. W. J. Allen, J.P.
Colonel R. T. G. Lowry, D.L.
Major J. C. Madden, D.L.

The Committee afterwards met, and took the preliminary steps that were necessary to give effect to the decision of the Grand Lodge.

In pursuance of a direction from the Committee, the Grand Orange Lodge for this County met in Armagh to-day, and unanimously passed the following Resolutions, to which we call your most serious attention:-

RESOLVED – "That the Grand Lodge of Ireland deserves our best thanks for taking up the case of oppressed Loyalists in the South and West; that we promise them our financial and other support; that our County Grand Treasurer send a contribution to the funds of the Emergency Committee as a first instalment from the Brethren in this County; and that all our District Lodges be directed to meet within a fortnight, and all our Private Lodges to meet within three weeks from this date to take such steps as may be necessary to give effect to the policy of the Grand Lodge of Ireland."

"That we hereby call upon all our District and Private Lodges to guarantee a contribution to the funds of the Orange Emergency Committee, such guarantee to be paid in four equal instalments, the first to be paid forthwith, the second after three months, and the others when called upon, to our County Grand Treasurer".

You will receive full instructions from the Officers of your District Lodge for the carrying out of the Resolutions, but meantime we send you form of guarantee, which you can fill up after your next Lodge Meeting, and return to Bro. Wright, our County Grand Treasurer, with the first instalment of the guarantee by your Lodge.

Masters of Lodges can render most valuable assistance by Summoning a Special meeting of their Lodges to consider the matter, and using their personal influence with the Members to subscribe liberally to the Guarantee Fund. As the movement is one, which should have the sympathy and support of all Loyalists, we appeal with confidence to our Brethren for Funds to enable the Emergency Committee to carry out its work.

Yours faithfully and fraternally,

JAMES H. STRONGE, Bart., County Grand Master.
GEORGE CROZIER, County Grand Secretary.

The second Home Rule Bill had only been defeated in 1893 when the Conservative majority in the House of Lords voted against it. In 1910 the Parliament Act was passed which reduced the powers of the House of Lords so that it could only delay a Bill for 2 years, after which the will of the Commons would prevail. Thus it seemed there was nothing which Ulster's Unionists could now do to prevent a third attempt at Home Rule from succeeding – nothing except their adopting unconstitutional methods such as forming their own 'virtual army' (Ulster Volunteer Force) and threatening civil disobedience with the ultimate threat of civil war.

With the encouragement of the Orange Order the Unionist clubs had begun to prepare for this eventuality in 1904 when the Ulster Unionist Council was formed (leaving the Southern Unionists isolated).

In 1911 Sir Edward Carson became the leader of the Ulster Unionists.

The County Lodge sent Carson the following address:-

TO THE RIGHT HON. SIR EDWARD CARSON, K.C., M.P.,
FROM THE GRAND ORANGE LODGE OF COUNTY ARMAGH.

Dear Sir,

In the name of all the Orangemen of the County of Armagh, whom we represent, we beg to give you a hearty welcome to Ulster on your arrival to open the campaign against home rule. In this grave crisis we desire to confide in you, as a leader, whose knowledge of Ireland, and particularly of the Loyalists of Ireland, peculiarly fits you to stand by us in our hour of danger and difficulty.

As you are aware in the year 1795 a number of men banded themselves together in this County for the protection of life and property against a people whom we have ever considered as rebels against English rule. After the Battle of the Diamond, where our cause was triumphant, our association was formed, and from a small beginning now flourishes throughout the length and breadth of the British Empire. In the past, as in the present, our members have always proved themselves to be loyal and faithful to their country and the empire, but today we find ourselves once more confronted with the enemy, who would have despoiled the Loyalists of 1795. We inherit their spirit; we are opposed to any scheming design, which will put the heel of the enemy on our necks. We refuse to submit, and are determined to resist home rule at all costs. We quite recognise the grave responsibility we place upon you, but if the courage and determination and the combined and concentrated force of the Orangemen of this County is of moral or physical support at this momentous period of our History, we assure you that you may calculate on the Orangemen of the County of the Diamond.

May almighty God give you wisdom and strength to lead us straight to victory, and save our beloved land from civil war, devastation and ruin.

(Signed on behalf of the County Grand Lodge)

James Stronge, Grand Master
William J. Allen, Deputy Grand Master
William H. Wright, Grand Treasurer.
George Crozier, Grand Secretary

Armagh, 23rd September, 1911.

In May 1912 the County Lodge resolved:-

"That whereas the Government of Ireland Bill would deprive us of the rights which we enjoy as citizens of the United Kingdom, and place us under the authority of the United Irish League – the authors of outrage and intimidation – and of the Roman Catholic Hierarchy who have recently promulgated theories characterised by cruel intolerance and by arrogant presumption, we deny the right of Parliament thus to dispose of our future, and we are prepared to take any steps that may be necessary to protect our liberties."

Perhaps Sir James Stronge who proposed this resolution had in mind, when he accused the Roman Catholic Hierarchy of intolerance and arrogant presumption, the issue of the "Catholic Bulletin" of March 1912, which declared "the time has come for action. The day of Ireland's missionary heroism is at hand to bring into the bosom of Holy Church the million of our separated brethren is a most attractive programme." (Quoted in J. Bardon's A History of Ulster page 423)

1912 will always be remembered for the signing of the Ulster Covenant on Ulster Day.

The County minutes record:-

"A special meeting of the County Grand Lodge was held in the Orange Hall Armagh on Wednesday 4th September 1912 at 3:15 pm

1. to consider the advisability of the brethren of the County attending en masse at the anti-Home Rule meeting to be held at Portadown on 25th September.

2. to consider arrangements for the celebration of Ulster Day and

3. to arrange for organisation and discipline.

The chair was taken by Bro. Sir James Stronge County Grand Master at 3:15pm and the vice-chair by Bro. James Gilpin, Deputy Master of Loughgall during the temporary absence of Bro. Allen, Deputy Grand Master.

All the Districts in the County were fully represented. The Lodge having been opened with prayer and a portion of scripture the County Grand Master moved:-

"that it is the duty of the Orangemen of the County of Armagh to do all in their power to make the meeting at Portadown on September 25th and the Ulster Day celebrations worthy of the Unionist cause, and to exert themselves to ensure that every Unionist in the County has the opportunity of signing the Covenant." The Resolution was seconded by Bro. Gilpin and passed unanimously.

On the motion of Bro. Crozier seconded by Bro. Foy it was resolved that the Orangemen of the various Districts of the County should attend in their full strength the public meeting against Home Rule in Portadown, that they should wear regalia and march in procession four deep each District being headed by a Union Jack or Bannerette or both, and by a band, but that no banners or big drums be permitted in the procession.

This photograph shows Sir James Stronge County Armagh Grand Master 1901-1921 Grand Master of Ireland 1914-1921 At a parade of U.V.F. volunteers in 1914

ULSTER DAY

Some of the brethren stated that Saturday the 28th could be an inconvenient day for the celebration of Ulster Day in their localities and asked if they could have the celebration on the 27th instead but it was stated that the day could not be changed as it was intended to have all the celebrations held throughout Ulster on the 28th, and that the services should be held in the various churches at such hour not earlier than 11 o'clock am as should be arranged by the various local committees, and the members of the congregation should after this go to such places as were appointed nearby to sign the covenant.

It was also stated that the committees of the Orange Society and of the Unionist clubs should work together conjointly to carry out the objects of the meeting.

ORGANISATION AND DRILL

It was moved by the County Grand Master seconded by the Secretary and resolved that a Committee be constituted of the District Masters and an other Brother to be nominated by each of them to provide more unity in the organisation of the drilled men in this County and that the committee meet some day in the first week of October to be named by the County Grand Master.

The railway arrangements for the Portadown meeting were left in the hands of the Portadown brethren.

It is worthwhile to record the wording of the Covenant signed by 237,368 men with a supporting declaration signed by 234,046 women (women were not allowed to sign the actual covenant because they were not expected to fight and in 1912 they did not have the vote).

THE ULSTER COVENANT

"Being convinced in our consciences that home rule would be disastrous to the material well-being of Ulster as well as the whole of Ireland, subversive of our civil and religious freedom, destructive of our citizenship, and perilous to the unity of the Empire, we, whose names are underwritten, men of Ulster, loyal subjects of His Gracious Majesty King George V, humbly relying on the God whom our fathers in days of stress and trial confidently trusted, do hereby pledge ourselves in solemn covenant throughout this our time of threatened calamity to stand by one another in defending ourselves and our children our cherished position of equal citizenship in the United Kingdom, and in using all means which may be found necessary to defeat the present conspiracy to set up a home rule parliament in Ireland. And in the event of such a parliament being forced upon us we further solemnly and mutually pledge ourselves to refuse to recognise its authority. In sure confidence God will defend the right we hereto subscribe our names. And further, we individually declare that we have not already signed this covenant.

God save the King.

The editor of the Observer newspaper described Ulster Day in Belfast in memorable words:-

> *"Through the masses, with drums and fifes, sashes and banners, the clubs marched all day. The streets surged with cheering, but still no disorder, still no policemen, still no shouts of rage or insult. Yet no one for a moment could have mistaken the concentrated will and courage of these people. They do not know what fear and flinching mean in this business, and they are not going to know. They do not indeed, believe it is possible that they can be beaten, but no extremity, the worst, will ever see them ashamed."*

In the villages and small towns of County Armagh the scene was very different on Ulster Day:-

> *"Here there was no hypnotic force of dense masses, no whirlwind of emotion, only the unadorned and individual action of those who had left their fields, and taken their lives and liberties in their hands laying them forth in the open sunshine as the measure of their resolve."*

The County minutes of 1913 and 1914 record no more references to drill and organisation. They merely record general Lodge business. Any reader would think that nothing unusual was going on in the community. The minute books of District and Private Lodges are also disappointing sources for information for these 2 years. The reason is not hard to imagine. The formation of the rifle clubs and the drilling clubs in to the Ulster Volunteer Force commanded by retired General Richardson, the gun-running at Larne and the distribution of German rifles throughout Ulster, were all strictly speaking illegal and were therefore not referred to in the minutes of Orange Lodges since they might fall into the hands of the Royal Irish Constabulary.

Sir Edward Carson gave some advice on illegal activity speaking in Newry on September 7th 1913:-

"We will set up a government. I am told it will be illegal. Of course it will. Drilling is illegal. I was reading as Act of Parliament forbidding it. The Volunteers are illegal, and the Government know they are illegal, and the Government dare not interfere with them. Don't be afraid of illegalities!"

A quotation from James Kane's book "For God and the King – the story of the Blackers of Carrickblacker" can give us a flavour of the events of 1914:-

"Many inspections of the Armagh Volunteers were carried out at various locations throughout the County. One such inspection took place on 10th January 1914 at Marlacco House, where King William had reportedly spent the night on his way to the Boyne. The Ahorey, Tandragee, Hamiltownsbawn and Clare Companies lined up and were inspected by their commanding officer Major Blacker. The overall proceedings were conducted by the Rev. R. J. Whan." (Rev. Whan was Worshipful Master of Tandragee District and a Deputy County Grand Chaplain in 1914).

On the night of 24 April 1914 the Clyde Valley sailed into Larne Harbour and unloaded 35,000 rifles and 5 million rounds of ammunition.

As James Kane states in his book on the Blacker Family:-

"In Portadown the companies were mobilised on the orders of Major Blacker in total secrecy and it must have pleased the major to see so many of his men answer the call. The men stood sentry at all roads into and out of the towns to await the arrival of their weapons. It is not hard to imagine the grim and silent determination of those men. As soon as the guns arrived they were quickly disposed of and stored in various locations throughout the town, most notably Orange Halls and in the houses of the Officers. The same scene was being repeated in Lurgan, Richhill and Tandragee."

By August 1914 an attempt by the Liberal Government to order the army at the Curragh to march into Ulster and disarm the U.V.F. had failed when the officers refused to obey orders. A last attempt to prevent Ulster Unionists setting up a Provisional Government for Ulster by a round-table conference at Buckingham Palace had collapsed and the scene was set for civil war. At this point the German army invaded Belgium and the First World War started.

Home Rule was suspended for the duration of the war with a promise that at least some of the Ulster counties could opt out. How many counties and for how long were unanswered questions until the war ended.

PART II 1914 – 1948

The Home Rule crisis passed without a civil war when the "Great War" in Europe started.

The Liberal Prime Minister, Herbert Asquith, told the House of Commons that the U.V.F.'s patriotic spirit had made the coercion of Ulster "unthinkable" and that Home Rule would not be implemented until the end of the war and amending legislation later on would make special provision for Ulster.

The 12th July Demonstration was held at Killylea in 1914. This was to be the last such demonstration until the war ended. Directions on how to observe the 12th during the war were given to the District Lodges as follows:-

Dear Brethren,

At the Half-Yearly Meeting of this Lodge, held in Portadown on Monday, 24th inst., the circular letter of 12th April, 1915, issued by our Grand Master, Bro.. Sir Jas. H. Stronge, to the County Grand Lodges of Ireland, was read and considered, in which he said that the Central Committee of the Grand Lodge had unanimously requested him to make suggestions as to the best manner of observing the 12th July this year; that it was only too likely that the war would not then be concluded, and the vital interests of our country would still be at stake; that many of us had already lost relations, and almost all of us had lost friends; and that by July thousands of Ulsterman would probably be at the front, where so many had fallen gloriously for their country, and as it was absurd to say that anything could be quite as usual this year, he thought that our celebrations should be modified to suit the circumstances of the time and the thoughts of the hearts of those who would be taking part in them, and that anything maintaining the orderly and semi-military characteristics of the celebrations would be appropriate, and anything emphasising their religious character would be especially appropriate; but, on the other hand, it was thought that on this occasion some of the festivity and some of the speech-making might be out of place. Having said so much, he left the matter to the best consideration of the County Grand Lodge, with the suggestion that no resolutions should be proposed, but that after a short address from the Chairman a short SERVICE OF INTERCESSION should be conducted by our Chaplains, commencing with the 90th Psalm and concluding with the National Anthem. And he also stated that he understood a great many of our Brethren were of the opinion that it might be better this year to observe Sunday, 11th July, instead of Monday 12th; and that if any County Grand Lodge should take this view he could see no objection to their arranging accordingly.

After several of the Brethren had exposed their views upon the subject, it was moved, seconded, and unanimously resolved:-

"That no County Demonstration be held on 12th July this year; that it be left to the several Districts to carry out the suggestions contained in the Grand Master's letter; and that in no case shall big drums be permitted, or banners be displayed; and further, that no Drumming Parties be permitted in the County during the continuance of the war; and that any Lodge disobeying this resolution be liable to suspension."

I was directed to notify the District Officers of the decision arrived at by the County Grand Lodge, and to request that they should see to its being carried out in their various Districts.

The Collections taken up at the Services arranged for should be devoted to the Enniskillen Orphan Society.

By order of the County Grand Lodge.

George Crozier,
COUNTY GRAND SECRETARY

In May 1916 the County Grand Lodge commented on the Rebellion in Dublin (the Easter Rising) by passing a resolution "That we desire to convey our heartfelt sympathy to the inhabitants of Dublin of all creeds in their sufferings and loss by the recent insurrection, we hereby declare afresh our loyalty to King and Empire, we venture hope that the lives and property of law abiding Irishmen will no longer be endangered in the vain hope of enabling a false appearance of unity; and we protest against the absurd suggestion of a portion of the English press that this is a favourable moment for the introduction of Constitutional changes."

The one event that all Orangemen remember in the First World War is the charge of the 36th Ulster Division on 1st July 1916 – the opening day of the Battle of the Somme.

As J. Bardon records "Blacker's Boys – men from the Armagh, Monaghan and Cavan Ulster Volunteers – returned with only 64 men out of 600 who had gone over the parapet." Most of these were Orangemen.

Captain Wilfred Spender, a staff officer with the U.V.F. and later on first Head of the Northern Ireland Civil Service, wrote a famous eyewitness account of the attack:-

"I am not an Ulsterman, but yesterday, the 1st July, as I followed their amazing attack I felt that I would rather be an Ulsterman than anything else in the world.

My position enabled me to watch the commencement of their attack from the wood in which they had formed up, but which long prior to the assault was being overwhelmed with shell-fire, so that the trees were stripped, and the top half of the wood ceased to be anything but a slope of bare stumps with innumerable shell holes peppered in the chalk.

It looked as if nothing could live in the wood, and, indeed, the losses were heavy before they started.

When I saw the men emerge through the smoke and form up as if on parade, I could hardly believe my eyes. Then I saw them attack, beginning with a slow walk over 'No Man's Land' and then suddenly let loose as they charged over the front two lines of enemy trenches, shouting 'No Surrender, boys'.

The enemy's gun-fire raked them from the left, and machine guns in a village enfiladed them on the right, but battalion after battalion came out of the awful wood as steadily as I have seen them at Ballykinler, Clandeboye, or Shane's Castle."

(Note: the Ulster Division charged from Thiepval wood uphill to capture a series of German concrete bunkers called the Schwaben Redoubt)

Grand Lodge forbade any demonstration on 12th July 1916 but in 1917 at the County meeting in May Rev. Whan proposed "that this County Grand Lodge instruct each District under its jurisdiction to carry out Rule 28 on the coming 12th July and arrange for a Public demonstration with bands, banners and regalia and so commemorate the anniversary of the Battle of the Boyne and also the memorable and splendid charge of the Ulster Division in France on 1st July 1916."

In 1917 Sir James Stronge's son was killed in action and a resolution of sympathy was sent to him at Tynan Abbey. He replied in a letter dated 2nd September 1917:-

"Dear Crozier, very many thanks for your sympathy. As you know what a fine and capable fellow my son was and how he drew everyone to him you can realise the pain his death causes to me and to all the family.

But if he was required for the cause we are thankful that he fell as he did instantaneously and at the head of his own dear Battalion of Transport men who would have done anything for him. They were taking water and ammunition to the men in the fighting line over a notoriously dangerous road and had been spotted by the heavy guns of the enemy. His dear wife is very brave about it. She and my second daughter hope to go back to the Ulster Hospital in France before long.

Yours very truly, James Stronge."

Another sign of the loss of men was the efforts made by the County Lodge to increase the amount of money paid to the Lord Enniskillen Memorial Orange Orphan Society because of the great number of children left with out a father.

At its half yearly meeting in November 1918 the County Lodge recorded "its deep sense of thankfulness to Almighty God who has given us complete victory in this most just war, the Lodge desires also to record its gratitude to the brave men through whose instrumentality the victory has been gained, and its satisfaction that the lives so freely given for justice and for country have not been given in vain."

Once the war was over, the political crisis returned and in 1920 Ireland was partitioned. The County Grand Lodge welcomed and supported the formation of the Unionist Government of Northern Ireland but was gravely concerned at I.R.A. attacks across the new border. The following letter was sent to every private Lodge in the County:-

THE PAVILION,

ARMAGH, 23RD NOVEMBER, 1920

Dear Sir and Brother,

At the November Meeting of the Grand Orange Lodge of this County the following resolution was passed unanimously, and I was directed to forward a copy of it to you and all concerned for your information and immediate action as the matter is very urgent. The swearing in of Special Constables is already begun, and it is most important that our loyal Brethren should give no cause to the enemy to triumph by showing any doubt or hesitation at this crisis in our history.

RESOLVED

"That we, the Officers and Members of the County Grand Orange Lodge of Armagh, wish to express our deep sense of gratitude to those among our Brethren who, during the present emergency, have proved that the old spirit of Orangeism is still alive among us, and who have secured our liberty during the last few months, and have achieved such marked success in protecting lives and property in this County.

"We welcome the opportunity which is now given us of ending once and for all in the Six Counties the lawlessness and sedition which has been urging our unhappy country towards the loss of so many loyal and innocent lives. And we call upon all loyal Orangemen to do to everything in their power – both by joining up themselves and urging others to do so also – to further the new Special Constabulary Scheme and make it a complete success. We suggest that those Brethren who, for physical reasons, cannot take part in active work should continue to supply hot refreshments at night for the men who are on patrol."

Please impress on the Members of your Lodge and on all Brethren and sympathisers who come into your sphere of influence that the offer now made to us is unique in the history of our Institution, and gives us the opportunity of establishing on a firm basis the principles to which we have pledged ourselves as Orangemen. Of any who hang back now it can be truly said that "he who is not with us is against us."

I wish to make quite clear three points to which some Brethren still seem to be in doubt:-

1. *Our Special Constables in the B and C Classes will be under their own officers, chosen by themselves; and, while co-operating with the Police, will not be required to take any orders from them or be in any sense under their command.*
2. *Men in remote districts who wish to join B class will not be asked to walk long distances to join a patrol. All should sign up for B or C; and if in any area it is found impracticable to form a B patrol the loyal Brethren will be put into Class C.*
3. *Services in Classes A, B or C will in no way interfere with any man's pension.*

Yours fraternally,

George Crozier,
COUNTY GRAND SECRETARY

As the I.R.A. attacks continued the County Lodge wrote again to the private Lodges in 1921 as follows:-

Grand Orange Lodge of County Armagh

ARMAGH

28th November, 1921

To the Worshipful Masters of the several Private Lodges.

Dear Brethren,

I herewith send you copy of the following Resolution which was unanimously passed at the half-yearly meeting of the Grand Orange Lodge of this County, held in Armagh to-day, namely:-

RESOLVED

1. *"THAT – considering the urgency of the present situation – we the Offices and Members of the County Grand Orange Lodge of Armagh, recognise the absolute necessity for the most careful and complete Re-organization of our Loyal Citizens. We heartily approve of the formation and objects of the Orange Black and Loyalist Association of Ireland, and urge all the Members of our Institution in this County not only to join the Association*

themselves, but to do all in their power to bring in all Loyalists who are not Members of our Order. We also approve of the Drilling and Instruction in the use of Arms, which has begun, and we charge our Brethren in each Private Lodge that it is their duty to prepare themselves for self-defence when the call comes."

2. *"THAT – we appeal to every Orangeman under our Jurisdiction to help to fight the Boycott of Belfast and other towns by ceasing to deal with any Merchant or Retailer who stocks any commodity from Southern Ireland, and by consistently asking for goods manufactured in the loyal portion of the British Empire."*

As the matters dealt with are urgent, I am directed to request you to bring the Resolution before the Members of your Lodge at the earliest possible date, and ask them to give their united and wholehearted support in having the Resolution carried out.

Yours fraternally,

George Crozier,
COUNTY GRAND SECRETARY

Michael Farrell and other Nationalist historians have described Northern Ireland as "The Orange State", claiming that Northern Ireland was run by Orangemen in the interests of Orangemen, but the minute books of the County Lodge show that there were many disagreements between Orangemen and the Unionist Government.

The first disagreement was over the Education Act proposed by Lord Londonderry (the first Minister of Education). Before the 1920's Education had been largely provided by the churches. The expenses of providing school buildings and salaries of staff forced the churches into transferring schools to the state.

Lord Londonderry's Education Act, which became Law in 1925 incorporated the findings of the Lynn Committee into Education provision and paid all teachers salaries in elementary schools. Schools transferred from church control were known as four and two schools (management committee composed of four people nominated by the transferors and two by the local educational authority).

This Act was attacked by both the Roman Catholic Church and the Protestant Churches and Orange Order.

Firstly the managers of Catholic schools stated that "the only satisfactory system of education for Catholics in one wherein Catholic children are taught in Catholic schools by Catholic teachers under Catholic auspices."

The Roman Catholic Church succeeded in getting another Education Act in 1930, which gave grants of 50% for building work for privately managed schools.

Protestant objections centred on the clergymen losing their control over teaching appointments to the 4 and 2 Committees and their demand for compulsory Bible instruction in state schools. The Roman Catholic Bishop of Down and Connor stated in response:-

> *"We cannot transfer any schools. We cannot accept simple Bible teaching. I wish to emphasize this point. Simple Bible teaching is based on the fundamental principle of Protestantism, the interpretation of sacred Scriptures by private judgement".*

These Educational matters were first raised in the County Grand Lodge in 1922 in a letter from L.O.L. No.94 (Armagh District), which resulted in a resolution:-

> *"That we the Grand Lodge of County Armagh do hereby enter our emphatic protest against the passing of the Education Bill now before the Northern Parliament, unless amended so as to secure the appointment of teachers of the same religion as that of the owners or trustees of the school, or of the majority of the children attending the school as in its present form it presents a serious menace to the Rights and Liberties of Protestants in the Six Counties and to the vital interests of the Protestant religion."*

In May 1926 the County Lodge discussed a motion from Richhill District:-

> *"That we the members of Richhill District L.O.L. No.2 desire to express our profound dissatisfaction with the Armagh Regional Committee in refusing to incorporate in the deed of transfer of Public Elementary Schools in this County to the Education Authority the clause providing that "Daily Biblical instruction should be given in these schools by the teaching staff." We regard the action of the Armagh Regional Committee as being indefensible in view of the Amending Bill to the Education Act passed in the Northern Parliament as the result of an Agreement between the Government and the Protestant churches in this area."*

Another serious disagreement between the Orange Order and the Unionist Government was over the question of Orange Halls being required to pay rates. In every decade beginning in the 1930's and continuing to the present day, the minutes of the County meetings show anger that Orange Halls in Northern Ireland were being crippled with rates whilst Orange Halls in the Free State were classed as community halls and were rate-free.

By 1950 the relationship between the County Grand Lodge and the Unionist Government had become so strained that a special County meeting on 31st July passed the following resolution:-

> *"We the officers and members of County Armagh Grand Orange Lodge are of the opinion that the present policy of our Northern Ireland Government is a betrayal of the trust reposed in it by the Orangemen and Protestants of Northern Ireland."*

So much for Farrell's exaggerated and insulting description of "the Orange state!"

At its half yearly meeting in May 1932 the County Lodge accepted the invitation of Tandragee District to hold the County 12th Demonstration at Poyntzpass. 1932 was a year of rising religious and political controversy and tension. De Valera's Fianna Fail (Soldiers of Destiny in English) had just been elected to government in the Free State and an economic war had begun with Britain. De Valera had signalled his intention to change the Free State Constitution and there were fears that the I.R.A. would be revived. In 1931 Orange parades were attacked in County Monaghan and County Cavan and in December 1931 Cardinal MacRory declared:-

> *"The Protestant Church in Ireland, and the same is true of the Protestant church anywhere else, is not only not the rightful representative of the early Irish Church, but it is not even a part of the Church of Christ."*

In June 1932 the Roman Catholic church held an International Eucharistic Conference in Dublin attended by the Papal Legate Cardinal Lauri who visited Newry amid scenes of religious fervour.

It was against this background that the Prime Minister of Northern Ireland, Lord Craigavon delivered his famous speech at the demonstration field at Drumbanagher, near Poyntzpass, in which he said:-

> *"Ours is a Protestant government and I am an Orangeman."*

This is nowadays so often quoted out of context and used to harm the Unionist cause and make propaganda for Sinn Fein.

In 1935 at the November County meeting the County Grand Master, Sir William Allen, "made touching reference to the death of Worshipful Bro.. Lord Carson. The Secretary was instructed to forward a letter of sympathy to Lady Carson. The motion was passed in silence, the Brethren standing." Carson was given a State funeral in Belfast and his body lies beneath a tomb in Belfast Church of Ireland Cathedral.

On 7th December 1935 Lady Carson replied:-

"Dear Mr. Rock, it was most kind of you to send me the sympathy of the County of Armagh Grand Orange Lodge, and I do appreciate it so very much indeed. Ulster really has been wonderful to me, and I will never forget you all. Yours sincerely, Ruby Carson."

The minutes of the half yearly County meeting on 20th November 1939 do not mention the outbreak of the Second World War at all. It had started on 3rd September 1939. The war was first mentioned at the meeting in May 1940 when it was decided to have no County Demonstration during the war and it was left to each District to make their own decision as to how to mark the Boyne Anniversary during wartime conditions.

In 1943 the Northern Ireland Prime Minister John Andrews retired and was replaced by Lord Brookeborough. The County meeting passed the following resolution:-

"That the County Grand Lodge of County of Armagh in Lodge assembled desire to place on record its sincere admiration and appreciation of the services rendered by Brother The Right Honourable J. M. Andrews for his long and devoted services to Northern Ireland during his terms of office as Minister of Labour, of Finance, and as Prime Minister, and for his unswerving loyalty to the maintenance of our connection with Great Britain. We tender to him our gratitude for his devotion to duty during the times of stress and war and we feel that the tribute paid to Ulster by the British Prime Minister Mr. Winston Churchill has been fostered by Mr. Andrews by his integrity of purpose and honourable conduct during this great world war."

The tribute to Ulster referred to is as follows:-

"This was indeed a deadly moment in our life, and if it had not been for the loyalty and friendship of Northern Ireland we should have been forced to come to close quarters or perish for ever from the earth....... we left the Dublin Government to frolic with the Germans and later with the Japanese representatives to their hearts' content."

(Winston Churchill: The Second World War, Volume 6 page 608)

In 1948 Sir William Allen died and the minutes record the following tribute:-

"Before proceeding with the business of the County Grand Lodge, the D.C.G.M. referred to the death of the County Grand Master; and the Members standing in homage directed that a record be placed on the minutes of the County Grand Lodge:-

This County Grand Lodge mourns profoundly the loss sustained by the Institution at large, and especially by this County, through the lamented death by accident of our beloved County Grand Master Lt. Col. Sir William James Allen, K.B.E., D.S.O., M.P., who for 20 years presided with universal acceptance and acclaim over this Grand Lodge, and whose presence and conduct in the Chair, both in Lodge and at the County Demonstrations, brought to the discharge of the high duties of his Office the most happy and harmonious worth, dignity and beneficent influence in our proceedings. Not alone as Grand Master and leader do we mourn him: he had our affectionate regard as a tried and trusty friend of every member of the loyal institutions, and a staunch and loyal exponent and champion of the finest traditions of Protestantism in this, the County of his birth – of which it was his pride to speak as "the County of the Diamond" which he loved so well and served so devotedly to his life's end. He had his desire, so often expressed, that he might die in harness; and his knightly Christian example and noble work will remain treasured possession. May this memory keep his image bright to inspire and carry us onward to maintain and extend the cause in which he nobly lived, which it was his chief ambition to serve, and in which he has passed to his well-earned reward.

PART III 1948 – 1981

John Peel retired as County Grand master in 1949 (died 1955) and the post was left vacant until R. J. Magowan of Portadown was elected in 1951.

In 1954 the property in Loughgall known as Sloan's House, where the first warrants were given out after the Battle of the Diamond, was purchased by the County Grand Lodge from the Jackson family. A small Orange Museum was created in the property – the rest being let to tenants.

The Armagh Guardian of July 7th 1966 contains the following article on the Orange Museum:-

DOLLY'S BRAE FLAG FOR ORANGE MUSEUM

Latest item of historical interest to go into the Orange Museum at Sloan's House in the village of Loughgall is a faded flag which was carried at Dolly's Brae on July 12th 1849.

The flag has had a most varied existence from that day when the Orangemen of County Down defied their opponents and marched over the hill near Castlewellan, thus directing attention to the right of assembly and procession.

Mr. Robert E. Bell, Oakland, California, U.S.A., is the person to whom Orangeism in Ireland is indebted for the return of this emblem to the land of its birth.

When Rev. Professor David Esler of Malone Presbyterian Church, Belfast, was in America a few years ago on the staff of the Presbyterian Seminary, San Anselmo, California, he got in touch with Mr. Bell, who inquired about the Orange Order in Ireland and so it came about that the flag was despatched to Mr. H. A. Cushnie, Brownlow House, Lurgan.

One of Mr. Bell's aunts gave him the flag on which is printed: 410 Rathfriland. Also printed on it is a compass and square and the words: Vide, Aude, Tace (See, Dare and be Silent).

Sometimes the minutes record a "less serious" side to the Order. For instance in 1959 a Lodge in Scarva had invited Sir George Clarke, Grand Master of Ireland, to the installation of their officers. However, this ceremony took place in November and not January as is the rule, which prompted an inquiry by a member of the County Lodge "Did he install the Officers ten months late or two months early?"

In 1962, fifty years after the signing of the Ulster Covenant, a Jubilee Parade was held to the Balmoral Show grounds in Belfast. The County Grand Lodge of Armagh accepted the invitation of Belfast County and all Districts attended the mammoth parade on September 29th 1962. The Prime Minister of Northern Ireland unfurled the largest Union Jack ever made at the Covenant Jubilee (last time flown at Carson's rallies). Before the parade the County Lodge organised a special service at St Marks Church in Armagh.

In 1964 the County Lodge opposed the Unionist Government's plans put forward by Home Affairs Minister William Craig to build a new city in the County. The following resolution was passed:-

"That this meeting of County Armagh Grand Orange Lodge protests in the strongest possible manner at the proposed development of a new City between Portadown and Lurgan, and we are unanimously convinced that it will be detrimental to the strong Orange interest in this County, and will eventually be responsible for over-throwing the Unionist representation in the Imperial Parliament.

We would point out that the Protestant population majority in this County is approximately 5000 and no doubt this will be considerably reduced once the project envisaged by the Government has become a reality. Thus we will have a strong Nationalist area between two loyal towns.

We respectfully call on the Government to cease forthwith with its plans for the New City and allow Portadown and Lurgan to extend their existing boundaries and develop according to proper standards of planning."

No need to record what happened next.

The County minutes record more quarrels with the Unionist Government over schools when in the 1960's small rural schools were closed. The minutes for 1964 record:-

> *"We, the Officers and members of County Armagh Grand Lodge, protest in the strongest possible manner to the closing of the following schools in this County, viz:-*
>
> *Cladymore, Madden, Temple, Cormeen and Middletown. It is true to state that these schools have been neglected by the County Armagh Education Committee for many years, and allowed to remain below the standard required in the regulations, so that eventually the committee would be in a position to formulate a re-grouping scheme. No doubt these schools have been the central point of education for many years and because they have served a useful purpose, the local people are determined, at all costs, to retain them.*
>
> *The closing of small Protestant schools throughout the County would be a disastrous and retrograde step and we respectfully implore the Minister of Education to stop its disruptive policy of concentrating on larger schools at the expense of the smaller ones.*
>
> *The loyalists have suffered enough frustration at the hands of our Unionist Government without incurring more disfavour."*

In 1965 the new Prime Minister Capt. Terence O'Neill and his wife visited Sloan's House and he and his wife were shown over the museum by the County Officers and Loughgall District Officers.

Also in 1965 worries were expressed about the Ecumenical Movement. A letter from Bessbrook District was read at the County meeting:-

> *"The ecumenical movement is of an overwhelming one-sided nature and our members are alarmed at the consequences if this Romeward trend were to continue. Our church leaders are bending over backwards to please their Roman counterparts with blind campaigns of unity. To many of our church leaders Protestantism is a dirty word, and anyone who sticks rigidly to the old principles of the Reformation, is branded a bigot.*
>
> *Whilst we believe that a more friendly spirit is essential in our mixed community, we must stress that on issues relative to our Religious Faiths, a strong stand must be taken."*

In 1966 worries were expressed at the County meetings about plans by Republicans to celebrate the 50th anniversary of the Easter Rebellion in Dublin – specifically a parade in Armagh at which a large number of Tricolours were flown. In retrospect, knowing what was to start in 1969 and continue for 30 years, could these celebrations of the Rebellion have re-kindled the spirit of militant Nationalism and contributed to the Civil Rights movement and the re-emergence of the I.R.A.?

In 1968 the County Grand Master, R. J. Magowan, died and a tribute was given at the County meeting by the Deputy County Grand Master Joseph Twyble:-

> *"Worshipful Brother Twyble expressed the great sense of loss felt by all the Brethren at the passing of our highly esteemed County Grand Master. Brother Magowan was an outstanding citizen and a leader of great ability. Brother Twyble recalled the many offices in public life, which Brother Magowan had held, including Lord Mayor and Freeman of the Borough of Portadown also Chairman of the Portadown and Banbridge Water Board. In the Orange Institution he held the offices of Deputy Grand Master of Ireland, County Grand Master of this County for 17 years, Worshipful Deputy Master of Portadown District and Worshipful Master of L.O.L. No.322 for many years. He was pleased to hear of the purchase of Bessbrook Town Hall by Bessbrook District and the Museum in Loughgall was a monument to his driving force."*

Also in 1968 the County Lodge supported the actions of Home Affairs Minister William Craig and the R.U.C. in seeking to control Civil Rights marches. In 1969 the present "troubles" began with the Hunt Report recommending the ending of the 'B' Special Constabulary. The I.R.A. re-emerged with the murder of 3 Scottish soldiers who accepted an invitation to a party in a house in North Belfast, only to be murdered. The minute books record that "resolutions were received from Tandragee, Armagh and Lurgan Districts expressing dissatisfaction with the Hunt Report, in particular matters concerning R.U.C. uniforms and the phasing-out of the 'B' Specials to be replaced by the unknown Ulster Defence Regiment.

The County were agreed that no change would take place in R.U.C. uniforms without the consent of the Rank and File of the R.U.C.

With regard to the "B Specials", the fact that opposition forces were not now welcoming the new Defence Regiment spoke for itself and members were satisfied that the security of the Province would be stronger than ever.

Knowing what was about to happen to the security of the Province in the next 30 years it is hard to read this extract from the minutes without feeling that many members of the County suffered from a great degree of complacency. However, in their defence, they did not have a crystal ball and could not see into the future. Also they were constantly re-assured by their unionist representatives.

As trouble continued and the I.R.A. Campaign developed fears were expressed at the County meeting that the Twelfth demonstration in 1969 might be banned. In 1970 the Unionist Government did in fact impose a 6 months ban on all parades (not including the 12th). At the County Lodge meeting the County Grand Secretary produced forms which he had received from Tandragee District incorporating the following statement:-

"we the undersigned members of the above Lodge being aggrieved at the present ban on parades will not tolerate any ban on traditional loyalist parades. We also request the Government to take all necessary steps immediately to restore Law and Order in Northern Ireland.' These forms had been signed by all private Lodge members in Tandragee District. As the ban referred to had now been lifted there was no further action taken."

Tension continued to mount and at the field in Portadown on 12th in 1971 some Orangemen had disrupted proceedings on the platform by shouting and demonstrating their strong feelings. The District Master of Portadown, Wor. Bro. Herbert Whitten complained about the conduct of four brethren and in a special hearing two members were suspended and two were expelled from the Institution. Also in 1971 the County discussed a resolution from Diamond Memorial L.O.L. (Loughgall District):-

"We the Loyal Sons of Ulster have pledged ourselves to maintain our constitutional position as an integral part of Great Britain at all costs. As the Republican forces increase their bombings and shootings in an all-out bid to achieve a United Ireland against the wishes of the majority and viewing with impunity the Hunt Report, disarming the R.U.C. and disbanding the trusted 'B' Specials, our only alternative would be to enlist a local defence force comprising of Orange Brethren to defend our property and homes."

Tandragee District wrote to request that Grand Lodge appoint a Public Relations Officer to appear on television to defend the institution, and Killylea True Blues L.O.L. No.630A sent a resolution to the County meeting which condemned:-

"The refusal of membership to the U.D.R. of able bodied loyal men with 20 years of faithful service in the Ulster Special Constabulary. The apparent slight on these men's character is preventing many Loyalists from applying for membership of the U.D.R. The Lodge also deplored that men with experience and knowledge of firearms were prevented from carrying arms in the R.U.C. Reserve and had to carry out duties unarmed along with inexperienced young Constables."

In 1972 Prime Minister Brian Faulkner again banned all parades for a time, much to the disgust of the Order, but then Edward Heath, British Prime Minister decided to abolish the Northern Ireland Parliament and institute a system of Direct Rule by Secretaries of State.

At the May meeting the County Secretary read a letter from Grand Lodge:-

> *"We unreservedly condemn the suspension of parliamentary democracy in Northern Ireland as a surrender to violence and civil disorder. We therefore demand the full restoration of the Parliament of Northern Ireland and the re-introduction of British standards of democratic legislative procedures."*

Also in 1972 the first parade in Portadown to be re-routed occurred when a traditional Junior Orange procession from Corcrain Orange Hall to Carleton Street had been turned on the orders of the R.U.C. area commander. Wor. Bro. Herbert Whitten Worshipful District Master of Portadown District had been given no reason for this decision. The County noted that this decision had broken an agreement with the authorities that there should be discussion with the various organising bodies of parades if it was considered necessary to re-route. The County Lodge was also shocked to learn that notice had been given to the R.U.C. by the Armagh Republican Clubs of their intention to parade through the City in view of the fact that:

1. Republican Clubs are banned organisations.
2. Their declared object is to protest against internment.
3. Their objectives are to gather support for the I.R.A..
4. The parade is not customary and will cause great offence to the peaceful and law-abiding citizens of Armagh.

At the November meeting in 1972 notice was given that a new newspaper – "the Orange Standard" – would start monthly publication on January 1973.

Also in 1972 the County was worried that unionist unity had been fractured and was informed that Grand Lodge had sent a telegram to Messrs Faulkner, Paisley and Craig "Immediate personal initiative and intervention demanded by you jointly – reference – formula for unity to prevent confrontation and possible militant consequences."

In 1972 Wor. Brother Twyble resigned as County Grand Master and Brother J. A. (Sandy) Anderson was elected.

In 1973 a referendum, known as the "Border Poll" was held. The County Grand Lodge contributed to a poster campaign to encourage a large turnout of voters.

MARCH 8TH

1702 DEATH OF WILLIAM III, PRINCE OF ORANGE
"of Glorious, Pious and Immortal Memory."

1798 INSTITUTION OF GRAND ORANGE LODGE OF IRELAND
"To organise the Orangemen of Ireland to defend King and Constitution."

1973 BORDER POLL

DEFEND THE CROWN AND CONSTITUTION THE DEMOCRATIC WAY

VOTE FOR YOUR BRITISH HERITAGE
(Issued by the Loyal Orange Institution)

W. Martin Smyth, Grand Master
Walter Williams, Grand Secretary
John Brown, Antrim
J. A. Anderson, Armagh
Hugh Radcliffe, Belfast
Samuel J. Cowan, Down
Brookeborough, Fermanagh
Robert Dickinson, City of Londonderry
Alfred E. Lee, Londonderry County
Jack Ashenhurst, Tyrone

GOD SAVE THE QUEEN

1974 was another tension-filled year with the formation of the "U.U.U.C." – United Ulster Unionist Council, the election of Brother Harold McCusker as M.P. for County Armagh, and the Ulster Workers' Council Strike which brought down the power-sharing Executive headed by Brian Faulkner on the issue of a Council of Ireland.

One member of the County Lodge spoke of the work of the U.U.U.C. Committee in the County, which had decided to support the Loyalist Strike, and gave details on various actions taken by the committee to alleviate hardship to the farming community as a consequence of the strike. The brethren were asked to spread the information in their districts.

Then in 1975 came a terrible blow to the Orange Order in County Armagh – the I.R.A. attack on Tullyvallen Orange Hall. It is best to quote the relevant portion of the minute book in full:-

9th September 1975

"An emergency meeting of County Armagh Grand Orange Lodge was held in Armagh Orange Hall on Tuesday 9th September 1975 at 3:00pm.

Rt. Worshipful Brother Joseph A. Anderson J. P. County Grand Master occupied the chair assisted in the Deputy chair by Worshipful Brother W. C. Moody M.B.E., J.P., Deputy County Grand Master.

The meeting was opened with prayer by Brother Rev. T. R. B. Taylor and Scripture reading by Brother Rev. W. S. Martin

The circular concerning the meeting was read by the County Grand Secretary.

The County Grand Master stated that this emergency meeting had been called following the massacre of the five of our Brethren in Tullyvallen Orange Hall and other Brethren from Newtownhamilton and Keady.

Rt. Worshipful Brother Anderson spoke of the great standing of all these Brethren in our Institution. Brother James McKee, J.P. Worshipful Master L.O.L. No.630 and also Deputy District Master of Newtownhamilton District was a man highly respected by all with whom he came in contact. He had been welcomed to the County Grand Lodge for the first time in May of this year. The County Grand Master paid tribute to the work of Brother McKee in Tullyvallen Lodge and silver band. His passing will be a severe loss to the area.

Brother Nevin McConnell, Secretary L.O.L. No.630 had put in a tremendous amount of work in the Lodge and in Newtownhamilton District, and he will be remembered as an industrious man in all his activities.

Brother John Johnston, Chaplain L.O.L. No.630 was a man of over eighty years of age. He lived in a strong Republican area but had always stood as a true Orangeman and loyalist.

Brother Ronald McKee, L.O.L. No.630 son of Brother James McKee, J.P. was following in his father's footsteps in the Lodge and Band where he had been leader of the Band. Brother Ronnie had been brutally shot whilst trying to escape through a window.

Brother William George Herron was a faithful and devoted member of L.O.L. No.630 and had been such for a long number of years.

The only crime these men had committed was their membership of the Orange Institution. The consequences of the foul act committed at Tullyvallen Orange Hall will be felt in this County Grand Lodge for a very long time. Words cannot express the feelings of our hearts at this time of deep sorrow.

Another member of this Lodge Brother William Meeklim had set up a very successful business in Newtownhamilton and was much loved and respected by people in the area. The details of his torture and murder were abhorrent.

Rt. Worshipful Brother Anderson referred to the wounded members of the Lodge who were still in hospital and expressed the hope that they would have a speedy and complete recovery from their injuries. Brother Anderson paid tribute to the member of the Lodge, also a member of the R.U.C. who had acted so courageously in firing at the I.R.A. murderers and indeed his action averted what might have been an even greater tragedy.

The County Grand Master then referred to the cold-blooded murder of Brother Joseph Reid District Treasurer of Keady District who had been murdered when he answered his door on 31st August. Brother Reid was a staunch Orange man who served the community well on the District Council and on the Ulster Defence Regiment.

Also Mr. Bertie Frazer of Newtownhamilton who had been murdered when leaving his farmyard at Ballymoyer. Mr. Frazer was a good family man who served Ulster in the U.D.R.

Worshipful Brother Anderson stated that all these murders highlighted the obvious lack of security in the South Armagh area and despite the fact of a deputation to the Secretary of State lead by Brother Harold McCusker M.P. no effort was made by Mr. Rees to have security tightened. He paid tribute to Brother McCusker for his work. Rt. Worshipful Brother Anderson extended the sincere sympathy of the County Grand Lodge to the families, relations and friends of all those who had been killed.

Worshipful Brother W. C. Moody, M.B.E. J.P. Deputy County Grand Master said that the County Grand master had spoken for all present and congratulated him on the leadership he had given over this difficult time.

The Brethren assembled stood to order in silence as a mark of respect, and the Obituary prayer was read by Brother Rev. Johns.

This was followed by a long discussion on whether or not members of the County Lodge should take part in a B.B.C. television programme.

Permission was given but at the next County meeting disgust was expressed when the B.B.C. did not show Orange contributions in full and instead edited them heavily and cut them drastically to a few seconds air-time. Orange feelings that the media coverage was unfair were to become a recurring theme.

As if Tullyvallen was not bad enough, the following year (1976) brought another I.R.A. massacre at Kingsmills, Bessbrook district.

The minutes record:-

"Rt. Worshipful Brother Anderson stated that he found words difficult to find to express County Grand Lodge abhorrence of the murders of our brethren and friends from Bessbrook and Glenanne who were callously shot down returning from their days work. He extended sympathy to the wives and families of all in that area."

In 1978 after spending 2 years researching the possibility, Brother Harold McCusker MP reported to the County Lodge that he could not proceed with a proposal to form an Orange Credit Union as it would have to be linked to the Irish League of Credit Unions and its money invested in Dublin. We should note that Orange Credit Unions were eventually formed, starting in 1989 with the Orchard Credit Union (see article on Credit Unions in this book).

The minute books, which I have read in preparation of this article, end in 1981. The period after this will be covered in separate articles in this millennium book.

Unfortunately I cannot end this article in 1981 with up-beat news. A special County meeting was called for 20th February 1981 to consider the murders of Sir Norman Stronge and his son James Stronge by the I.R.A. and the burning of Tynan Abbey.

The County Grand Master, Brother J. A. Anderson paid tribute to Brother Rt. Honourable Sir Norman Stronge:-

"He had been speaker of the Parliament at Stormont for a long number of years and had always been a staunch unionist and loyal Orange and Black man.

The County Grand Master had known him for 28 years. Sir Norman was a highly respected member of the community. We could not afford to lose people of such calibre.

He compared the loss to the Institution to the Queen losing her cousin, Lord Mountbatten, in the Eire murder, or the Prime Minister's loss of Airey Neave. He regretted the loss of both father and son and the destruction of Tynan Abbey."

A long discussion on security followed. Two faults, which contributed to the murders, were identified:-

1. Failure to keep the same troops in the area long enough to get to know the terrain.

2. Insufficient R.U.C. strength in border areas and stations.

No criticism could be attributed to the R.U.C. and R.U.C.R. who came on the scene at Tynan Abbey. Overall criticism could be levelled at the army officers who seem to give border security a low priority.

It was decided to send a deputation to see the Prime Minister, Margaret Thatcher, in London.

Also in 1981 Danny Morrison, Sinn Fein's Director of Publicity stated at his party's annual conference

"Who here really believes that we can win the war through the ballot box? But will anyone here object if with a ballot box in this hand and an Armalite in this hand we take power in Ireland?"

Was a new phase in the terror campaign about to begin?

WHAT ARE YOU?

Are you a loyal Orangeman and worthy of the name
Of William Prince of Orange, immortal honoured fame?
What is your daily practice, which is the part you play?
Do you respond to duties' call and tread the narrow way?

Was it through love and loyalty that you a stranger came
To cross the rugged mountains in search of Jordan's plain?
Where the waters stood divided and the chosen found a way
Was it to aid such principles you joined the grand array?

Was it for sake of earthly gain you joined the glorious throng
Of William Prince of Orange who conquered at the Boyne?
Do you accept the righteous robe that made all nations free
And care not for the principles that gained such liberty?

Do you uphold the principles for which our fathers died,
Or when the enemy is in view are you the one to hide?
Have you attained the golden steps, Faith, Hope, and Charity,
Or do you stand at Rome's command to lap and bend the knee?

These are simple questions, to each your answer give
The world will prove it's value by the life you try to live
If you're a would-be Orangeman then choose some other sect,
But if a worthy Orangeman you're one of the Elect.

END

An Orange Ball at Killycopple L.O.L. No.345

THE DISTRICTS OF COUNTY ARMAGH GRAND ORANGE LODGE

W. H. Wolsey states in his book "Orangeism in Portadown District" published in 1935:-

> *"It is interesting to note that the order of the Districts goes back to June 6th, 1814. On that date at the half-yearly meeting of the County Grand Lodge, held in Henry Walker's Portadown, it was unanimously agreed that each District should draw for their different places, when the lot fell as follows:*
>
> *Portadown 1st, Richhill 2nd, Loughgall 3rd, Tandragee 4th, Armagh 5th, Lurgan 6th, Camlough 7th, Killylea 8th, Newtownhamilton 9th, Blackwatertown 10th and Keady 11th.*

The first six mentioned and Newtownhamilton retain the numbers received in 1814, but Killylea is now 7th, Keady 8th, Markethill 10th and Bessbrook 11th."

PORTADOWN DISTRICT L.O.L. No.1

Portadown has always been recognised as one of the greatest strongholds in Irish Orangeism and that has been the case since the earliest days of the Order .

In fact, no other District, with the possible exception of Loughgall is more steeped in the traditions of the organisation formed after the Battle of the Diamond a few miles from the town.

Portadown was little more than a village in 1795 when the Battle of the Diamond took place, but it was poised for great expansion with the industrial revolution of the early 19th century just over the horizon.

The village of Portadown was surrounded by the rich rolling countryside of central Armagh, and it was among the farmers and later the weavers of the surrounding townlands that Orangeism took deep root.

Memories of the 1641 massacre at the Bann Bridge were still strong in the Portadown area. No other part of Ulster had suffered more from the Irish Rebellion than Co. Armagh, where the English settlers were put to the sword and cast out into the wilderness to starve in the forests which harboured wolves and wild boar in the early 1600s.

The massacre at the Bridge of Portadown was, according to a chronicler of the time, responsible for the deaths of upwards of 200 Protestants. In Bro.wn's " Account of O'Neilland Barony in 1632" it was stated that Portadown had a "fair wooden bridge nearly 1,000 feet in length."

It was a carefully planned and executed attempt to exterminate the Protestant settlers and Bagwell attributes the success of the horrific enterprise to one Captain Manus O'Cahan, a chief actor in the drama.

Many of those who died had received passes of safe conduct from Sir Phelim O'Neill, but O'Cahan drove all the prisoners into the river. Those who could swim were shot or forced back into the water.

At that time the River Bann followed a course close to the town side of the present Bowling Green, and when this sports arena was being laid down sixty years ago human remains were unearthed, believed to be those of the martyrs who perished at the hands of the Irish insurgents.

Listen to the deposition of Catherine Cook, wife of a Portadown carpenter who said:-

"On December 2 (1641) a large batch of prisoners sent from either Loughgall or Kilmore to Portadown were drowned in the River Bann. This was the second batch sent to Portadown; the first having been despatched at the

beginning of November.....one Roman Catholic priest Dr. Daly, preached so vehemently against the prevailing massacres that in the end he had to fly for his life."

Sir John Temple, Master of the Rolls, and one of Her Majesty's Most Honourable Privy Counsellors (1812) wrote:-

"The Popish priests of Ireland had incited the Irish papists to destroy the Protestants without warning. There were one thousand men, women and children carded out at various times in several troops and all successfully drowned at the Bridge of Portadown which was broken down in the midst, and so the Rebels, drowning them and forcing them on, threw them into the river. This number was deposed and taken 22 August, 1642."

Contemporary accounts of this vile deed state that the unfortunate Protestants were treated "in a most barbarous manner," Christians "driven on to the place of their sufferings like swine, and if any were slack they sometimes pressed forwards with their swords and pikes often hastening on the rest either by killing or wounding some of their fellows on the way."

Other similar depositions relate that unfortunate victims were flung headlong into the river "Brought like sheep or beasts to the Bridge of Portadown."

Mrs. Elizabeth Price, wife of Captain Robert Price, Turkarry, "in the town and County of Armagh" swore a deposition that five of her children -Adam, John, Anne, May and Jane, were with 100 other Protestants, one of the parties from Armagh, Loughgall and other places, sent away with passes from Sir Phelim O'Neill with the promise to be safely conveyed over to their friends in England.

But, says Mrs. Price, "Captain Manus O'Cahan brought them or rather drove them like sheep or beasts to the Bridge of Portadown, and there forced or threw all those poor prisoners into the water together with the deponent's five children and there and then drowned most of them."

Within Co. Armagh it was estimated that 4,000 Protestants lost their lives in the 1641 Rebellion.

Thomas and Elizabeth Green gave evidence that "the rebels at several times murdered, killed and destroyed the most part of the Protestants of the Parish of Drumcree being about 300, and indeed most of the Protestants in all the County thereabouts did they kill and destroy by drowning, hanging, burning, the sword, starving and other deaths exposing their slaughtered bodies to be devoured by dogs, swine and other ravenous creatures:-

" And the deponent Elizabeth saw the dogs feed upon those dead carcases. Jurat November 10. 1643."

As Orangemen and members of the Royal Black Institution parade along Bridge Street in Portadown on their days of celebration they and those who line the streets as spectators would do well to remember those of their kith and kin who perished over three and a half centuries ago in what must be regarded as Ireland's most tragic days of shame and infamy.

By the late 1700s, the North Armagh area had been transformed by the hard work of the farmers, those descendants of the settlers who survived the 1641 massacre, and who returned with the army of Oliver Cromwell who crushed the rebellion.

Peace and relative tranquillity prevailed, and the area became prosperous. The outstanding English evangelist John Wesley, visited the area several times in the 1700s and found it to be settled and prosperous. He made many converts in Portadown and district.

However, the conflicts of the secret societies which abounded in Armagh and Tyrone in the later 1700s affected the Northern part of the County, and Protestants became alarmed at the rise of militant Roman Catholicism, combined with the general lawlessness.

The Protestants of County Armagh mainly Anglican and Methodist, were loyalist to a man, and were largely unaffected and unimpressed by the rise of republicanism in the ranks of their Presbyterian co-religionists in Antrim and Down.

The Society of United Irishmen had few followers in Armagh, and while the denominational differences had something to do with this - Presbyterians felt a sense of grievance over the treatment they received from the Crown - the main reason was probably due to demographical and historical reasons.

The Scottish planters of Antrim and Down did not suffer the same terrible effects of "ethnic cleansing" at the hands of the rebels in 1641 because Scottish armies under General Munroe arrived quickly to save the Presbyterian Plantation from the fate of the English Protestants of Armagh, Tyrone and parts of Londonderry and Fermanagh.

The Protestants of Antrim and Down also had overwhelming numerical superiority over the Roman Catholics. Armagh on the other hand was a cockpit county where Protestants and Roman Catholics were roughly equal in number, so the incursion of the Defenders into mid- Armagh from the southern part of the county and also from Cavan, Leitrim and other areas was greeted with great alarm.

The alarm bells of 1641 sounded loudly for the Armagh and Tyrone Protestants, so when the United Irishmen rose in rebellion in Antrim and Down in 1798 they got little support from their Protestant co-religionists in the interior of the Province.

On the 29th February, 1796, the Protestants of the Dean Blacker estate in the neighbourhood of Portadown, met to consider what measures should be adopted in reference to threatening papers posted in the district. It was unanimously resolved that the disturbed condition of the country called for the exertions of every honest man to protect himself and his neighbour, and all present pledged themselves to do their utmost to prevent illegal meetings thereafter, and to give information to the nearest magistrate against every person who violated the peace, no matter what his profession. A little more than a fortnight later, on the 16th March, the Protestants of Lurgan and its neighbourhood assembled in the courthouse of that town, and, under the presidency of Mr William Brownlow, passed resolutions condemning the outrages which continued in the county. The examples set at Portadown and Lurgan were followed on the 17th and 18th of the same month by the tenantry of the Manors of Legacurry and Mullalelish, who met at Richhill. An association was formed of the Protestants of the parishes of Drumcree and Seagoe, who deprecated the efforts to spread discontent, condemned the correspondence of the United Irishmen with the French, declared at the hazard of life and fortune to support and defend the King George the Third, against all foreign and domestic enemies, and resolved to discourage and oppose all treasonable practices. These Associations, naturally, formed a basis for the spread of the Orange Order.

The spread of the Orange Institution from the very outset and the hold which it got on the loyal people of the County Armagh is shown by the fact that eleven months after the Battle of the Diamond, on 21st September, 1795, there was formed on 21st August 1796, a Portadown District Lodge, with 23 private Lodges. A year later there were 27 Lodges. The numbers in 1796 were 7, 8, 9, 10, 13, 18, 19, 20, 25, 31, 35, 40, 56, 58, 78, 80, 89, 99, 107 , 172, 174, 318 and 417. The additional Lodges in 1797 were 516, 831, 948, 755. It will thus he seen that practically all the Lodges in existence in 1796 are still prospering, although they may not all be in the districts in which they were formed.

BLACKER - A PIONEER ORANGEMAN

The Orange Institution has had few more colourful personalities in its 205 years existence than Colonel William Blacker of Carrickblacker, Portadown.

In his Diaries, extending to seven volumes, written in his own distinctive handwriting, he has left on record a wide variety of his views and opinions on a host of subjects, ranging from theology to local history.

Blacker has left us some valuable historic material relating to the formative years of Orangeism - he established the first Orange Lodge to sit in Trinity College in Dublin and the initial meetings were held in his own room there.

He describes in some detail the second demonstration of the Orangemen in Co. Armagh. It took place on the Twelfth of July in Lurgan in 1797, less than two years after the formation of the Order at Loughgall. But a more serious side to Blacker's Orange activities was to follow several years later. By 1833, when the Party Processions Act was in operation, Dublin Castle took steps to make known that Orange parades would not be permitted. The Ribbonmen were out on St Patrick's Day (March 17) and the Freemasons paraded on St. John's Day, the latter producing anger among the Government. Then on the Twelfth of July the Orangemen from Portadown and Lurgan paraded to Carrick, the home of the Blacker family, Colonel William having by this time been recognised as the "Bard of Orangeism".

As the parade entered the estate they were "graciously received" by the ladies of the Blacker family, and the Colonel's nephew, Mr. Stewart Blacker, all of whom, with the servants, wore "Orange favours".

As a magistrate for Co. Armagh Blacker reminded the brethren of the danger of such meetings held in defiance of the Act and he advised them to disperse at once. This advice they accepted immediately. When he said they should be on their way out in 15 minutes, some of those present replied. "Five minutes will do, sir". Fourteen of the processionists were arrested and committed to undergo trial at the Assizes. Eleven were eventually set free and three were bound over.

Subsequently a Government Inquiry was held to investigate the Orange demonstrations at Carrickblacker, Lurgan, Portadown, Tandragee and Ballyhegan, a townland near Portadown where there was a riot on the Twelfth. The outcome of the whole affair was that Colonel Blacker was deprived of his Commission of the Peace by the Lord Chancellor on the bidding of Mr. Chief Secretary Littlelow.

As a protest a leading Co. Armagh country gentleman, Colonel William Verner, was so dissatisfied with the treatment meted out to Blacker that he resigned his Commission.

The following year 187 Orangemen were arraigned for having walked on a Twelfth of July parade. In due course the right of lawful assembly superseded the party Processions Act (it expired in 1845) and public parades by "both sides" provided the people of this country with the opportunity to mark their respective celebrations by parading on their "set occasions."

TWELFTH DEMONSTRATIONS IN PORTADOWN SINCE 1886

A "Twelfth" of July demonstration in Portadown has always been regarded as something special. All down the years from the formation of the Orange Order at the Diamond in 1795, the town has regularly played host to the county demonstration, and invariably these have been huge and spectacular.

Portadown is rightly regarded as one of the cradles of Orangeism a district rich in Orange tradition and folklore, handed down from father to son.

Along its streets in 1886 paraded the men of County Armagh who were resolute in their determination to resist the implementation of the Home Rule Bill, a measure which would have brought loyal Ulster into a Rome-dominated State.

In 1910, as the clouds of war began to appear on the horizon, and as Ulster prepared to resist the enforcement of another attempt at Home Rule, tens of thousands of loyalists crammed into Portadown to see a mighty County demonstration. The ranks included many of the fine young men of County Armagh, who just four years later were to earn glory in the ranks of the 36th (Ulster) Division, at the Battle of the Somme.

Many of those splendid young Orangemen were to answer their last roll-call on July 1st 1916, at the Battle of the Somme, a day that is forever etched into the history of Ulster.

The Somme decimated the ranks of Ulster's finest young men who gave their all for King and Country, and there was a special sadness in homes all over the province that Twelfth.

For the first time since 1796, there were no fifes or drums on the streets of Ulster, as the people mourned their loved ones, and as a mark of respect, the Orange Institution abandoned its celebrations that year.

The following year, the districts from Portadown and Lurgan celebrated together at Drumgor, which lies roughly half-way between the two towns. The Orangemen marched out from each town, to hold a joint demonstration on ground that is now taken up by housing estates in the centre of the new city of Craigavon.

It was not until 1927 that the County rally was held in Portadown again, and the previous year the celebrated Ulster painter, Sir John Lavery painted the fine portrait which hangs in the Ulster Museum Art Gallery-"The Twelfth of July in Portadown". He sat upstairs in a public house at the foot of the town and painted the vivid scene as the Lodges marched down from Carleton Street.

The practice of rotating the Twelfth demonstration venue between the various Districts in the County was now well under way and by the time the Lodges of the 11 districts next converged on Portadown it was 1935 in the heart of the "depression" just before the years leading up to the Second World War.

That first postwar Twelfth held on July 12, 1945, was one greeted with rejoicing by tens of thousands of people who crammed the streets in the town centre and right along the parade route to Shamrock Park. It was the First 12th demonstration held in Portadown since the outbreak of the Second World War in September, 1939, and the colour and pageantry was something the people had waited for six long years to see once again. That parade was an emotional and nostalgic one, and for many people there was a mixture of tears of delight and sadness. Delight that the Orange parades had appeared once again to brighten the lives of a population starved of colour and gaiety, and sadness at the fact that many young men who had last walked the streets of Portadown with their Lodges had paid the Supreme Sacrifice. Indeed, the war was not completely over, because another month was to elapse before the atomic bomb saw unconditional surrender by Japan. But victory over Germany had been achieved, and some of the men taking part in the parade still wore their Army and RAF uniforms under their orange sashes.

For many of the young people who watched that splendid procession it was their first sight of an Orange parade, and it was a marvellous event. The speeches in the Field matched the mood of a nation which had endured so much and fought through to victory. There was thankfulness and gratitude to Almighty God for victory, and there was sadness at the loss of so many lives. There was also the determination that such a war should not he needed again to ensure liberty and peace.

Northern Ireland's vital part in the securing of victory was also mentioned, especially Sir Winston Churchill's famous tribute "But for the loyalty of Northern Ireland!" a reference to the key role of the ports of Londonderry and Belfast. The neutrality of the Irish Free State, and the fact that the Southern premier, Eamon De Valera, had called at the German Embassy in Dublin to offer his condolences on the death of Adolf Hitler were also stressed. Britain was considerably weakened by that war and had paid a colossal price, but as the words on the Edgarstown Arch proclaim ."One Fleet One Empire", -the British Empire was still intact.

When the next county Armagh Twelfth demonstration was held in Portadown in 1951, things had not changed a great deal in the material sense. Britain was still feeling the effects of food rationing and shortages, and had lost India, Ceylon and Burma which had gained their independence.

Labour had been in power since 1945, but Prime Minister Attlee and his Ministers were friendly disposed towards Northern Ireland, and had made it clear when Eire became a Republic in 1949 that Northern Ireland would not be incorporated in any united Ireland against the will of the majority of its people.

The Festival of Britain had proved a big success that year, and Portadown was more gaily bedecked than ever for the 12th parade which was a huge success.

Portadown was again the choice for the County demonstration in 1954, and there was an influx of young men into the ranks of the Order that year. Britain had a new Monarch -Her Majesty Queen Elizabeth the Second having been crowned the previous year following the death of King George the Sixth. There was a spontaneous outpouring of loyalty to the Queen, and the speeches at Shamrock Park where the demonstration was held, reflected the pride in being subjects of the young Queen and the enthusiasm for the British Commonwealth of Nations.

It was 1962 before the Orangemen of the County of the Diamond paraded out the Armagh Road, returning through Edgarstown. It was a colourful procession which made its way through the town -one town with many new shop fronts and an air of prosperity which reflected Portadown's growing affluence and that of Northern Ireland in the Sixties. The Northern Ireland Government had been vigorous and successful in promoting new industries, while local authorities, like Portadown Borough Council, had provided thousands of new houses.

Northern Ireland had survived an I.R.A. campaign from 1956 to 1962, this uprising having been finally defeated a few months before the 12th demonstration.

It was 1971 before Portadown hosted its next County spectacular, and as the thousands of Orangemen paraded the streets on their way to a new field at Loughgall Road, there was an air of determination in the part of the massed onlookers. It reflected the growing effects of the Civil Rights and I.R.A. campaign which had begun three years previously.

Portadown had experienced some of the strife, but the Troubles were to really hit the town the following year when murders and intimidation began a movement of population which was to polarise large parts of the town.

By the time the next parade was held, in 1982, radical changes had taken place in Northern Ireland. Stormont had gone, and the Troubles had intensified, with murders and destruction of property almost a daily event.

In 1993 the Twelfth returned to Portadown a few weeks after a bomb devastated the main Street

Wor. Bro. Harold Gracey, District Master, in welcoming the visiting Brethren, stated:-

> *"Portadown is but the latest in a long line of cities, towns and villages which have experienced the wicked actions of the I.R.A. as they try to bomb and shoot the Ulster people into a United Ireland. It will be the determination of the people of Portadown to rebuild their town centre and to quickly demonstrate to the enemies of this Province that their cruel and evil campaign will flounder on the rocks of Ulster resistance in which the Orange Institution as it has in the past, will play a key role."*

In 1999 the County demonstration was due to go to Killylea, according to the rotation of Districts, but the County Lodge decided to switch the venue to Portadown as a protest at the continuing stand-off at the Drumcree Church Parade. Many predicted a low turn-out because of the tension following the decision of the Parades Commission. In the event the parade was as large as ever, but there was a massive number of followers and spectators. The day passed off peacefully.

COLONEL SAUNDERSON AND THE BRIDGE AT PORTADOWN

For upwards of 94 years the statue of Colonel Edward James Saunderson has stood sentinel at the "top of the town" in Market Street, Portadown. Complementing it beside the main entrance to St. Mark's Parish Church is the War Memorial to the gallant men who in two World Wars defeated the might of the Kaiser and Hitler. The Saunderson statue is a splendid example of the skill of the artist who designed and brought to fruition this memorial of a distinguished Ulsterman and parliamentarian who espoused the Unionist Cause and defended it tooth and nail, both in Ireland and in the Palace of Westminster. No wonder he is seen with one foot trampling on a representation of the Home Rule Bill!

Colonel Saunderson was born in 1837 at Castle Saunderson, between Clones and Cavan. In early life he espoused the Unionist Cause with vigour and flair, being elected M.P. for North Armagh in 1885, a position he held until his death in 1906. At the time of his first nomination he was eagerly sought to represent a seat in Co. Antrim, but after he attended a rally of Unionists and Orangemen in Portadown his mind was fixed on North Armagh, and so it was to be. His wholehearted dedication to Unionism was matched by his allegiance to the Orange Institution, and he made his mark as a doughty champion of both in the Parliament of the United Kingdom of Great Britain and Ireland, as it then was. The memory of this stouthearted Co. Cavan man remains as fresh today as ever, and on each Twelfth an Orange sash is draped around the shoulder of "the Colonel" who served the Orange and Unionist Cause with such distinction and loyalty.

Below his feet on the statue is this inscription:-

Colonel Edward James Saunderson
M.P. for North Armagh 1885-1906
Born 1837, Died 1906
A Devoted Servant of his God and his Country

The development of the Newry Canal and, more importantly, the Railway network in the 19th Century, led to the growth of Portadown as a commercial centre. It was not, however, as a commercial centre which Colonel Saunderson referred to but rather as the symbol of a developing sense of identity. In the present situation in Northern Ireland it is this significance which the Unionist people ought to be emphasising.

When Irish Nationalists argue that Northern Ireland is not a legitimate State, or that Ireland ought to be united because it was one State prior to 1920, it is a gross distortion of history. The concept that a State rested upon the wishes of its inhabitants and derived it's existence from their sense of identity, the concept of Nationalism, was a 19th Century development. As this concept was applied to Ireland so, at the same time and in direct reaction to it, the concept arose of a community which rejected inclusion in the developing Irish Nationalism.

It was this growing sense of identity to which Saunderson referred in his 1893 rejection of Home Rule:-

"No man who comes to Belfast will laugh at the Ulster Loyalists. When all is said and done, whether or not the House of Lords reject this Bill, I say in the name of my people I reject it. You may occupy the House of Commons for years to come with academic debates about the merits of this Home Rule Bill but I say in their name I reject it ...Home Rule may pass this House but it will never pass the Bridge at Portadown!"

A DISTRICT WITH MANY FINE HALLS

Nearly a dozen of Portadown District's 32 Lodges meet in the main hall in Carleton Street. It was not the first hall in the District. Derrinraw Hall was opened on the 16th January, 1873, and in the same year the Baroness von Steiglitz (a member of the Blacker family) laid the foundation stone of the Carleton Street hall. The prime mover in the project was Rev. W. Devenish, but his removal to Liverpool caused the operations to be discontinued and no one seemed to feel themselves responsible for finishing the work. However, in 1881, Bro. Joseph McCaghey was elected District Master and under his guidance the hall was opened on 10th April 1882.

Carleton Street Orange Hall is a hub of activity, being used most nights during the week by members the Loyal Orders, as well as young people making use of its recreational facilities. On the 12th and 13th July the Hall is packed by Orangemen and members of the Black Institution before they leave for their respective demonstrations. The brethren crowd in to collect their banners, pay their dues, or exchange a bit of "crack" with friends and talk about past demonstrations. Important improvements have been carried out to the Hall since the last county demonstration in 1982, and these reflect the, importance of what is one of the busiest and most important Orange Halls in Northern Ireland. Portadown District, however, has many Orange Halls, both inside and outside the boundaries of the town. In addition to Carleton Street there are other Orange Halls inside the town at Corcrain, Edenderry, Clounagh, Seagoe and Levaghery.

The latter hall is actually the meeting place of a Lodge which belongs to Lurgan District - a reminder when Portadown was much smaller than it is today and Levaghery was then in the rural area.

Seagoe Orange Lodge also belonged to Lurgan District for many years, but only transferred to Portadown District within the past 20 years. A few years ago Bocombra also switched to Portadown from Lurgan, another move which made obvious sense as the result of population trends and the expansion of Portadown.

Edenderry and Clounagh Orange Halls have been greatly improved in recent years, but the brethren of Corcrain have been hampered by the fact that their hall is the subject of almost unceasing attacks by republican elements. Fewer Orange Halls have come under greater attack than Corcrain, and it has not been easy for the brethren of the L.O.L. No.339, but they have shown commendable courage and fortitude, refusing to surrender to the demands of republicans that they should quit an area which was once a Loyalist stronghold but in later times has been greatly affected by population changes.

The country Lodges which belong to Portadown also take a pride in their halls, and a number have carried out important improvements. Battlehill is an example, there the brethren of L.O.L. No.395 have an excellent building with modern amenities. Likewise Ballygargan has a relatively new building.

There are fine halls dotted throughout the lovely countryside close to Portadown – Breagh Kilmoriarty, Derrycarne, Kilmagamish, Derrykeevan, Derryneskin, Derrinraw, Drumherriff and Bocombra.

On the Armagh side of Portadown there are the halls in the Protestant strongholds of Clonroot, Derryhale, Kilmore and Drumnahuncheon, while in the Tandragee direction there are the fine halls at Ballylisk, Brackagh and Ballyworkan. Brackagh is one of the renowned drumming centres of Portadown District, and on a summer night the sound of the Lambeg drifts over the countryside towards Portadown, proof of the fact that preparations for another Twelfth are underway. Portadown District is a fine mixture of urban and rural Orangeism, and its flourishing condition is reflected in the care lavished on its many Orange halls and the fact that they are a focal point for community activity, not just confined to the Orange and Black Institutions.

There are 140 Orange Halls used for Lodge Meetings in County Armagh, valued at around £15 million. This does not include Brownlow House (Lurgan District) as it is impossible to estimate the present value of this historic building.

DISTRICT MASTERS OF PORTADOWN DISTRICT L.O.L. NO 1

1796-1807	John Burleigh	1854-1855	Thomas Dawson
1808-1812	Richard Hunt	1856	Daniel Chapman
1812-1815	Henry Chamney	1856-1859	Robert Anderson
1816	Thomas Joyce	1860	John E. Bro.wn
1817-1819	William Cregan	1861-1880	Robinson Ruddock
1820-1823	Curran Woodhouse	1881-1885	Joseph M'Caghey
1824-1825	Laurence Ruddock	1886-1891	Rev. Andrew Leitch
1826-1829	Daniel Bulla	1891-1905	W. J. Locke, JP
1830-1835	John Hamilton	1905-1926	W. H. Wright
1836-1837	John Overend	1926-1944	Major D. G. Shillington, (D.L., M.P.)
1838-1839	Rev. Charles King Irwin		
1844-1845	James Armstrong	1944-1955	Dr George Dougan, M.P.
1846-1849	Daniel Bulla	1955-1968	R. J. Magowan, O.B.E., J.P.
1850	Rev. Henry de L. Willis	1968-1981	Herbert Whitten, J.P., M.P.
1851	William Holland	1982-1985	John Brownlee
1851-1853	James Searight	1986-	Harold Gracey

THE DAYS WHEN THE BRETHREN TRAVELLED BY TRAIN

The serious cutbacks in the railways of Northern Ireland in the 1950s and 60s deprived many of the towns and villages of County Armagh of their rail link. That has been regretted by many people, and not least members of the Orange fraternity who have memories of travelling to county demonstrations by train.

The bus companies do a commendable job, and in many respects the journey by this mode of travel is more comfortable and more convenient than was the case when trains were used. But there was something special about those journeys by rail when the brethren poured into the railway station and packed the platforms as they waited for the trains to pull in and take them to their destination. For some years after the Second World War the Orangemen of Portadown paraded to the former station in Watson Street and boarded their trains for Armagh, Lurgan, Tandragee, Keady, Armagh and Richhill.

One of the advantages of the bus is that it can decamp passengers fairly close to the demonstration venue. Many Portadown brethren can recall the long walk from Madden station to Tandragee in the mid-1950s on a searing hot day when it seemed ages before the parade reached the town.

Then there was the 12th in Bessbrook in 1957 when the Orangemen arrived at the model village to find Ulster Special Constabulary men guarding the great viaduct against a possible attack by the I.R.A..

The axing of the line to Armagh ended the possibility of travelling to the Primatial City or to Keady and Richhill by train. Markethill had lost its rail links from the 1930s, and now the only demonstration venues which are convenient for rail journeys are Portadown and Lurgan.

The transfer from train to bus has gone so smoothly that it is unlikely that the railway will ever figure as largely as it once did on 12th demonstration days.

But for many Orangemen and Loyalists the nostalgic memories will remain of that rush into the station to try to get on the first train from Portadown to Armagh, and the long wait by those who failed to, as they waited in the station for later departures. There are the memories of the Standard Bearers hoisting the great Orange banners into the guard's van, of the overworked ticket collector trying to cope with hundreds of tickets proffered to him at the same time, or the embarrassed guard getting a train packed with Orangemen on the way to its destination by waving a green flag!

Four members of Portadown District have been murdered by terrorists in the recent "troubles":

Bro. Trevor Holland, L.O.L. No.273, age 36,
Shot dead from a passing car while standing outside a café in West Street in 1973.

Bro. Alfred Doyle, L.O.L. No.7
Sergeant in the U.D.R., murdered in 1975.

Bro. Walker Whitten, L.O.L. No.40, age 73,
Died 3 months after being shot from a passing motorbike.

Bro.. James Wright, L.O.L. No.127, age 48,
Killed by a car bomb outside his home.

THE PRIVATE LODGES OF PORTADOWN DISTRICT

L.O.L. No.7 BREAGH LEADING HEROES

In Sibbett's History of Orangeism it is recorded that:-

> *"Mr. Thomas Lecky, of Breagh, a most determined leader, who charged the rebel position at the Battle of the Diamond, obtained No.7, which afterwards went to Portadown District. According to the tradition, he owed this good fortune to his persistent flourishing of a blackthorn stick over the heads of those assembled in Mr. Sloan's parlour."*

The Lodge was to settle with the building of its own Orange hall at Breagh in 1891 but prior to this the Lodge is recorded as sitting at Diviney in July 1887 before moving to Breagh in October 1887.

In 1932 the Lodge unfurled a banner featuring King William crossing the Boyne on the front and the 'Secret of England's Greatness' on the reverse. These scenes were repeated on the Lodge's next banner which was unfurled in 1954. The Lodge's next banner, featuring the Biblical scene of 'My faith Looks Up To Thee' on the reverse, was unfurled at a ceremony held on 21 May 1971.

During the 'Troubles' the Lodge was to suffer the loss of Bro. Alfred Doyle, a sergeant in the Ulster Defence Regiment who, along with two friends, was brutally murdered by republican terrorists on 3 June 1975. The three men had been returning home from a dog show in the Irish Republic when their car was ambushed on the border near Killeen, County Armagh.

The late Bro. Isaac G. Hawthorne JP, MP who died in December 1992 served as Worshipful Master of the Lodge from 1956-58. Bro. Hawthorne was a former Chief Whip in the Northern Ireland Parliament at Stormont.

Members of L.O.L. No.7 unfurled a new banner in June 1995. The banner, featuring a depiction of Jesus walking on the water and a portrait of King William III, was unfurled by Mrs. Sommerville whilst the dedication ceremony was performed by the Reverend John Pickering.

L.O.L. No.8 STAR OF ERIN, DRUMHERIFF

Following the Battle of the Diamond, Richard Robinson, Timnakeel, received the first warrant in the house of James Sloan at Loughgall. In 1796 the Lodge was recorded as sitting in Drumheriff. It also sat at Ballyfodrin where in 1829 it had as its Master John Todd. The warrant was renewed to Thomas Crockett, W.M. in 1891 and the Lodge was meeting in the house of Samuel McCoo in 1892. The following year, 1893, the Lodge was meeting in the house of William Sparkes, Cornamuckley, but by the end of 1900 was again back at Drumheriff.

The new Orange hall was erected in 1912 and at the time Samuel Smyth was the Lodge's Worshipful Master.

L.O.L. No.9 THE EARL OF BEACONSFIELD PRIMROSE LEAGUE, CLOUNAGH

No.9 first sat at the Grange with John Winter as its Master up to 1815. In 1819 the Lodge received authorisation to move to the Dobbin and during the next forty years the Lodge was known as the Derryhale or Dobbin Lodge depending on its meeting place. By 2 February 1829 the Lodge's Master was noted as John Watson. The warrant fell temporarily dormant for some fourteen years but by 1862 it was operative again with Thomas Hoy as its Master. By 1864 the Lodge was known as Artabracka L.O.L. No.1883 saw a further move to Derryhale.

It was in 1896 that No.9 assumed the title as The Earl of Beaconsfield Primrose League. By this time the Lodge was sitting in Portadown and by 1904, under Worshipful Master, James Uprichard, Clounagh Orange Hall was built.

The late Bro. George Hanlon served with the Royal Navy during the Second World War. He saw service in the hazardous Arctic convoys bringing supplies to the Russians. Bro. Cecil McKinney also saw service during the war as a member of the Royal Ulster Rifles and Parachute Regiment.

The Lodge's current banner, featuring a painting of Benjamin Disraeli, the Earl of Beaconsfield, the Prime Minister of the United Kingdom during the 1870s, was unfurled in the 1960s.

Clounagh Orange Hall was extensively renovated after a boiler explosion and was reopened in 1988.

L.O.L. No.10 GREENISLAND TRUE BLUES, DERRINRAW

In 1796 No.10 was recorded as sitting at Richmount. During the period 1823 to March 1825 it was also recorded as meeting at Glenanne and up to 1904 in Markethill District. In the year 1829 the Master was recorded as Mark Berry and by 1856 the Lodge was sitting at Derryvore with Alex Trotter as its Master. The place of sitting of the number moved from Kilmore to Derryvane around 1864 before moving to Richmount, Ballyoran, Edgarstown and settling at Derrinraw about 1870. The Lodge sat in the house of William McFadden before the Orange hall was built and opened on 16 January 1873. In 1875 Thomas A. Woodhouse was the Worshipful Master of the Lodge and the warrant was renewed to John Maguire W.M. on 12 May 1894. Wolsey noted in his book *Orangeism in Portadown District* that:

> *"John McNally walked from Derrinraw to the Red Lion to see Robinson Ruddock to get No.10 warrant. James Taylor, a stone-cutter, cut the stone for the Hall (the oldest in Portadown District) and gave it to the Lodge free of cost."*

The hall at Derrinraw, dating from 1873, is thought to be the oldest purpose built Orange hall in County Armagh. Unique features of the hall include an original framed portrait of Queen Victoria, a Lodge warrant from 1896, a Lodge seal, possibly dating from the late 1790s and probably most unique of all – original gaslight fittings within the hall.

L.O.L. No.13 THE RISING SONS OF WILLIAM, DERRINRAW

In 1796 No.13 was recorded as sitting in Drumcree with John Flavelle as its Master. By 1819 the Lodge has moved to Kilmagamish with John Atkinson recorded as Master on 2 February 1829 and it returns to Drumcree in 1844. The Registry of Lodges for 1856 names the Master of the Lodge as John Abraham during which year it was meeting at Derryall with Robert Bird as Master. Having moved to Derrinraw in 1880 the No.13 warrant was renewed by John Forbes W.M. on 26 June 1891.

L.O.L. No.13, the smallest Lodge in the District, is also another of the numerous drumming Lodges in Portadown.

L.O.L. No.18 GOLDEN SPRINGS, BRACKAGH

The No.18 warrant was first recorded as meeting in Portadown in 1796 with its Worshipful Master as John Lutton. For a number of years from 1838, when the Lodge had a membership of twelve brethren, the Lodge was meeting in the Mahon area to the extent it became known as the Mahon Lodge. In 1842 it was meeting at the house of Robert Wright, Worshipful Master, at the Mahon. By the year 1860 the Lodge had moved to Brackagh meeting in the home of James McKeown.

The new hall was erected at Brackagh in 1914 and in 1923 Mr. and Mrs. Maginnis provided an organ for the hall as religious services were held in the hall from time to time. Also, in 1923 a new banner was obtained by L.O.L. No.18.

In 1943 a memorial tablet was erected in Brackagh Orange Hall by the officers and members of L.O.L. No.18 and R.B.P. 265 in memory of the Late Sir Knight and Bro. John Toal 1891 to 1942.

A new banner featuring a painting of King William III on horseback was unfurled on 22 May 1992.

On 13 October 1993 a tablet was unveiled in memory of the late Sir Knight and Bro. John G. Toal who had served in the office of Worshipful Master from 1942 until 1993, a period of fifty-one years.

Brackagh is one of the major Lambeg drumming Lodges within Portadown District.

L.O.L. No.19 BALLYWORKAN TRUTH DEFENDERS

The first recorded meeting place of No.19 is at Ballyworkan in 1796 with Arthur Huston as Master. On the 2 February 1829 the Master of the Lodge was William Gillespie, and in 1856 the Lodge was sitting in Ballyworkan with John Cullen as Master. In the years 1875 and 1891 the Master was recorded as James Miller, Portadown.

Unlike many other Lodges of the time No.19 does not appear to have moved around different parts of the surrounding countryside. In fact, it is noted that the Lodge has always met around Whiteside's Hill up to 1923 where, like most other Lodges, it met in private houses. In 1923 the house of John Stewart, in which the Lodge had met for many years, was purchased and turned into a suitable hall.

In 1937 L.O.L. No.19 unfurled a new banner, the ceremony was carried out by Sister Miss N. Wright of Mullavilly, the sister of the late W. H. Wright former District Master of Portadown, with Bro. the Rt. Hon. Major D. G. Shillington D.L., M.P., District Master, presiding.

During the Second World War Bro. Taylor Tweedie made the Supreme Sacrifice when he was Killed in Action at Monte Casino, Italy.

The Lodge's present banner features paintings of the 'Fortunate Escape of King William' and the burning at the stake of Latimer and Ridley. Ballyworkan is another of the many drumming Lodges within the District.

L.O.L. No.20 ERIN'S ROYAL STANDARD, KILMAGAMISH

No.20 was working under Worshipful Master William Hall at Derryanville in 1796. Membership records show that by 1814 the Lodge had thirty-nine members, showing as increase to sixty-six by 1816. In 1819 the Lodge was meeting at Kilmagamish and in 1829 the Master was Curran Atkinson. In 1880 the number had become known as Foy L.O.L. but in 1884 the name was changed to Waterloo Verner Heroes.

The Forsythe family would appear to have had a strong connection with No.20 as it was recorded in 1874 that the Lodge was paying James Forsythe 4d per week for sitting in his room in Foy. Indeed in 1890 the Lodge was still meeting at Forsythe's at Derrymattery. In the same year the Lodge meeting place moved to Mr. McFall's in Drumena but only for a short period because the following year 1891 it had moved again this time to the mill in a house of William Forsythe. The year 1893 saw the Lodge meeting at Kilmagamish, 1902 at Corbackey and in 1910 back at George Forsythe's at Kilmagamish. The new Orange hall was opened on 13 September 1913.

Members of the Lodge unfurled a new banner on 12 June 1993. The banner features a painting of Drumcree Parish Church on the front and a depiction of King William III landing at Carrickfergus on the reverse.

L.O.L. No.22 BOCOMBRA TRUE BLUES

No.22 Warrant originated in Lurgan District. On 2nd February 1829 it was recorded in Lurgan with Henry Dynes as Master. The year 1825 records Thomas McDowell as Master and by 1856 the Lodge was sitting at Bocombra with Thomas Malcolmson as Master. In the year 1891 Thomas McDowell of Lurgan was again noted as Master of the Lodge.

Bocombra Orange hall was opened in 1908.

This Lodge transferred to Portadown District in 1992.

L.O.L. No.25 WINGFIELD VERNER'S CRIMSON STAR, PORTADOWN

No.25 has continually sat in Portadown since 1796. Initially known as The Boyne Club of Loyalists No.25 the Lodge had as its first Master James Dawson. In 1854 the Lodge changed its name and became known as the Calimotte Orange Lodge. The Master in 1856 was Thomas Henry and in 1869 the Lodge was meeting in the house of John Williamson at Woodhouse Street.

David Clayton, Clounagh, who died in 1927, was for many years chaplain and led the Lodge on the Twelfth on his own white horse. Duplicate warrants were issued in Counties Down and Londonderry in 1856.

L.O.L. No.25 meets in Carleton Street Orange Hall. Bro. Harold Gracey, the Worshipful Master of Portadown District is a member of this Lodge.

L.O.L. No.26 CHURCHVIEW, SEAGOE

No.26 warrant was first issued to Lurgan District in 1798. 2 February 1829 shows the warrant with a Joshua Cherry, Lurgan, and a duplicate with Banbridge District. On the morning of 12 July 1848, L.O.L. No.26 was presented with a beautiful stand of colours by Mrs. Saurin (nee Warburton, the sister of General Warburton. A famous Australian explorer and the wife of the Reverend James Saurin, the Rector of Seagoe.) In 1856 No.26 was still with Lurgan District and in 1875 Henry McCrory was Master and two duplicates were working in Banbridge. 1891 shows the Master again as Henry McCrory.

In 1897 the foundation stone for a new Orange hall at Seagoe was laid by Baroness Von Stieglitz a member of the well-known Blacker family. The Baroness had kindly donated the land on which the Orange hall was to be erected.

In 1972 L.O.L. No.26 transferred from Lurgan District to Portadown District.

The members of L.O.L. No.26 unfurled a new banner, featuring a painting of the nearby Seagoe Parish Church, on 26 June 1992.

L.O.L. No.31 BIBLE AND CROWN DEFENDERS, KILMORIARTY

On the 6 August 1796 this warrant was taken out by Abraham Hart with a membership of over fifty. The following year the Lodge was meeting at Tottens Hill with Joseph Morrison as Master. During the next period of years the Lodge had a number of name changes. In 1813 it was known as the Mullentine Excelsior Lodge and in 1882 became known as Kilmoriarty Excelsior Lodge when John Summerville was Master. A further name change resulted in 1886 to Derry Rossmore Scarlet Star and the final change of name to Bible and Crown Defenders came about in 1905. In 1856 the Lodge was meeting at Mullentine with Benjamin Ford as Master and by 1875 the Master was William Lawson. During the 1920s membership of the Lodge was up to seventy.

Kilmoriarty Orange Hall was opened on Easter Monday 1912.

On 24 May 1985 the members of L.O.L. No.31 unfurled a new banner which featured a portrait of their late Worshipful Master, Bro. Tom Woods. The unfurling ceremony was performed by his son, Bro. Tommie Woods.

The Pride of the Birches Accordion Band accompanies L.O.L. No.31 on parade.

Bro. Private James Magee of L.O.L. No.31 served during the Great War. He was killed in action. The Lodge has a photograph of Bro. Magee, in full service uniform, which was taken shortly before he left for the Front.

The Lodge's original warrant, issued in 1796, is in the Orange Museum in Loughgall.

L.O.L. No.35 ST AIDEN'S TRUE BLUES, KILMORE

No.35 is one of the warrants issued on the day of the Battle of the Diamond to George Innis, Grange, O'Neilland. In 1796 the Lodge was still meeting at the Grange with Worshipful Master Richard Robinson but by 1820 it was meeting at Ballywilly. The year of 1856 notes the meeting place as Anahoe and James Pierson as Master. In 1875 John Haughton was Master. On the 24 April 1905, Easter Monday, an Orange hall was opened on a site given by the late Rev. Richard Johnston.

Kilmore Orange Hall was the venue for a dedication ceremony on 24 April 1992 when members of L.O.L. No.35 unfurled a new banner featuring a painting of Kilmore Parish Church.

L.O.L. No.40 HERBERT WHITTEN MEMORIAL, PORTADOWN

This Lodge was formed in 1796 at the Grange as the Erne Temperance L.O.L., its first Master being Laurence Ruddock. By 1856 it was still meeting at the Grange with Worshipful Master, William Taylor. In 1901 it was meeting in Portadown with W. J. Locke, J.P. Master, also District Master of Portadown District. Following his death in August 1905, a resolution was passed at the September meeting:-

> *"That we express our deep sorrow on the death of Bro. W. J. Locke, W.M. of this Lodge. He was Master of this Lodge during the many years it worked in Portadown, and we always found him to be not only a loyal and earnest fellow-worker but a true and faithful friend. He was greatly attached to the Orange Institution and worked Zealously in its interests and the Institution, and especially our District, will greatly miss him who for so many years has been our tried and trusted friend."*

W. H. Wright was secretary of the Lodge until his death in 1921. He was also District Master of Portadown District. Following his death the Lodge became known as W. H. Wright Memorial. In 1932 Herbert Whitten was elected secretary of the Lodge. He also became District Master of Portadown District in 1968. Bro. George Dougan, Worshipful District Master of Portadown from 1944 to 1955, was a member of L.O.L. No.40 before his transfer to L.O.L. No.56.

After the death of the Worshipful District Master, Bro. Herbert Whitten, the Lodge was renamed to perpetuate his memory. In June 1984 a new banner featuring a portrait of the late Bro. Herbert Whitten was unfurled by members of the Lodge.

The Lodge is accompanied by the Star of David Accordion Band on the Twelfth of July.

L.O.L. No.40 meets in Carleton Street Orange Hall.

L.O.L. No.56 PRINCE OF WALES, PORTADOWN

No.56 has never left Portadown District. Thomas Buntin was the first Master of the Lodge. On the 1 July 1851 it was decided that the Lodge should be called Temperance L.O.L.. In 1856 James White was Master. At the time there were two other L.O.L. No.56 warrants operating in Co. Cavan and Co. Londonderry. The Portadown warrant fell dormant during the period 1862-1864 but in 1864 the warrant was reorganised under the name of Prince of Wales with Worshipful Master, Abraham Harvey. In 1870 a presentation was made by the Lodge of a bridle and saddle to the Rev. Albert J. Ard, curate of Drumcree, following the presentation of a horse by the parishioners of Drumcree to him. On the 11 July 1878 the Lodge name was changed to Portadown Conqueror but in 1883 it reverted back to the Prince of Wales. Mention is made of the fact that there was a Prince of Wales Conservative Flute Band. At the 1884 demonstration in Newry L.O.L. No.56 was headed by their brass band. The Grand Master of the time, Sir Edward Wingfield Verner, took the Lodge and band out of their place in the procession and put them in front of the County Grand Lodge of Dublin, asking them to lead the entire procession of 40,000 Orangemen through the streets of Newry to the place of meeting at Altnaveigh.

L.O.L. No.56 meets in Carleton Street Orange Hall.

L.O.L. No.58 COLONEL SAUNDERSON'S SILVER STREAM, PORTADOWN

From 1796 to 1832 No.58 sat at Ballinteggart. The first Master of the Lodge was James Ferguson. In 1834 the Lodge was now sitting at Kilmoriarty with James Ruddell as Master. In the same year a problem seems to have arisen due to a duplicate 58 Warrant. On 3 September the Grand committee of G.O.L.I. resolved:-

> *"....that No. having been originally been given to the first mentioned District and that a duplicate having been illegally trafficked by the other districts resolved that No. 58 Portadown District be the only Lodge acknowledged as sitting under a Warrant of that Number and that all others having that No. to be declared cancelled."*

On 2 January 1883 the number was restored after being dormant for a period of time by Joseph McCaghey District Master, and W. J. Locke Deputy District Master. At the time six members were present.

Four members of the Lodge served in His Majesty's Forces during World War II. They were Bros. R. J. Whyte, F. Todd, R. H. Bunting and R. J. Jones.

The Lodge was renamed after Colonel Edward James Saunderson, a loyal Orangeman and the Unionist M.P. for North Armagh. The Lodge's two previous bannerettes have featured portraits of King William III and Colonel Saunderson. A portrait of Colonel Saunderson is featured on the reverse of the Lodge's current bannerette which was unfurled on 18 April 1989. The bannerette was presented to the Lodge by members of the Wylie family and features a portrait of the late Bro. R. J. Wylie, P.M. on the front.

L.O.L. No.58 meets in Carleton Street Orange Hall.

L.O.L. No.78 BIBLE AND CROWN DEFENDERS, DERRYCARNE

In 1796 No.78 was meeting in Portadown with Miles Atkinson as its Master. In 1809 the number fell dormant for a short time before being taken out again in 1810 with Henry Chamney as Master. He was to remain as Master to 1816 when it again fell dormant. In 1821 the warrant was reopened with William Irwin, the District Secretary becoming Worshipful Master of the Lodge. By 1844 the Lodge was meeting at Derrycorey and in 1856 the Lodge was now meeting at Derrycarne with Robert Johnston under a new warrant 'The Warrant having been carried off to Australia a renewal was granted 2 February 1849'. In 1890 the Lodge was given permission to use the name Bible and Crown Defenders.

The Lodge opened a new hall in a ceremony which took place in 1911.

In 1994 two members of the Lodge received presentations to mark their 50 years' membership of the Lodge. Bro. Samuel Dowd, Worshipful Master of L.O.L. No.78 and Bro. Thomas Forbes, his deputy, received 50 year Membership Certificates and inscribed Bibles from the Worshipful District Master Bro. Harold Gracey. Both men joined the Lodge as teenagers in 1944.

The current banner of L.O.L. No.78 depicts, as their name suggests, a Bible and Crown on the front, whilst on the reverse is depicted the Biblical scene 'My Faith looks up to Thee'.

Recently members of the Lodge purchased Derrycarne Primary School as new accommodation for the Lodge. The members are now embarking on an ambitious renovation programme for the hall.

L.O.L. No.80 STAR OF THE NORTH, BALLYLISK

In 1796 the Lodge was meeting at Ballyworkan with William Wright as Master but by 1819 the meeting place had moved to Drumnakelly. The year 1856 saw William Mateer as Master with the Lodge sitting at Mullahead. In 1829 the warrant was in the name of William Brownlow, Portadown and in 1875 in the name of George Laverty.

Ballylisk Orange Hall was opened on 12 July 1920 when the brethren of L.O.L. No.80 played host to the County Armagh demonstration.

In 1938 the Lodge unfurled a new banner featuring King William III crossing the Boyne on the front and 'The secret of England's greatness' on the reverse.

The Lodge's current banner, which features a depiction of David slaying Goliath, was unfurled in 1975.

L.O.L. No.81 DERRYHALE

Warrant No.81 first appeared in Portadown District records in 1800 with William Hunniford as Master.

In 1856 the Lodge was sitting at Derryhale and Robert Anderson was Master. The Lodge was still noted at that location in 1875. Prior to the building of its own hall for meetings in 1899 the Lodge had met in the houses of John McQuillan, Mullalelish; Hector Teggart, Derryhale; Thomas Tougher, Derryhale; and William Mckinney, Lisavague.

On 12 July 1922 the County Armagh demonstration was held at Derryhale on the occasion of the opening of Derryhale Orange Hall.

L.O.L. No.89 RECHAB'S TRUE BLUES TOTAL ABSTINENCE, PORTADOWN

No.89 was meeting in Timnakeel in 1796 with William Dillon as Master. The warrant moved to Portadown in 1820 with Daniel Bulla becoming Master in 1882. By 1844 the Lodge was meeting in Battlehill but the following year the meeting place had moved to Derryhale. In 1856 the Master was Thomas Hoey and at this time the place of sitting was noted as Artabracka. The number was to fall dormant from 1884-1867 when it appears at Cock Hill, Tartaraghan, with William Gardiner as Master. The number was to again have a period when it was dormant from 1884-1889 when William Best of Killycomain became Master. It was in 1893 that the Lodge took the name of Rechab's True Blues.

W. H. Wolsey, the author of *Orangeism in Portadown District*, was a member of this Lodge fulfilling the post of Worshipful Master in 1945 and again in 1953. During World War II the following brethren saw active service in His Majesty's Forces: John Campbell (H.M.S. Centurion), Fred Harvey (Royal Air Force), Harry McKerr and C. H. Rock.

In 1943 Bro. R. J. Hewitt was appointed S.D.C. of the Ulster Special Constabulary in Portadown.

In 1959 W. H. Wolsey became Mayor of Portadown. L.O.L. No.89 which sat in Carleton Street Orange Hall became dormant in the late 1980s.

L.O.L. No.99 JOHNSTON'S ROYAL STANDARD, PORTADOWN

The first mention of No.99 is in 1796 at Clonamola with John Erwin as Master. In the year 1810 the Lodge was meeting at Leganny but by 1856 it had moved to Baltylum and had as its Master, Bro. William Weir. During the years 1862-1870 the Lodge was known as William Street Orange Lodge and its Master was James Albin. By 1874 the Lodge was meeting in Obins Street and the Worshipful Master in 1875 was Joseph McCaughey. The number fell dormant for a short period but was revived in 1881 with William Jackson as Master. In 1882 the Lodge took the name of Royal Standard which was extended to William Johnston Royal Standard in 1893. At one stage L.O.L. No.99 had its own band and Lambeg drums.

In 1937 a new banner was unfurled by Sister Mrs. Shillington, the wife of the District Master. The banner featured a portrait of Lord Carson, who had died in 1935.

William Baxter, Portadown's oldest surviving veteran of the Battle of the Somme, was a member of this Lodge. He died in 1993. Bro. Tommy Speers, a Royal Air Force veteran, who took part in the Normandy landings in June 1944, laid the wreath at the town's War Memorial on the occasion of the District's pre-Twelfth Orange parade commemorating the 50th Anniversary of D-Day. Tommy, a Past Master of the Lodge died shortly after this event.

L.O.L. No.99 meets in Carleton Street Orange Hall.

L.O.L. No.107 SIR EDWARD WINGFIELD VERNER'S TRUE BLUES, KNOCKNAMUCKLY

This warrant was first noted in 1796 sitting at Drumnakelly with Henry Jackson as Master. By 1819 it was sitting at the Dobbin and the following year had moved to Kilmoriarty where William Hyde was Master. The years of 1845 and 1846 saw the Lodge sitting at Corcrain and Artabracka, respectively, the latter of which it was to remain at to 1867. The Lodge was on the move again in 1868 when it moved to Ballygargan. The title of Verner's True Blues was granted in 1883. The Lodge was renamed Sir Edward Wingfield Verner's True Blues on the death of the County Grand Master of Armagh, who was the son of Sir William Verner. The original hall was opened on 5 November 1894.

Sir Edward Wingfield Verner's True Blues unfurled their banner on Friday 8 July 1977. Mrs. Anna Haire unfurled the banner, which was donated to the Lodge by her Brother, Bro. George Duke, in memory of his father, Bro. Richard Duke, who was secretary for 47 years. The previous banner was destroyed in the terrorist attack the year before.

Ballygargan Orange Hall was destroyed in a terrorist attack on 28 March 1976. On the morning of 28 March the Worshipful Master, Bro. Eric Davison, received a phone message from the police, asking him to open Ballgargan Orange Hall to enable the army to make a routine check. He arrived about 11.00 a.m., opened the door, went through the main hall and into the kitchen with the soldiers. On returning to the main hall there was an explosion and he was thrown across the room. The trapdoor to the roof space was booby trapped and one soldier, Corporal Donald Traynor, was killed. The Lodge lost a lot of artefacts, including photographs, furniture and banners. Upon reaching the road the Worshipful Master was informed that the police had received a message on the confidential phone saying arms were being stored in the hall. A floral tribute and letter of sympathy was sent to the family of the dead soldier. On 11 April a retiring offering was taken up in the three local churches – Knocknamuckley Parish Church,

Bluestone Methodist Church and Newmills Presbyterian Church. The Lodge met in the Victory Hall, Drumnacanvey, kindly loaned by Carrickblacker Guiding Star R.B.P. 503, until the new hall was built.

L.O.L. No.107 is another of the major drumming Lodges within the District.

L.O.L. No.127 KING WILLIAM'S DEFENDERS, PORTADOWN

The warrant No.127 originally sat in Tandragee District. In 1795 the warrant was granted to James Quinn of Mullahead and the Lodge was still sitting at this location by 1832. The warrant No.127 was to move to Portadown in 1890 where it took as its meeting place Parkmount. The Lodge moved to Carleton Street Orange Hall when the new portion was built to the hall. The Lodge became known as King William's Defenders in June 1900 and previous to this it had been called Verner's Golden Star. No.127 is one of those Lodges within Portadown District which has become synonymous with the area in which it once sat. It is often referred to as 'Parkmount' or 'The Walk' Lodge.

Edward McCann was the Master of the Lodge up to 1912 and in the early 1920s membership of the Lodge numbered seventy. No meetings were held by the Lodge from 1914 to 5 July 1918 due to the Great War and the large number of brethren who were away from home on active service with the forces. The Master reopened the Lodge on 5 July 1918 as a number of disabled brethren had returned home and wished the Lodge to be active again.

During World War Two Bro. David Gillis, who was serving with the Royal Air Force, was Killed In Action over Germany on 22 June 1940.

On 8 July 1955 the Lodge unfurled a new banner featuring a portrait of King William III and a depiction of the Mountjoy breaking the boom.

In 1990, as part of the celebrations to mark the tercentenary of the Battle of the Boyne, the brethren of L.O.L. No.127 were accompanied on parade by a goat. Parkmount Junior L.O.L. No.150 accompany the senior Lodge on parade.

L.O.L. No.127 meets in Carleton Street Orange Hall although the Lodge retains close links with the Parkmount area of Portadown. Castle Avenue in the Parkmount area was the natural choice as a venue for the unfurling and dedication of the Lodge's new banner in 1991.

Bro. Stanley Thompson, the current District Treasurer, is a member of this Lodge.

L.O.L. No.161 WESLEYAN TEMPERANCE, PORTADOWN

Warrant No.161 was established in Loughgall District in 1798 with James Sloan as Master. In early demonstrations L.O.L. No.161 carried a silk flag, bearing the Royal Coat of Arms, which had been originally presented to Lt.-Col. Robert Camden Cope and his troop of Volunteers in 1782 by the Colonel's daughter.

In 1856 it was still at Loughgall with James Woods as Master. The warrant fell dormant for a period of thirty years before coming to Portadown District in 1933. The Lodge was opened by James Dermott, Portadown District Secretary, and David Rock, Asst. District Secretary, on Monday 6 March 1933. The first Worshipful Master of the Lodge was Thomas Caddell. The Lodge took as its title Portadown True Blues.

From its inception again in 1950, Wesleyan Temperance has had a strong Methodist membership. It was mainly members of that denomination who restarted the Lodge.

For the past forty-five years Wesleyan Temperance L.O.L. No.161 has played a leading and influential part in the affairs of Portadown District L.O.L. No.1.

The Lodge banner for some thirty years had on one side a portrait of John Wesley, founder of Methodism. It had provided 161 with a unique and immediately recognisable place in the Portadown Orange parade.

Incidently, the portrait of John Wesley which adorned the 161 banner for many years is now framed and much admired in the lecture hall of Thomas Street Methodist Church.

Changing circumstances, not least social conditions, meant a decline in numbers in the 1970s and early 1980s but there is a great loyalty and resilience on the part of 161 brethren and in recent years the Lodge has been making its mark once again with numbers on the increase and several brethren making an impact at District Lodge level, notably Bro. David Burrows, Deputy District Master, Bro. Nigel Dawson, District Secretary and Bro. Rev. Duane Russell, District Chaplain.

In the 1950s and '60s, men prominent in civic and business affairs who were members included names like Robert Williamson, a Mayor of Portadown, Councillor John George McCann, Victor Reavie – whose café in Thomas Street was the venue for the Lodge Twelfth dinner – and Councillor Ernest Downey.

The name Wright has always been to the fore in 161 and at one time four Brothers of that family were members – Bros. Dick Wright, still a very active member, Earl Wright, who played a leading role in trade union and civic affairs, and the late Bros. Eric and Jim Wright. The Lodge also has brethren in its ranks who rendered outstanding service in local government and two of those were the late Bros. Ken Jones and Billy Robinson.

L.O.L. No.172 ST SAVIOUR'S TRUE BLUES, CLONROOT

In 1796 this Lodge number was meeting at Canoneil with Master George Morrow. Before coming to Portadown District in 1848 the Lodge was meeting at Artabracka in 1820 and Mullahead in 1832. Two years after coming to Portadown District the number fell dormant and remained so to 1854 when it was given to Daniel Chapman at Drumnahuncheon. By the following January the warrant was again dormant. In July 1869 the first mention is made of the Lodge being known as St. Saviour's True Blues and 1875 John Robert Logan of Portadown is noted as Master. The Rev. C. K. Irwin (Jun.), a member of 172, was a Deputy Grand Chaplain of Ireland in 1872. Clonroot Orange Hall was erected in 1884.

The Lodge's current banner, featuring a portrait of the late Bro. James McBroom and a painting of St. Saviour's, The Dobbin, was unfurled in 1964.

L.O.L. No.273 THE RISING SONS OF PORTADOWN

In June 1902 L.O.L. No.540, sitting in Carleton Street Orange Hall and formed in 1899 exchanged their warrant for that of No.273. They carried across with them the name Christian Volunteers. J. A. Haire was the Worshipful Master and G. Matchett was Deputy. This Lodge continued to function until 1962 when the warrant became dormant.

After a period of seven years the dormant warrant No.273 was reconstituted on 5 November 1969 under the name The Rising Sons of Portadown. The Master at the Lodge's reconstitution was Bro. Robert Jones. Since its reconstitution L.O.L. No.273 has continued to sit at Carleton Street Orange Hall.

On Friday 25 June 1971 L.O.L. No.273 unfurled its banner at a service of Dedication in Carleton Street Orange Hall. The banner depicts the scene of the drowning of the Protestants in the River Bann 1641.

The Rising Sons of Portadown was the first Lodge in Portadown District to carry the Bible in a glass case when on parade. In August 1976 the Lodge members opened their new Lodge room in Carleton Street Orange Hall.

L.O.L. No.322 R. J. MAGOWAN MEMORIAL TEMPERANCE, EDENDERRY

The earliest recorded mention of warrant number 322 is found in the 1798 Minute Book of the Grand Orange Lodge of Ireland, but no other information is given.

On 30 May 1895 a duplicate warrant was issued to Bro. John Black of Portadown on the formation of Lord Arthur Hill's L.O.L. No.322 sitting in Carleton Street Orange Hall (Arthur Hill was the late Unionist M.P. for West Down). This Lodge functioned until 1905 when the members decided to merge with Dr. Kane's Crimson Star L.O.L. No.417.

The inaugural meeting of Edenderry Temperance and Benefit L.O.L. No.322 was held on 13 May 1907 at Carleton Street Orange Hall with Bro. David Bright being installed as the Lodge's first Worshipful Master a position he held until 1913. The Lodge's first banner was unfurled in 1909 and featured King William III on the front and the Biblical 'Good Samaritan' scene on the reverse. This scene has been depicted on all the Lodge's banners ever since. The cost of the banner was £13.

During the Great War many brethren served in the forces including W. J. Adair, Thomas Stewart, Thomas Hyde, James Chambers, Sandy Orr, David Boyd, James Johnston, William McClatchy, David Medlow, Robert Callison and James Gilliland. Bros. Chambers and Johnston were serving with the 36th (Ulster) Division and were wounded at the Battle of the Somme.

The foundation stone for Edenderry Orange Hall was laid by Mrs. W. H. McCammon on 20 April 1920 and on 19 September 1925 the hall was officially opened.

The Second World War saw many Edenderry men again volunteering for service namely Joseph Gibson, Walter Curry, Gardiner Atkinson, Charles Johnstone, William Hewitt, Frank Radbone, Henry Kane and Frank Magowan, the son of R. J. Magowan. Bro. Kane was lost at sea on 21 June 1940 when his ship was torpedoed by a German U-boat.

In 1947 Bro. R. J. Magowan was elected as the first Mayor of the Borough of Portadown and two years later he received the O.B.E.. A new banner, the Lodge's third, was unfurled in 1955. March 1968 saw the end of an era with the death of R. J. Magowan, Worshipful Master of L.O.L. No.322 since 1934 and the District Master of Portadown since 1955. The Lodge was renamed the R. J. Magowan Memorial Temperance L.O.L. No.322 in memory of the late Worshipful Master and a new banner bearing this name was unfurled on 12 July 1971.

In 1982 Bro. John Brownlee became the second member of L.O.L. No.322 to serve as W.D.M. of Portadown District. A member of L.O.L. No.322 for fifty years, Bro. Brownlee died in 1995.

L.O.L. No.339 CORCRAIN PURPLE ROCKET

This warrant first came to Portadown District in 1897 to replace No.533. L.O.L. No.533 had been opened on 14 May 1894 by William J. Locke, District Master. It was decided at this meeting that the title of the Lodge would be Corcrain Purple Rocket L.O.L.. The word Temperance was not introduced until the following meeting. The first Master of L.O.L. No.339 was John Anderson. Erected as a memorial to the Late Bro. W. J. Locke, District Master of Portadown, Corcrain Orange Hall was opened by Mrs. C. Johnston on 4 November 1911.

A number of memorial plaques have been erected in the hall in memory of past members of the Lodge. On 30 June 1956 a memorial plaque was erected in memory of the Late Bro. John Wright for services rendered to the extension of the hall. Another was erected in memory of the Late Bro. Thomas Uprichard for services rendered to the hall and Lodge from 1923-79. A plaque of Past Masters of the Lodge was presented by the Milligan family in memory of the Late Bro. Cecil Milligan a member of the Lodge for forty-six years who held the offices of Treasurer 1983-84 and Deputy Master 1985-86.

The members of the Lodge unfurled their present banner featuring paintings of King William leaving Belfast Castle and the Biblical scene 'My Faith looks up to Thee' in 1977. The old banner was donated to a Lodge in County Monaghan.

Throughout the period of the 'Troubles' Corcrain Orange Hall has been subjected to countless attacks by republicans. The hall has been daubed with paint and slogans, attempts have been made to set the hall on fire and cars belonging to members have been tampered with. No other Orange hall in Portadown has been on the receiving end of so many wanton and sectarian attacks. From 1985 there have been four arson attacks on the hall. A serious attempt to cause damage took place on 11 June 1994 when a security grill was broken off a window and a fire started in the Gents' toilets.

Corcrain L.O.L. No.339 held a special service on 15 May 1994 to commemorate the 100th Anniversary of the formation of the Lodge.

L.O.L. No.352 DERRYKEEVIN TEMPERANCE

Warrant No.352 came to Portadown District in 1896 when the officers and members of L.O.L. No.817 exchanged their warrant for L.O.L. No.352. L.O.L. No.352 was recorded in Lurgan District on 2 February 1829 and again in the Register for 1856.

L.O.L. No.817 was opened on 13 February 1886 by Rev. A. Leitch, District Master. It was known as Maiden City Fortress Temperance L.O.L.. In 1825 L.O.L. No.817 was meeting at Derrylard with Richard Best as Master. In 1896 the Master of the L.O.L. No.352 was John Cooper who had also been Master of L.O.L. No.817. On 9 September 1898 the Lodge minutes record that 'the office-bearers decided to keep their positions' but the minutes were left unsigned and sometime later warrant No.352 was handed in. Warrant No.352 was to be taken out again on 2 January 1933 when the name adopted was Derrykeevin Temperance L.O.L.. The Lodge was opened and the officers were installed by Major D. G. Shillington M.P., District Master, Portadown District. The first Worshipful Master of the Lodge was Bro. Joshua Crockett and he was followed by Jacob Benson who took over in 1934. Bro. Benson occupied the chair until 1980 when he was succeeded by Bro. Samuel G. Benson.

Members of the Lodge erected as Orange hall in 1936 on land kindly donated by Thomas Trueman and within the hall is a plaque in memory of Thomas Trueman. The opening ceremony was performed by Lord Craigavon, the Prime Minister of Northern Ireland.

On 11 April 1950 the members of the Lodge unfurled a new banner, featuring paintings of King William III crossing the Boyne and the 'Secret of England's Greatness'. The Lodge unfurled a new banner in June 1994.

The District Chaplain, Bro. George Robinson, is a member of this Lodge.

L.O.L. No.371 APPRENTICE BOYS, DRUMNAHUNCHEON

This warrant was first recorded in 1798 with William Hill as Master. By 1856 the number was in Lurgan District, sitting at Balteagh, with William Robinson as Master and in 1875 the position remains unchanged. With the coming of 1887 the warrant was recorded as in the hands of Richard Hobson and on 24 October of the same year the Lodge was opened by the District Master, William J. Locke, at this meeting Richard Hobson was elected as Worshipful Master. The hall used by the Lodge was opened in 1910 and in the early 1930s membership of the Lodge was recorded at seventy.

Within the hall are two memorial tablets in honour of Lodge members who served during the Great War and to those members who made the supreme sacrifice for King and Country. Those members who were Killed In Action were: A. Doherty, J. Courtney, A. Graham, T. Troughton, A. Loney, J. Taylor and J. Black.

In June 1936 the Lodge unfurled a new banner, featuring a portrait of King William III on the front and a depiction of Saul sparing David's life on the reverse.

The Dobbin Parish Hall was the venue for the unfurling and dedication of a new banner on 9 July 1993. The banner features a portrait of the late Bro. Richard Hobson and a painting of the baptism of Jesus.

Bro. Tom Quinn, a Past Master of the Lodge and one of the oldest Orangemen in the District, was presented with a Bicentenary Jewel by the District Master, Bro. Harold Gracey, at the annual Boyne Anniversary service at St. Saviour's, The Dobbin, in 1995. Later members of L.O.L. No.371 presented Bro. Quinn with a special certificate making his seventy-five years' membership of the Lodge.

There is a strong tradition of Lambeg drumming within this Lodge which has always been accompanied by drums on the 12 July. The last few years have seen a large influx of new young members into the Lodge which augurs well for the future of the L.O.L. No.371.

L.O.L. No.395 BATTLEHILL

No.395 was taken out by the Master and members of No.948 in 1895. The Lodge was first known as Eldon L.O.L.. Warrant No.948 was initially established in 1796 at Magarity with the then Master Thomas Bradshaw. During the period 1823-1827 the Lodge was meeting at Crowhill. By 1845 No.948 was meeting at Cranagill but in 1850 the number had ceased meeting. On 6 October 1851 the warrant was handed to Alexander Trotter but on 7 June 1852 he lodged it with the District Lodge. The following year in October 1853 the warrant was to be taken out again 'to be held in Corcullentrough' and by 1856 it was at Drumlellum before being returned, in 1857. In 1867 the warrant was working again and in the late 1800s the Lodge was meeting at Clonroot. James Hyde was Master in 1895 with the Lodge meetings held in Mullan's house, Clonroot in an area known locally as Hivy Gap. When No.948 finally ceased working in 1895 James Hyde became the Master of the new L.O.L. No.395.

When William J. Magee took over as Worshipful Master the Lodge moved to the 'Walk' area of Battlehill and erected a tin hut in Kelly's field in which to hold meetings. This move was necessitated after Mullan's house in Clonroot was burned down with the loss of the Lodge banner and one or two Lambeg drums.

A number of brethren from L.O.L. No.395 served during the Great War of whom four did not return, a Lambeg drum featuring a portrait of Lord Kitchener was dedicated by the Lodge to their memory. Bro. Robert Devlin, who was later to occupy the deputy chair, served in France. The Lodge has a photograph of him in his army uniform and also retains his service medals.

In 1930 Ballintaggart School House became vacant. Captain Lindsay of Hannavale House, another neighbour and Orangeman, became aware of this development and decided action was needed. He summoned Harry Grey W.M. of L.O.L. No.395 and Bob Devlin D.M. to a meeting and between them agreed to buy the school house for use as an Orange hall. The school house was bought from the Reverend Mr. Hogarth, Rector of St. Saviour's, at the Dobbin, for the sum of £175.

A new banner for L.O.L. No.395 was unfurled on 12 July 1936. The banner featured paintings of King William III crossing the Boyne and 'The Secret of England's Greatness'.

On Easter Monday 20 April 1981 the brethren of Portadown District assembled at Carleton Street and headed by the District Master, Bro. Herbert Whitten, paraded to Battlehill on the occasion of the re-opening of Battlehill Orange Hall.

The Lodge's present banner was unfurled on 11 July 1987. The front features a portrait of the late Captain R. H. Lindsay of Hannavale House, who was instrumental in organising the purchase of Ballintaggart Old School House for use as Battlehill Orange Hall.

In 1994 two flags were presented to the Lodge by Mrs. Kathleen Power and her daughter Pearl, in memory of her late husband Bro. Joseph Power, Past Master of the Lodge and late District Lecturer of Portadown.

L.O.L. No.417 DR KANE'S CRIMSON STAR, PORTADOWN

No.417 first met at Ballinteggart in 1796 with Robert Kinney as Master. In 1823 the Lodge was meeting at Mulladry but in 1850 it ceased working for a time. 1856 shows Daniel Magee as Master and the Lodge sitting at

Corcullentrabeg but by 1860 the warrant had been handed in again. In 1865 the Lodge was again working at this time under the name of Tavanagh True Blues, Portadown, and John Leckey was Master. The year 1888 saw Portadown's L.O.L. No.417 called Ranfurly Royal Purple Banner with Robert Courtney as Master. In 1896 the Lodge changed its name to Dr. Kane's Crimson Star and in 1905 No.417 amalgamated with No.322 but retained the warrant No.417.

L.O.L. No.417 unfurled their current banner on 20 May 1983. The ceremony was performed by the late Bro. Harold McCusker M.P.. The front of the banner is adorned with the Bible and Crown, with the All-Seeing Eye, whilst the reverse pictures King William III crossing the Boyne.

L.O.L. No.417 meets in Carleton Street Orange Hall.

L.O.L. No.500 HARMONY, PORTADOWN

On 24 September 1828, this warrant is recorded in Monaghan, Co. Monaghan with Rev. H. L. St. George as Master. In the Registry of 1856 the Lodge was still at Monaghan with Master Edward Smyth and in 1891 it was renewed to Joseph Lester Worshipful Master. The warrant was cancelled at the outbreak of the First World War in 1914. Warrant No.500 came to Portadown District on 14 June 1944 when the warrant was taken out in the name of Joshua Ward, Worshipful Master. The Lodge sat in Carleton Street Orange Hall.

Harmony L.O.L. No.500 became dormant in 1984.

L.O.L. No.608 PORTADOWN EX-SERVICEMEN'S

Warrant No.608 is another of the warrants that came to Portadown from southern Ireland. On 4 November 1828 it is recorded at Ballymaehigh, Co. Cavan with William Byers as Master. By 1856 it was still in Co. Cavan this time at Ballyjamesduff with Thomas Hawthorn as Master. In 1875 the Master was recorded as Rev. Snegde Taylor and although the warrant was renewed in November 1897 it was to be cancelled on 17 December 1930.

Portadown Ex-Servicemen's Lodge was formed on 14 February 1946 at a specially convened meeting of Portadown District. L.O.L. No.608 met for the first time under the new warrant on 8 September 1955. Since 8 September 1955 each meeting has begun with the Worshipful Master saying the Ex-Servicemen's Salutation followed by one minute's silence.

In June 1961 the old standard, which featured Battle Honours of World War Two, was handed over to the County Grand Deputy Master, Bro. W. Gracey J.P..

On 5 July 1962 a new standard, featuring the Battle Honours of World War Two was unfurled by the Lodge. The chairman at the meeting was the W.D.M., Bro. R. J. Magowan O.B.E., J.P..

On 11 April 1963 it was agreed by members of the Lodge that members and former members of the Territorial Army and the Ulster Constabulary be allowed to join the Lodge.

Bro. A. Rusk, a well-known personality in the town, joined the Lodge in 1964 on transfer from L.O.L. No.99. A former sergeant in the Royal Artillery, Bro. Rusk served in France with the British Expeditionary Force where he was evacuated from Dunkirk in 1940. Later in the war Bro. Rusk took part in the Normandy landings, seeing service in France, Belgium, Holland and Germany.

In 1965 the late Bro. W. Cardwell joined the Lodge on transfer from L.O.L. No.339. Bro. Cardwell had served with Lord Louis Mountbatten in South-East Asia and was a member of the Burma Star Association of which Lord Mountbatten was President. (A portrait of Lord Mountbatten is featured on the current standard of the Lodge.)

Portadown Ex-Servicemen's L.O.L. No.608 has the honour of leading all parades of Portadown District L.O.L. No.1. This tradition began in 1969 when the Lodge headed the Boyne Anniversary Church Parade to Drumcree. The following year the W.D.M., Bro. H. Whitten, again asked L.O.L. No.608 to lead the District church parade and also to lead the procession on 12 July.

L.O.L. No.608 has the eminent distinction of having provided no fewer than four mayors and one chairman of the two local government areas of Craigavon and Armagh. The mayors of Portadown who have been members of L.O.L. No.608 are Bro. Edward Cassells, Bro. Alfred Martin, Bro. Frank Dale and most recently Bro. Brian Maguiness who served as Mayor of Craigavon for the year 1994-95. In addition Bro. George McCartney was elected as chairman of Armagh District Council.

L.O.L. No.608 sits in Carleton Street Orange Hall.

RICHHILL DISTRICT L.O.L. No.2

The original name for Richhill was Legacorry, and in 1664 there were 20 houses in the village. Around 1681/82 permission was granted to Major Edward Richardson to hold a Saturday market and three fairs per year. The fairs were held on Shrove Tuesday, St. Swithin's Day and St. Francis Day. New orchards were being planted at this time and houses were springing up along the road sides.

In 1688 a party of the local Volunteer Light Dragoons left to take part in the Relief of Derry, and in 1690 part of the Williamite Army camped at Legacorry, en route to the Battle of the Boyne. We are told that much cider was consumed by soldiers in the spring of that year.

By 1736 Legacorry had become known as Richhill, probably so named by Edward Richardson or his wife. As one writer commented, "it was most appropriately named, in so much as it commands a full view of a country rich in pastures, plantations, orchards and grain fields".

Just across the road from the "Twelfth" field is Course Lodge, and it was adjacent to here that the famous Richhill Races were held each July for five days. It seems that Richhill in Race Week was the place to be. It attracted people from all classes, they arrived on foot and in carriages drawn by from one to six horses. Racing started each day at three o'clock to the accompaniment of ballad-singers, fiddlers and other side shows. Each morning was taken up with cock-fighting, a very popular sport at that time. It is a well known fact that the fighting never ended in the cockpit as the owners and their supporters often re-fought the contest in one of the many public houses in the village. Hunting with hounds was another popular sport at that time and unlike the cock-fighting still takes place, the surrounding countryside during the winter months echoing to the sound of the beagles and their handlers.

A Market House was built in the Square by William Richardson in 1753. It became a very important centre of the brown linen trade where in 1804 sales averaged at least £500 per week, despite rival markets in both Armagh and Portadown. The construction of a new road from Armagh to Belfast which by-passed Richhill triggered the decline of the weekly market and the three fairs. So it was that the Market House was converted into the Present Parish Church in 1837. It is interesting to note that in a census in 1814 Richhill had 161 dwellings, six more than Portadown. Occupations included hand loom weaving, straw platemaking, shuttle-making, wood turning and spademaking.

By 1835 the three Miss Richardsons, who now owned the estate, and were described as excellent landlords, had built many new country schools on the estate, Mulladry and Derryhale being two examples.

With the coming of the railway in 1848, again by-passing Richhill the village became even more isolated. With the markets having died out and the advent of weaving factories most of the hand looms became redundant and the population decreased. Occupations too were changing and the village now had two tanneries and a fruit preserving factory.

Moving into the 20th century Richhill became famous as a furniture making centre with at least four fairly large factories producing all kinds of household and office furniture. This trade is still very much in evidence with the manual skills and the machinery having changed to produce the type of furniture in demand for modern homes.

Modern homes are something Richhill has in abundance. Over the past thirty years the population has spiralled and the "Best Kept Village" of the sixties is now in the small town category. Even the centre of the village has not escaped the developers with the greatest changes being evident in the vicinity of the War Memorial. Here new self contained flats for the elderly have replaced the once impressive Legacorry House. The old Congregational Church cum Orange Hall has now been converted into a Day Centre for the handicapped.

Richhill Castle. Ancestral Home of the Richardsons

Built between 1664 and 1669 Richhill Castle is steeped in history. It stands on the site of an earlier dwelling erected by Francis Sacheverall, a planter from Rossbye in Leicestershire in 1611.

In 1610 Sacheverall had received two portions of land, 1000 acres in each, called Mullalelish and Legacorry and decided to live on the latter. He declared himself to be worth £300 a year and brought over from England with him, three masons, one carpenter, one smithy, nine labourers, two women four horses and a cart. Before his death in 1649 Sacheverall had sold the Mullalelish portion to Sir William Alexander, a Scottish speculator who was later honoured with the title "Earl of Stirling".

Francis Sacheverall's son and heir, also called Francis, and his wife Dorothy had only one child, a girl named Anne, who married Major Edward Richardson in 1654. Major Richardson was M.P. and High Sheriff for Armagh. Through this marriage Legacorry became the property of the Richardson family and the present castle was built.

The Richardsons originally came from Pershore in Worcestershire, and a branch of the family later settled in Rossfad, Ballinamallard, Co. Fermanagh.

Edward and Anne Richardson had two sons, William and John. William was M.P. for Armagh when King William III camped at Scarva. He married Elizabeth, daughter of Lord Chief Justice Reynell in 1695, they had no family. John Richardsons grandson, also called William, followed his great-uncle into politics and served as M.P. for Armagh for many years.

This William Richardsons first wife, Dorothy Munroe, was the celebrated Dolly Munroe, who at seventeen was acclaimed the most beautiful girl in all Ireland. When she went to visit her aunt, Lady Loftus, in Dublin, she was the object of such admiration that she could not walk in the Mall because of the crowd of undesired worshippers. Instead she had to rise at 6am and take her exercise in St. Stephens Green to ensure some privacy. Dolly and William were married in 1775, but sadly she died, childless, in 1793.

William Richardson's second wife however, bore him three daughters, Elizabeth, Isabella and Louisa, who collectively inherited the village, now called Richhill, and the rest of the estate. It is recorded that these three ladies were remarkable for their charity to the poor of the neighbourhood, and generously supported many worthy causes. Only the youngest, Louisa, was married. Her husband, Edward Bacon, was High Sheriff of Armagh and as she had no family the estate passed to the Rossfad Richardsons after her death in 1881.

In the early part of this century the castle was the residence of Major Robert Gordon Berry and there are some stories surrounding him involving secret passages, skeletons and a grave in the castle grounds. After the establishment of the Government of Northern Ireland in 1920, the castle became the property of the Northern Ireland Education Authority. During the 1930s it was occupied by a Mr. Sam Hewitt, whose main claim to fame was the invention of an egg washing machine.

Architecturally Richhill Castle is described as a two storey building with a gabled attic in a high pitched roof. It consists of a centre range plus a wing at each end with Dutch gables. There are four similar, but smaller gables on the centre range, and on the inner face of each wing. It is typical of many mansions built throughout Europe in the 17th century .

According to one famous archaeologist, Francis J. Biggar, "the glory of the place is the extended range of iron gates and railings at the main entrance to the castle." No finer specimen of wrought ironwork remains in Ireland today," he said. These gates were made by the Thornberry Brothers of Armagh in 1745, they were eighteen to twenty feet high and topped with the Richardson family's Coat of Arms.

Unfortunately you cannot see these magnificent gates in Richhill today. In 1936 they were removed by night to Hillsborough Castle, then the residence of the Governor of Northern Ireland, which was being renovated after a fire in 1934. In spite of a storm of protest from local councillors and the people of the village at this high-handed move by the Civil Service, the gates were never returned. One consolation, I suppose is that they are being well looked after, and over the years many thousands of people have admired them at the front of Government House as they visited the historic conservation Village of Hillsborough.

At present the castle and five acres of woodland is owned and occupied by three families of Lyttles, and is also the headquarters of their Land Surveying business. It is to their credit that they have not changed the exterior, though some modernisations have been carried out to the interior.

Orangeism in Richhill and District

The first reference to Orangeism in the Richhill area is of two meetings held on the 17th and 18th of March 1796, attended by the tenantry of the manors of Legacorry and Mullalelish. At this meeting Orange Associations were formed to protect the Protestant people of this district against the outrages being continued throughout the country .The following resolution was unanimously passed:-

> *"That every honest man should protect himself and his neighbour against the present outrages, and give information to the nearest magistrate against every person who violates the peace, no matter what his profession. We also pledge at the hazard of life and fortune to support and defend the King, George the Third, against all foreign and domestic enemies. We further resolve to discourage and oppose all with their treasonable intent"*

At the turn of the century Richhill District L.O.L. No.2 consisted of seven Lodges and held its meetings in the Parochial Hall. The oldest District records show that in 1936 total membership was 170 made up thus: No.11 Ballyleany 23, No.47 Hamiltonsbawn 30, No.54 Cloughan 22, No.79 Sleepy Valley 10, No.114 Rockmacreaney 34, No.312 Irish Street 12, and No.665 Parochial Hall 39.

The next Lodge to get into difficulty was L.O.L. No.79, their warrant was handed in to the District on April 28th 1937 by Bros. G. Kennedy and F.

Hewitt, six pounds was also handed over which was to be used to maintain their former hall, a tin hut in Sleepy Valley. Permission was granted to Greenview Dart Club to use the old L.O.L. No.79 in return for a rent of six shillings per quarter. This hall was later sold in June 1942 to a Mrs. Morrison from Markethill to be used by the Y.M.C.A. and can now be seen in use as a cattle shed on the Ballygroobany Road.

In January 1942 a committee was formed to negotiate the purchase of Richhill Congregational Church which they did successfully, their bid of £300 being accepted on the 18th of May. Bro. Bob Buckley was appointed caretaker and being a handyman spent many hours repairing and improving the property. One pew was given to L.O.L. No.47 and the rest were sold. The new hall was used regularly by the following organisations, Greenview Dart Club, Richhill Part Flute Band, The Home Guard, L.O.L. No.665 and R.B.P. 113. The last two paying a charge of 50 shillings per year. Note that the April 1944 electric bill came to £1-6s-7d, or £1.33 in todays money.

With parades resuming after the Second World War, the new bannerette purchased for £10 in 1940 was unfurled in July 1945, by Past District Master Bro. William Nellins. The previous summer a new drum bearing General Montgomery's portrait was unveiled by his mother, for L.O.L. No.11 at Ballyleaney. The banner formerly carried by L.O.L. No.79 was sold to Derryhennett L.O.L. No.37 in 1946. The District had a choice of "Twelfth" venues in 1945, having been invited by both Portadown and Armagh, they decided to go to Armagh as train times were more suitable. A similar situation arose in 1946 between Markethill and Armagh, again the latter was chosen. The county returned to a single demonstration in 1947 with Tandragee District as host.

Until 1959 the Annual Service was held in the Parish Church every year, but changes had been suggested in 1957 and in 1960 it was agreed to go to the Presbyterian Church, since then the District Service rotates around the Church of Ireland, Presbyterian and Methodist Churches. Richill Conservative Part Flute Band headed this Parade every year since records began until 1966 when they disbanded. After that Hamiltonsbawn and Rockmacraney were invited on alternate years to lead the parade on the Sunday before the Twelfth.

Although the selling of the Orange Hall by L.O.L. No.665 in 1993 surprised most people, in fact, they first discussed this action over thirty years ago. The District Hall had been handed over, free of charge, to them on 26th of April 1950, with clauses covering future use, sale, or event of "665" ceasing to exist. On 21st of January 1961 they reported to the District meeting their intentions to sell, a proposed exchange for the Masonic Hall was also mentioned. Later L.O.L. No.665 let their hall to a religious body for £50 per year and the situation eased for the time being. But the issue didn't go away and on 29th January 1986 it was again reported that L.O.L. No.665 was looking a buyer for their hall. This buyer was eventually found, and at a special meeting on the 13th February 1993 the District Lodge gave their approval to L.O.L. No.665 to proceed with the sale" and their plans to build a new hall next door, on ground which they already owned.

In order to save money the warrant No.312 was handed in after the October meeting in 1962, L.O.L. No.312 had been dormant for some years. Their last known meeting places were the old school-house beside the Parish Church and in rooms at what is now "Ye Olde House Bar" in Irish Street.

An interesting contradiction happened in the late nineteen sixties. In January 1965 a letter of confidence was sent to Rt. Hon. Terence O'Neill, Prime Minister, after his meeting with the Eire Prime Minister, Sean Lemass.

Grand Lodge had also expressed pleasure at Prime Minister O'Neill's action and hoped it would lead to better trade relations with Eire. Four years later however, the District Lodge had changed their opinion and the following resolution was passed, "that this Lodge has no confidence in the Prime Minister of Northern Ireland, Capt. Terence O'Neill". This attitude was also apparent in 1972 when it was rumoured that all "Twelfth" parades would be banned. As Richhill were the hosts that year it was unanimously agreed that they would hold a rally, irrespective of whether the rest of the county came or not!

A new District bannerette was unfurled in July 1966 by Bro. Hamilton Hawthorne, W.D.M., and dedicated by Canon John Cockrill, it cost £19. The effects of rampant inflation can be seen here because twelve years later in 1978 another new bannerette cost £60. It was unfurled by Bro. James Nicholl, W.D.M. in June and dedicated at the Annual Service in July.

The "Twelfth" has come to Richhill Village in the years 1892, 1905, 1919, 1925, 1936, 1963, 1972, 1983 and 1994. There was also a demonstration in Hamiltonsbawn in 1819. At the "Twelfth" in 1983 an Orange Arch was erected in the Village. Made in 1939 by Bro. Billy Forbes at a cost of £5, it was originally erected each year outside Cloncore Orange Hall on the Dungannon-Birches road. After a road widening scheme due to the building of the motorway, it was then too short for the site and was put into storage. There it remained until 1983 when Bro. George McAdam, a native of the Birches, along with the District Officers successfully negotiated its transfer to Richhill. After repainting, mainly carried out by Bro. James Gwynne of

L.O.L. No.114, it was erected on the 2nd of July beside the War Memorial. Bro. McAdam was also instrumental in bringing another of Bro. Forbes' arches to the district. This arch came from Derrykeevin and was first erected outside his premises, "The Bawn Inn", sixteen years ago.

A new bannerette was unfurled in 1990 as part of the Tercentenary of the Boyne celebrations, which included a parade of fancy dress, floats and a detachment of the Williamite army, to the recreation ground on the New Line where sports and side-shows entertained the crowds.

Since the start of the recent period of Terrorist violence in 1969 (universally called the "Troubles") three Brethren from this District have been murdered.

Bro. Hugh Turbitt, L.O.L. No.11,
R.U.C. Constable, killed in 1978.

Bro. Jackson Hogg, L.O.L. No.47,
shot while returning to his car in Armagh City car park, after work.

Bro. Paul Bleakley, L.O.L. No.665,
Private in the U.D.R., blown up in the Glenanne UDR base in 1991 while on guard duty.

In addition one Brother Orangeman from L.O.L. No.47 had a sister killed on a train by a bomb while returning home from work for the weekend and another Brother from L.O.L. No.114 lost his daughter when she was killed by a bomb, on a train from Belfast.

THE PRIVATE LODGES OF RICHHILL DISTRICT

BALLYLEANEY PURPLE STAR L.O.L. No.11

The first written record we have of L.O.L. No.11 appears on 9th August 1796, less than a year after the Battle of the Diamond. The entry appears merely as a list of fifty-three names, the first of which is a Brother William Jackson.

The list of names makes interesting reading as a lot of them would no longer be regarded as familiar Richhill names, such as Sprent, High and Whitley. There was even a Captain Charles Henry Porter of the 23rd Light Dragoons at that time stationed at Armagh.

It would appear that in those early days L.O.L. No.11 had a strong and boisterous membership as fines would seem to have been levied at regular intervals for various misdemeanours some as trivial as arriving half an hour late and smoking in the Lodge rooms.

Detailed minutes of meetings are available from 1911. In 1912 it is noted that brethren took part in drill movements as many of them had joined Sir Edward Carson's Ulster Volunteers. In October 1913 it was proposed by Brother George Running and Seconded by Brother T. Magowan that L.O.L. No.11 become a temperance Lodge. It was also around this time that the Lodge started to hold meetings in the Temperance Hall, Tandragee Street, which had been rented from Mr. D. W. Kane for thirty shillings a year.

Two brethren are mentioned in the Lodge minutes as having been killed in action. They were Brother Alexander McKee and Brother John Creaney.

After the Great War the Lodge membership began to rise. In October 1918 a bed was sponsored by the Lodge in the U.V.F. Hospital, Belfast, for the sum of five shillings in the memory of Lieutenant James M. Armstrong. In March 1921 L.O.L. No.11 moved to Ballyleaney and a new hall was opened in 1923.

In Post War years membership of the Lodge remained fairly static until the early 80's when new housing developments in Richhill brought an influx to the population which has resulted in the Lodge steadily growing in membership and has peaked at round 60 brethren. Wor. Bro. Matthew Clarke, District Master, is a member of this Lodge.

HAMILTONSBAWN GUIDING STAR L.O.L. No.47

This Lodge was formed in 1796 one year after the Battle of the Diamond. It first sat in a house or barn belonging to a Martin Albin of Markethill Road, Hamiltonsbawn, also known as Barrack Hill. The first W.M. was John Beck. The Lodge then moved to sit in a room in Beck's house. In the other end of this house was Beck's pub or tavern, which today is known as the Bawn Inn.

Although no official records of the Lodge exist until 1862, other evidence is available to prove that the Lodge was active since 1796. There is evidence that the warrant was renewed in 1799, 1817, 1824 and 1899.

In 1819 Portadown and Richhill Districts held their 12th of July demonstration in Hamiltonsbawn.

In the early years of the 20th century it was decided to build an Orange hall, although no mention of an Orange hall appears in the minutes until 1913. It must have been planned for a number of years beforehand as fund raising dances and socials were held in Albin's Barn on Barrack Hill Hamiltonsbawn, from 1902 onwards. James Glenny Fergus and Joe Clydesdale raised money for the building of the hall when they worked as overseers on the Pennsylvania rail-road, by collecting from the workers each pay-day. The hall was built in 1914 on a site donated by James Glenny Fergus, and later Bro. Hugh Fergus donated more land to build a kitchen and toilets. The hall was built by voluntary labour and after the foundations were laid the complete brickwork was built to the square on one Saturday with six horses and carts drawing bricks to the builders. Prominent among the builders were Jacksons, Whittens, Fergus, Parks, McLoughlins and Andersons.

The Lodge set out from their new hall on the 12th July for the first time in 1915, in the words of the then Secretary "the Lodge left without either flag or music".

Until 1925 the Lodge carried a flag and their first banner was purchased in along with Deacon poles for £33. Between the Wars the Lodge gained a reputation for Lambeg drumming but in 1945 J. Nicholl and J. Jackson put the drums down in the Hall and said that the Lodge either train drummers or start a band. The first band used accordions but they got soaked at the Twelfth in Portadown in 1946 so the Lodge started a silver band instead. Practice began in 1947 with Dick Irwin as tutor. Hamiltonsbawn Silver Band has gone from strength to strength and now has over 30 members and is in great demand for parades, church services, concerts and fetes.

Wor. Bro. Alexander Nicholl, Deputy District Master, is a member of this Lodge.

The Village of Hamiltonsbawn

Hamiltonsbawn takes it's name from John Hamilton, a nobleman from East Lothian in Scotland, who was granted a tract of land by King James I in the year of 1619. He brought with him 30 soldiers and 26 families, to hold possession of and to work the land. John Hamilton built a Bawn, (a fortified farmhouse surrounded by an 18-feet high defensive wall). This lime and stone building stood outside the present village on the road to Markethill, and the village grew up around the junction of the Armagh-Tandragee Road and the Richhill-Markethill Road.

During the rebellion of 1641 the Bawn came under attack from a raiding party led by Owen Roe O'Neill in which it took a severe pounding and was almost destroyed.

Hamilton's daughter married into the Acheson family of Markethill, (the Achesons were later elevated to the peerage as Earls of Gosford in 1806). Arthur Acheson and his wife wanted to rebuild the Bawn but couldn't decide whether it should become a Malthouse or a Barrack. After lengthy debates between them and their friend Dean Swift work started in 1729 to build a Barrack.

It is said that Dean Swift was very impressed by the hardworking people of Hamiltonsbawn and wrote a humerous little poem about the village as follows:

"Newry town for mice and rats,
Armagh city for dogs and cats,
Hamiltonsbawn that keeps no Sunday,
For every day is an Easter Monday."

By the end of the 19th century Hamiltonsbawn was a thriving community with over one hundred hand loom weavers working in their own homes. There were also two very famous hire fairs held each year on the 26th of May and the 26th of November, except Sundays, when servants were hired for six months at an agreed wage. It became a local school holiday because the children were needed to help bring the animals to the fairs, they also had a rhyme which went:

Twenty sixth of May, The 'Bawn fair day,
If wc don't get a holiday, We'll all run away.

In the early nineteen thirties the hiring fair had died out, but its passing was mourned by one local at least who wrote:-

"It was a gran' hirin' fair they used till have here, but who needs servant boys now? Shure the young fellas now wud rather drive a bus or go till Ameriky or one of them foreign places, than feel the reigns atween their fingers. Aye it's a hard life the farmers have but its good till be alive an in the fiel's with the horses at times. Ye have a guess as till how the saysons go when yer in the open. Not but what they've changed too. I doubt whether it wus wise till alter the clock. Shure what has foolish man till do with God's own time?

But mind ye I'm not denyin' the long evenin's is good for them that has time till skite about, but what about the mornin's an the dew on the grass, an nothin' a doin' at all, at all, until it's nearin' the middle of the day".

There are no churches actually in Hamiltonsbawn at present, the last known church was a Presbyterian congregation which met for worship in a building on the site where 43 Main Street is now situated. This building had also been used as a school in the past, and L.O.L. No.47 met there, prior to the existence of the present Orange Hall. The Presbyterians built a Meeting House of their own at Druminnis and moved there in June 1842.

CLOUGHAN CRIMSON STAR L.O.L. No.54

The first record of a Warrant for No.54 is in 1798 and the first W.M. was John Foster.

The present warrant for L.O.L. No.54 was issued to James Morrison on 28th May 1898.

The Lodge initially sat in the home of James and Bessie Gates. It then moved to the house of John Scarr which was a short distance from the site of the present hall.

The Stronges of Tynan Abbey owned Hockley Lodge and they provided land and financial support for the construction of a purpose built hall in the townland of Hockley close to its border with Cloughan. In accordance with their wishes the hall was named Hockley and Cloughan Protestant Hall. It was opened in 1899. The deeds were later passed to the Lodge.

In May 1947 the Lodge gave permission for a new R.B.P. to sit in the hall and some of the Lodge members were founder members.

The Lodge concerned itself with the welfare of its members and their families from early times, examples are, registering suitable members for the National Insurance Act in 1912 and a payment made to help a member who was hurt in an accident in February 1923. In September 1938 the Lodge decided to present a Bible to any member who got married and since then quite a number of presentations have been made.

Members of the Lodge served in the 36th Ulster Division during the First World War and a number of them fell in action. In 1920 the Lodge commissioned a banner from Belfast depicting the Battle of the Somme based on the painting by J. P. Beadle. The names of the Battles at which the brethren had fought were included on the Banner namely the Somme, Kamel, Thiepval, Messines, Ploegst, Wyshaete, Kemmel and St. Quentin. After the war the Lodge made a donation to the endowment of a memorial bed for the late Bro. J. Stronge at the U.V.F. Hospital.

This support for the armed services continued during the Second World War. While some of the brethren served in the Armed Forces, the remaining brethren ran events to raise money for the Red Cross and the Soldiers Comforts Fund.

The Lodge has also shown interest in political events ranging from a petition to both houses of parliament about the budget in 1909, signed by all members, to the present protests against the Anglo-Irish Agreement.

Through its history the Lodge has had many esteemed members who have given long service. Some of those from past years were Bro. John Morrison P.M. who attended the Lodge without absence for 66 years until July 1938 when he was affected by ill health. Bro. George Robinson, a member for 70 years and W.M. for 30 years until his death in August 1940 and J. K. Hamilton who received the M.B.E. in 1973 and had held various offices in the Lodge up until his death later that year.

ROCKMACRANEY TEMPERANCE L.O.L. No.114

The warrant for this Lodge was originally issued to Bro. Thomas Hutchinson in 1823. No records are available for the first years, but the Lodge met at Hockley. Another known meeting place was a loft at a farmhouse in the townland of Mullinasilla. This farmhouse is now occupied by Miss May Irwin.

In 1867, Orange parades were banned by the Government, but L.O.L. No.114 refused to comply and broke the ban. The W.M. Bro. Michael Mallon was arrested and brought to court, where, it is said, the R.M. remarked that he had a very unusual name for an Orangeman.

On the 6th September 1909 the warrant was renewed and issued to Bro. Christopher Graham and the Lodge then moved to the present property at Rockmacraney. It was formerly a dwelling house occupied by the Haire family, and was known locally as the "Haire's Den".

The Orange Hall was officially opened on the 5th November 1913. In 1961 an extension comprising of a kitchen and storerooms was built onto the original ball, an work being carried out voluntarily.The roof for this extension came from the old R.I.C. barracks in Irish Street, Armagh, which was given to the Lodge on condition that they removed it themselves and knocked down the walls before they left the site.

In the early part of this century Rockmacraney had a flute band which ceased to function in 1927. On the "Twelfths" of 1928-1930 two pipers from Markethill were hired at a cost of £3-10s-0d plus train fares to the demonstrations and back. These two pipers were not available in 1931 and Battlehill Pipe Band met the Lodge at Killylea railway station and lead them to the field.

Walking behind a Pipe Band must have appealed to the brethren of L.O.L. No.114, because in October of that year they started their own Pipe Band with the assistance of Bro. Edward "Ned" Pearson from the Battlehill Band who then transferred to L.O.L. No.114. Bro. Samuel Pillow is the only remaining member of the Lodge who was present at the inaugural band practice, and remembers that the bands first outing was to the opening of Mullabrack Orange Hall.

Over the years the Pipe Band has had several successes in the contest arena, most notable being two All-Ireland Championship wins in 1965 and 1966, under the late Pipe Major Bro. Albert Albin who retired in 1969. In 1989 the Band moved to premises of their own when they purchased the old Wastelands Primary School building.

It was decided in 1932, that the new Pipe Band be dedicated to the memory of four brethren from L.O.L. No.114 who had paid the supreme sacrifice while serving their King and Country in the Great War of 1914-18. They were: Bro. Thomas Albin, killed in action at Ypres in Flanders; Bro. Frank Best, killed in November 1918 serving with the North Irish Horse; Bro. Harry Hynes and Bro. John Neville, 36th Ulster Division, both killed in action on 1st July 1916 at the Battle of the Somme.

Three other members also served during the Great War: Bro. William Allen, North Irish Horse, Bro. James Quinn, Royal Irish Rifles, and Bro. Thomas McMurray. The minutes of the March meeting in 1916 record that the six serving brethren should receive a present of cigarettes.

The banner carried by L.O.L. No.114 depicts Saul trying to kill David.

Nowadays the Lodge assembles in Richhill on the "Twelfth" morning, this is a far cry from the days when they used to walk from the Hall to either Richhill or Hamiltonsbawn railway station in the morning, take the train to the demonstration and walk back again in the afternoon.

RICHHILL TRUE BLUES TEMPERANCE L.O.L. No.665

The warrant of L.O.L. No.665 dates back as far as 1823 when it was first issued to a Mr. Philip Kelly in the Markethill District. Records show that in 1835 the warrant was then held by the Charlemont District, which is now non-existent. During the next twenty years the warrant went dormant, but was again re-issued in 1856 in Glenanne, of the Markethill District. The following forty years once again saw the warrant going dormant until it was again re-issued to Worshipful Master, John Colvin of the Richhill District; where the Lodge sat at Ballynahinch under the name of "Boyle's Blues". In 1889 the warrant was again re-issued to John Colvin and the Lodge transferred to the Church of Ireland Parochial Hall and was re-named Richhill True Blues Temperance. The Lodge sat in the Parochial Hall until the mid 1940s whereupon it moved to the Congregational Church at the War Memorial when Richhill District acquired the old church as a District Hall.

In the 1950s the District gave the hall over to the Lodge where they continued to sit until 1993. At this stage it was deemed necessary to agree to the sale of the hall because of disrepair, hence the hall was sold in September 1993 and a new Hall was built.

LOUGHGALL DISTRICT L.O.L. No.3

Loughgall District L.O.L. No.3 consists of 22 Lodges stretching across an area from near Armagh through and around Loughgall Village beyond Annaghmore and The Birches to the shores of Lough Neagh. It covers parts of Co. Armagh and intrudes into Co. Tyrone.

Loughgall, situated in a verdant and fertile valley, and recently designated a Conservation Area has changed little over the years. There are many listed buildings with Georgian and Regency architecture which add to the distinctive appearance of the village. The surrounding area, noted for its orchards and famous Bramley apples, is often referred to as "The Garden of Ireland." It is recorded that quartermasters with King William's army purchased large quantities of cider here in 1690 for the refreshment of the troops.

It is known that a religious settlement existed in Loughgall from the ninth century although it was not until the restoration work following the Civil War of the 1640's that the settlement took on the appearance of an English village. The Old Court House (1776) in Main Street has been restored and is now a centre for antiques. Across the street is James Sloan's house where the first Orange warrant was signed in blood following the Battle of the Diamond on the 21st September 1795. Part of the house is now the Orange Museum.

The oldest structure in the village is the ruins of the old church in the graveyard and it serves as a stark reminder of earlier conflicts. Loughgall has suffered over the years and most latterly during the Troubles at the hands of terrorists.

As Loughgall strides towards the future the village is delighted with Armagh City and District Council's ambitious plans to develop part of the Manor-Estate into a country park with leisure facilities and golf course.

1995 was an important year for the village for it was the bicentenary of both the Orange Order and St. Luke's Church of Ireland Parish Church. The District Officers, working closely with the County Lodge officers and the then County Grand Master and Loughgall Brother, Rt.Wor Bro. Norman Allen, planned a mammoth Orange parade in Loughgall to celebrate the Bicentenary of the Battle of the Diamond. Starting at the Diamond Memorial Orange Hall and passing the two Winter family cottages and the recently –erected memorial to the Orangemen who fell in the Battle, an estimated 30,000 brethren paraded behind their District Bannerettes into the Field where a mock battle was fought by the Scarva Brethren, and returned home via Loughgall village, passing Sloan's House and the saluting platform.

Many people thought that such a large parade along narrow country lanes could never be successfully carried out and anyway where could hundreds of buses be parked?

The Loughgall brethren managed to overcome all such problems and the parade was a major success.

In this age of the motor car, people with more leisure time and the interest in visiting sites important for understanding our heritage, it was realised that the site of the Battle of the Diamond was not easily recognised. The Late County Grand Master, Rt. Wor. Bro. Norman Hood promoted the idea that the site should be clearly marked by the erection of a monument. Indeed he suggested that this had been a serious oversight since the Centenary Celebrations of 1895.

Suggestions for the design of the monument were accepted by the County Armagh Diamond Committee. The contract for the cutting of the stone in black ebony granite was awarded to Messrs Cheevers of Armagh. The contract for the construction of the base was awarded to Bro. William Neill and the railings to Bro. James George of Cabragh. The monument was unveiled by Most Wor. Bro. Charles Ferrel, Imperial Grand Master on Thursday 21st September 1995 and was dedicated by Most Wor. Bro. Rev. Martin Smyth, Grand Master of Ireland.

The inscription reads:-

THIS MONUMENT IS ERECTED
BY THE COUNTY
GRAND LODGE OF ARMAGH
TO COMMEMORATE
THE BICENTENARY OF
THE FORMATION OF
THE ORANGE ORDER AFTER
THE BATTLE OF THE DIAMOND
ON THE 21ST SEPTEMBER 1795

Each year the District is indebted to the various Churches where the brethren join in religious services. For the four Sundays preceding the 12th July the following Churches play host to Loughgall District and visitors from further afield:

Cranagill Methodist Church
Grange Parish Church
Tartaraghan Presbyterian Church
Cloveneden Presbyterian Church
Tartaraghan Parish Church
Loughgall Parish Church
Milltown Parish Church
Annaghmore Parish Church.

A Parade and Service is also held in September each year to commemorate the Battle of the Diamond. We are grateful to Lodge Nos.85, 118 (Loughgall District) 35 (Portadown District) each year for organising what is probably the most relevant service in the Orange Institution.

The parade passes the site of the battle on its way to the Diamond Memorial Orange Hall, where the organising brethren are always delighted to welcome visitors.

Seven members of Loughall District have been murdered by terrorists in the present period of "troubles"

Bro. George McCall, L.O.L. No.1287
murdered in 1975

Bro. Eric Lutton, L.O.L. No.1287
murdered in 1979

Bro. James Hewitt, L.O.L. No.85
murdered in 1980

Bro. Melvin Simpson, L.O.L. No.1287
murdered in 1984

Bro. Stephen McKinney, L.O.L. No.36
murdered in 1988

Bro. John Griffiths, L.O.L. No.36
murdered in in 1989

Bro. Eric Smyth, L.O.L. No.36
murdered in 1994

The Diamond

Tucked away in the peaceful townland of Grange - O'Neilland is the historical 'Diamond'.

Open hostility on the part of the Roman Catholics or Defenders towards their Protestant neighbours began around 1791-92.

This came to a head in the Summer of 1795 when Protestant Orange Boys (a club started in Tyrone in 1792 by James Wilson - a near relative of Daniel Winter) heard of the Defenders plan to burn all the Protestant homes in the Richhill, Kilmore and Loughgall districts. The Protestants prepared themselves for action and they concentrated from various quarters to a position at the Diamond.

The early hours of 21st September 1795 was the climax of a 3 day struggle from opposite hills overlooking the Diamond Crossroads. The Defenders on Faughart Hill (Tullymore), The Orange Boys and their allies on the Diamond Hill (Grangemore). A farmer named Daniel Winter and his sons owned the field of action between the two hills, the ancestral home in the farmyard and the property at the Diamond Crossroads.

During the battle, the property at the Crossroads was burned and became uninhabitable.

Daniel Winter and his sons defended their property as long as possible, having to retreat to the Diamond Hill when the thatch was fired.

"Capt" McGarry of Whitecross had taken over the leadership of the Defenders from Quigley who had been associated with the truce. At first light, shortly after 5a.m. on the Monday morning the Defenders stole down into the valley hoping to catch the Winters asleep. However the Cottage was stoutly defended and a furious battle raged for its possession.

James Wilson, had he been a less able commander, would have been tempted to go to the Winter's immediate assistance but he held his ground and waited.

Inevitably the thatch of the cottage caught fire and before long Dan and his sons were forced to give up the fight and withdraw. There were no doors at the back but the windows afforded an escape route. The Orange Boys gave covering fire while the Winters came up the hill to join them on the top.

Meantime according to Sibbett's account "the Cottage was completely wrecked. All the contents, which mainly consisted of drink and victuals, for he carried on the joint business of a publican and a grocer, speedily disappeared. The whiskey and the beer, as faithfully recorded, were run off, the barrels that held them were knocked into staves, the bags of meal and flour, and the supplies of tea and sugar were scattered on the street, the webs of linen and piles of yarn were thrown everywhere, the furniture was smashed, and the roof of the house was torn away!"

The neighbouring cottages which had been vacated by their terrified occupants were also ransacked by the mob. The scattered Defenders now proceeded in a disorganised mass up the hill behind the cottage led by McGarry.

At the top a field hedge hid the Orange Boys from view. On the hedge tradition relates some hats had been placed to allow the Defenders some target practice and waste their powder and ball.

About 100 yards back from the hedge - the effectual range of a "Brown Bess" musket, stood the Orange Boys in ranks.

Rev. John Brown writes 'The Protestants who had served in the Volunteers stepped out, dressed their line according to the drillbook, and fired a destructive volley from their commanding position and from close at hand, directly into the disorganised mob of Defenders. This won the battle, the Defenders poured back through the Diamond, still under heavy fire'. Sibbett relates "The Ballyargan Boys, at a given signal, led a strong contingent down the slope and violently engaged the enemy. Hand to hand fighting ensued in the Diamond proper, with the result, in less than half an hour, the Defenders were routed'.

Various Orange Historians relate how young Blacker was now approaching with reinforcements from Portadown and from another direction, about sixty invalid soldiers from Charlemont, headed by Mr. Atkinson and Captain Killeney. The Defenders in their flight left behind them white and green banners, rude weapons, tattered uniforms and a variety of religious emblems. The gun which Quigley had fired also fell into the hands of the victors, along with his rallying standard, a white flag with a border of green shamrocks and in the centre a painted representation of the Virgin Mary presiding as a goddess: 'The Queen of Heaven". It had an inscription reading:-

"Deliver us from the heretic dogs and we will be free".

The carts brought to transport the plunder were now employed to remove the Defenders who had fallen in the struggle, numbering forty eight, included

Capt. McGarry. Many were interred in the old burying ground in the neighbourhood of Ballygawley.

How many were wounded in the rebel host no one but themselves could tell; but they were roughly estimated at 50.

Tradition passed down the Winter family line from Daniel c 1730, one of the founding fathers of the Orange Society, is that the first embryonic meeting of The Orange Society as we know it took place in the ancestral home in the farmyard 100 yards from the Diamond Crossroads.

Following the battle, the main leaders including James Wilson, Daniel Winter and James Sloan needed to get away from the throng to plan and think. They needed a representative readily available to act for the whole body. James Sloan was chosen as Secretary. He was an educated man, a former schoolmaster, who owned an Inn on the main street in Loughgall.

Discussion took place to outline the new organisation and it was decided to hold further discussion later in the house of James Sloan. In the actual room where these founding fathers met, are to be seen old muskets and pikes as well as an old sword found many years ago in the thatch. All had been used at the Battle of the Diamond. Heavy lead shot has been found recently in the roof space of this famous house.

When Daniel Winter was making enquiries and getting reports in favour of union amongst Protestants for the new organisation, he and his son Daniel were living, in the house better known as the Birthplace of Orangeism "Dan Winters House" The Diamond. The house and land are still owned by direct descendants of the much celebrated Dan.

Warrant No.1 was secured by James Wilson, of the Dyan, near Caledon, in the County of Tyrone.

No.2 was given to Thomas Sinclair, of Derryscollop, County of Armagh. He became a Lieutenant in the Churchill Corps of Yeomanry, and discharged the duties of an inspector under the Irish Linen Board. He was a substantial farmer and linen manufacturer; took part in the Battle of the Diamond; and held the position of Master of the Lodge until his death.

No.3 passed to Mr. Bartley, of Derryaughill, between the towns of Moy and Blackwatertown, respectively situated in Tyrone and Armagh. He was a master tailor, and was so proud of his prize, and so anxious to communicate the news to his neighbours, that he swam across the Blackwater River, always swollen in winter, in order to take a short cut to his home.

No.4 fell to Mr. Lockhart, of Knocknacloy, in the County of Tyrone.

No.5 was allotted to Robert Irwin, of Kinnego, in the County of Armagh. The informant was his son James, an old Orangeman, who said his father was initiated behind a ditch.

No.6 went to a resident in Killylea, Co. of Armagh, but his name has not been discovered.

No.7 was given to Thomas Lecky, of Breath, in the County of Armagh. He was a man of resolute character, a leader at the battle of the Diamond; and among the first to undertake dangerous enterprises. It was he that inflicted severe punishment on O'Neill in Loughgall fair. Among the old people in the neighbourhood the tradition is that Lecky arrived at Sloan's house when No.7 was about to be made out for another person. Lecky, however flourished an immense blackthorn stick in his hand, declaring he would disperse the meeting if he did not get the Number. Therefore, it was assigned to him for peace sake. This Lodge, in the beginning, often met in a lime kiln.

No.8 passed to Richard Robinson, of Timakeel, and is still in the Portadown District, but not at Timakeel.

No.9 was issued to a man in the neighbourhood of Portadown, but we are unable to discover his name.

No.10 became the property of George Templeton, one of the three who stormed Faughart Fort.

No.28 fell to James Sloan. Among the members were Mr. John Hardy, agent to the Cope estate and his three sons. The Number sank and rose again three or four times, and was called in and lay dormant until James Stothers took it up in lieu of a later Number. It went to Bond Hill, near Cran-na-gael, and thence into Cran-na-gael, and is working well in Loughgall District. One of the original members was Mr. John Bates, of Ardea.

No.35 became the property of George Innis, who kept an inn in Grange O'Neilland, not far from the Diamond.

No.40 was given to Robert Ruddock, whose descendants are members of No.7.

No.85 was given to Henry Spencer, of Causnagh, near Loughgall. He was one of the joint secretaries to the early meetings in Sloan's. The first treasurer was William Preston of Derrycrew, grandfather of the late Sir John Preston, of Belfast.

No.118 was given to Bernard Lamb, formerly of Druminis near Hamilton's Bawn, and subsequently of Castleraw, near the Diamond. He was the other joint secretary to the first meeting in Sloan's. "Diamond Dan" was a member of this Lodge.

This is all that could be ascertained about the distribution of the Loughgall Warrants in the County of Armagh. The first Masters of Lodges, or their Brothers or sons, were at the Battle of the Diamond, and they were not forgotten, not even when they had left the County to reside elsewhere.

LOUGHGALL

Have you ever been an Orange man on the Twelfth day of July,
Have you stood and watched the brethren as proudly they marched by,
Have you heard your Masters orders, have you heard your Chaplain call,
Put on your Orange sashes boys we're leaving for Loughgall.

It is a lovely little village the finest ever seen,
Surrounded by sweet countryside and fields of grasses green,
Our Orange Banners floating outshine the rebels all,
As we proudly march in memory to the village of Loughgall.

We numbered twenty thousand as proudly we march down,
The streets we've known from childhood through the streets of Portadown,
We have walked them all from childhood but now we do recall,
This glorious Twelfth when we all march to the village of Loughgall.

You have heard of old Dan Winter so many years ago,
He formed our lovely Order he proudly watched it grow,
He said we'll stand for Ulster we'll stand and never fall
And cry out "No Surrender" when we're marching through Loughgall.

But he is dead and gone now and I hope in Heaven above,
Up with his great Grand Master in that great land of love,
But I know that on this glorious Twelfth he will surely see us all,
As we proudly march in memory to the village of Loughgall.

I know that far across the sea in a palace fair and bright,
Our noble Queen is watching, for she loves this glorious sight,
She even sent a Telegram God speed one and all,
You Protestants of Ulster as you're marching through Loughgall.

THE PRIVATE LODGES OF LOUGHGALL DISTRICT

LIEUTENANT SINCLAIR'S RISING SONS L.O.L. No.2

In March 1798 L.O.L. No.2 had 63 members. David Blevins was W.M. Bro. Blevins was succeeded by James Verner as W.M. but we have no record of the exact date. Bro. Verner who was the son of Thomas Verner the first Grand Master of Counties Tyrone, Fermanagh and Londonderry remained W.M. in 1829 by which time the Lodge was meeting in Derryscollop.

The Register of Warrants for 1856 shows that the Lodge met at Derryscollop.

The Register of Warrants of 1875 and 1891 show Robert Emerson to be the W.M.

KINNEGO L.O.L. No.5

In 1870 the Lavery family gave the ground for Kinnego Orange Hall. It was called the Salt Box because it was so small.

The Lodge mostly consisted of Irwins at this time. After a few years younger men joined the Lodge but the older men would not permit the younger men to hold office. The younger men then left and formed a Lodge of their own which was held in Irwins' barn in Kinnego. After some years the original Lodge which sat in the hall was reduced to four brethren and because of this the younger brethren were then asked back to the hall.

In 1917 the Lodge formed a flute band which was instigated by James Roleston who is the grandfather of the present Bro. W. Roleston.

In 1938 land was acquired from W. Brownlee who is the Grandfather of the present secretary Bro. C. Brownlee, and this land was used to extend the hall to its present size. The first banner of No.5 depicted a portrait of Sir James Lonsdale. Wor Bro. Isaac Walker, Inside Tyler to the County Grand Lodge is a member of this Lodge and still going strong, never missing a County meeting at the age of 93 years young!

BALLINARY CHOSEN FEW L.O.L. No.14
(in past times called Derryanagh)

The Lodge has been working since the formation of the Order in 1795, with the first recorded membership coincidentally being 14. The Lodge meets in it's own Orange Hall at Ballinary.

While many names on the register have relatives still living in the area and on the present books, many more have long since left the district. The Jacksons, including relatives of General "Stonewall" Jackson of American Civil War fame have always until recently been prominently identified with the Lodge, having provided Officers in various posts over the years.

One of the Lodges' proudest claims is that of the Late Bro. Robert Brennan holding the position of W.D.M. of Loughgall District for many years as well as W.M. of the Lodge. He was also prominent in R.B.P. District Office. After he died Loughgall District L.O.L. presented a Bible in his memory to Milltown Parish Church for use in the Pulpit. Ballinary has his portrait painted on their banner.

The present banner has a picture of the aforementioned Church as the Lodge is located within the Parish. Other names having family connections within the Lodge are Abrahams, Bullers, Haughs, McClellands, Smyths, Taylors and Woods.

Drumming has been a popular interest within the Lodge, and after a lapse for a number of years it is enjoying a revival with some younger members showing a keen interest.

The Lodge's most successful drum, the "Long Hair", bearing a portrait of King William III with flowing locks (hence the name) was recently restored. The drum was purchased with a donation from a Lodge member who emigrated to America.

LOYAL SONS OF JOSHUA L.O.L. No.21 DERRYADD

L.O.L. No. 21 while not claiming a warrant on 'the First day' is nevertheless justly proud to be counted among the very earliest Lodges registered in Co. Armagh in 1795. Like practically all the formative Lodges in the Institution their meetings first took place in the homes of Lodge members or in that of the Worshipful Master.

It was almost 50 years before the Lodge had a regular meeting place being granted the use of a room in the local school house at Derryadd. In 1876 the Lodge was given possession of the school house by Bro. William Verner, local landlord, County Grand Master, and Member of Parliament for Co. Armagh. This single-storied thatched dwelling was developed into a permanent meeting place and soon became one of the first established rural Orange Halls in the County.

It has been home to L.O.L. No.21 ever since, being also the meeting-place of 'Pride of The Birches W.L.O.L. No.200 and 'The Birches Branch Club, Apprentice Boy's of Derry.' Today within the family of Lodges which make up Loughgall District, L.O.L. No.21 can look back on two centuries of Orange history with pride, its 35 active members stepping into the next century with confidence.

ORR'S MILL TRUE BLUES L.O.L. No.28 CRANAGILL

Warrant No.28 was originally given to James Sloan, the first Secretary of the Orange Order, in 1795 soon after the Battle of the Diamond. The number went dormant three or four times but was kept within the District. The present Lodge No.28 was formed among the workers of Orr's Linen Mill on the Acheson Estate. The mill is still standing, although now derelict.

The Lodge meets in it's own Orange Hall, built in 1903 and once part of the Linen Mill complex. Their banner has a painting of the Battle of the Somme and is usually headed by Lambegs on the Twelfth.

GRANGE TRUE BLUES L.O.L. No.36

The history of this Lodge is rather sketchy, however what can be established from records is that L.O.L. No.36 would have been one of the first Lodges formed after the Battle of the Diamond in 1798, the W.M. was a James Sloan, Loughgall and at that time they were meeting as they still are in Loughgall district. This is also referred to in the "History of the Royal Arch Purple Order" (pages 38 and 51). Could this James Sloan be the one in whose home the Orange Order was formed?

The next reference we can find is in the Register of Warrants for 1829. The W.M. then was an Adam Sloan, again in 1856 when the Lodge then met in Greenan, Loughgall, the W.M. was a James Taggart. (Greenan is the area of the old Loughgall Limestone Quarry on the Armagh Road).

In 1875 the W.M. was a William Conn, and in 1881 and 1891 Robert Conn was the W.M. Close to the Grange is the townland of Annacramp, and in the Orange hall there is a Certificate with "Annacramp True Blues" thereon.

In more recent times names associated with the Lodge were the Todds, Orrs, Georges and Saundersons.

On a sadder note the Lodge lost three of their members in the present troubles

Bro. Stephen McKinney,
U.D.R., 25/9/88;

Bro. John Griffiths,
Prison Officer, 4/5/89;

Bro. Eric Smyth,
Ex-U.D.R., 28/4/94.

RISING SONS OF WILLIAM L.O.L. No.48A DERRYLEE

This Lodge is recorded as first meeting in private dwelling houses in 1824.

It now meets in it's own Orange hall at Derrylee, which once was an old schoolhouse. The Hall was renovated in 1955.

The Lodge is led by Derrylee Flute Band which is a Blood and Thunder type band.

Bro. Derek Greenaway is the present District Secretary and holds office in the County Lodge as Deputy Grand Treasurer. He is often called-upon to also perform the duties of a lay chaplain.

DERRYCORRY PURPLE GUARDS TEMPERANCE L.O.L. No.52

The history of L.O.L. No.52 can be traced back almost to the Battle of the Diamond itself.

In the 1835 Parliamentary enquiry Col. William Blacker stated that in July 1796, (ten months after the Battle of the Diamond) that 90 Orange Lodges existed in Ireland. L.O.L. No.52 is listed in the first Grand Lodge of Ireland Minute Book in 1798 under the Worshipful Master William Lightbody.

In the early years the Lodge may have been known as Tullyroan as shown on the Original Stamp and for some reason now sits with a warrant from one of the old Ardress Lodges. It is unknown how this warrant arrived in Derrycorry Orange Hall or the whereabouts of L.O.L. No.52's own warrant. In the Grand Lodge report of 1894 an application from L.O.L. No.52 to have their original warrant returned was granted. The warrant to be returned to the Worshipful Master at this time James A. Gilpin. The

Worshipful Masters name on the warrant was Richard Gilpin. This would indicate that this warrant would have been first issued when Richard Gilpin was Worshipful Master of L.O.L. No.52, between 1859 and 1867

The subject of Home Rule was the major topic for discussion during the period around the turn of the last century. So much so that in March 1893 it prompted the Lodge to pass the following resolution:

That we the members of Derrycorry Temperance L.O.L. No.52, in Lodge assembled protest against the Home Rule Bill introduced to Parliament by the Grand Old Meddler, handing us over to be ruled by Priests and their gang of followers and we pledge ourselves to stand firm in to the cause for which our fathers died and never submit to popery.

In November 1906 following the death of Colonel Saunderson, a letter was written to L.O.L. No.52, still in Lodge possession, from his wife Lady Helena G. Saunderson thanking the Lodge for their support and resolution of condolence.

In 1913 the Lodge sent notices out to all members advising them to attend for drill, to be held regularly every Thursday night in Derrycorry Orange Hall.

At present the Lambeg Drums are not used on the Twelfth, however in the past they were a focal point of the Lodge, so much so that when a new drum was ordered at the start of this century there was to be "no expense spared" in the purchase of same. The two most popular drums, the "Cock drum", at one time said to be "the best drum in Ireland", and the "Sir Henry Wilson" along with a plain shell are still on display within the Orange Hall.

ANNAGHMORE CROWN DEFENDERS L.O.L. No.53A

Early records of this Lodge are scarce but we do know that the lodge was formed sometime before 1877.

In those days there was on occasions, confusion over the numbering of the warrants, and two were issued to number 53. The matter was resolved simply by giving the Annaghmore Lodge, the number 53A. As was common to all Lodges, at the outset, the over the shoulder sash was the norm, but some time later 53A changed to the distinctive blue collarette.

The Lodge met originally in the Parochial Hall, formerly the School, at the invitation of the Rector, the Reverend G. L. Sweeney. This arrangement was most convenient until the arrival of the new Rector, the Reverend T.

Kingsborough in 1886. In the "Parish History" we read of an eventful Vestry Meeting on 26th April,, 1887, at which "a deputation from the local Orange Lodge (L.O.L. No.53) was informed that they could no longer meet in the Parochial Hall. It was then pointed out that the former incumbent, the reverend G. L. Sweeney, had allowed them to meet in the Parochial Hall:- Mr. Sweeney looking round the Hall, said, "Boys, this is a nice comfortable Hall and a nice place for some other purpose." At the close of the meeting the Lodge officers were invited to remove their property, but we read, "They refused and threatened that they would break open the door on the following Thursday." On that tense note the Secretary recorded that "the Meeting closed with the Benediction." The Rector made sure that he had the last word!

After that verbal skirmish, the Lodge members resolved to build an Orange Hall, which was completed later that year. Its Centenary was celebrated with a special service on 26th September, 1987.

In the late 1970's an extension was built unto the hall as well as a new kitchen, and toilets, the ground for this was kindly given by the late W.Bro. William Woods. The prime mover in getting this work done was W.Bro. Joseph Campbell, who was then the Worshipful Master, and who is now the Deputy County Grand Master.

SUMMERISLAND L.O.L. No.66

Originally known as Clanmain L.O.L. No.66, the Lodge was formed in 1848 and first met in the house of the W.M. Bro. J. Elliot.

It became known as Summerisland in 1864. The Lodge also had a Junior L.O.L. No.38 in the 1940's.

CLONCORE GUIDING STAR L.O.L. No.84

In the famous Parliamentary enquiry of 1835 Colonel William Blacker stated that in the month of July 1796, some ten months after the Battle of the Diamond, 90 Orange Lodges existed in Ireland. In the first Grand Lodge of Ireland Minute Book of 1798 the number has risen to around 700, in which L.O.L. No.84 is listed as having twenty three members under J. J. Dodds, W.M.

It is almost certain that in the early years the Lodge met in Ardress Orange Hall, now demolished. This is shown on the original stamp. Why they moved to Cloncore is unknown. One theory is that most members moved to Cloncore to work as tenants on the Wakefield Estate where it is thought they held their monthly meetings in the dwelling house of James Vennard, Derrinraw, now the Harrison family home.

In 1891 landlords Charles Stafford Wakefield and Edward Thomas Wakefield, being ardent supporters of the Orange Institution, gave the existing site, consisting of "twenty five perches and six yards English Statute measure", to be used for the construction of an Orange Hall.

The foundation stone was laid on Easter Monday 1891 and the opening ceremony held on the 5th November the same year. A presentation trowel used for laying the foundation stone still sits in the hall today.

As with the present day, Orange Halls were also attacked by republicans during the early troubles. In September 1920 following warnings, it was proposed that the gates were to be kept locked and an all night guard placed on the hall. Each member took their turn, also acting as a neighbourhood watch.

In 1954 it was realised that the existing hall was too small to meet the needs of a thriving Lodge and was in need of extensive repairs.

One family whose name is synonymous with Cloncore Orange Hall is the Forbes family of Derrykeevan. Right from its construction in 1891, to the present day, they have led by example, from fund raising for repairs to meticulously preparing the hall for the July celebrations. Wor. Bro. T. D. Forbes is District Master of Loughgall District.

The "Orange Hall" in Cloncore has now become an integral part of our community. Not only has it been used for Lodge meetings, but also as a mission hall, a temporary school, a cinema, Boys Brigade meetings and a playschool. The Secretary was even contacted during the Second World War asking for the use of the hall as a dispersion centre for evacuees.

Dedication towards the Lodge is even shown in the folklore. Stories such as:- In the days when the monthly dues were one penny, one member who was not well off was unduly worried because he did not have his dues for that month's meeting. Tending his garden he noticed a single penny among the sods, and immediately proclaimed that "God must indeed be an Orangeman" and attended that night's meeting.

Here in Cloncore, despite having been led by a band on a few occasions, we have remained faithful to the "Lambegs". Even at the turn of the last century, when a new drum was ordered, it was "to be the best that money can buy". Every member may have their own point of view, but one thing is certain, the homecoming of L.O.L. No.84 from the Twelfth of July celebrations has been heard throughout the surrounding countryside for over one hundred and fifty years.

THE DIAMOND MEMORIAL L.O.L. No.85

This Lodge is the closest to the scene of the Battle of the Diamond. The Diamond Memorial Orange Hall is sited at the summit of the hill to the rear of the Diamond Cross-roads where the two properties defended by the Winter family in 1795 are situated and still in the possession of the Family.

Since the huge Bicentenary parade in 1995 which started at the Orange Hall, the battlefield has been signposted by the Council as it is a major tourist attraction. Both the Winter cottages have been restored and re-thatched and Mrs. Hilda Winter not only welcomes day visitors but often opens the cottage in the evenings for Orange Lodges to hold a special meeting in Dan Winter's parlour. This has been so successful that it has drawn Lodges from England and Scotland.

Wor. Bro. Norman Allen J.P. is a senior member of this Lodge. Bro. Allen D.G.M.I. is a Past District Master and a Past County Grand Master.

The Late Wor. Bro. D. J. Allen was a Deputy Grand Chaplain of Ireland. Bro. Ronnie Allen has served as a Councillor on Armagh District Council.

The Lodge helps to organise the annual Diamond Memorial Service in September. Sadly this Lodge has suffered in the recent "Troubles."

Bro. James Hewitt
murdered in a car bomb in Portadown in 1980.

Bro. Ronnie Allen
injured in an I.R.A. ambush in 1973.

CROWHILL CHOSEN FEW L.O.L. No.97

This Lodge is named after the Townland where the Lodge originally met.

It now meets in it's own Orange Hall at Teaguy, which was opened in 1904. Teaguy's banner has a painting of the Open Bible and Crown.

The Lodge maintained an accordion band for many years but sadly numbers declined and the band folded in 1996.

CLANTILEW BIBLE AND CROWN DEFENDERS L.O.L. No.101

The first Minute Book of Grand Lodge dated March 1798 lists Warrant No.101 as being operative in Loughgall District with 30 members, the W.M. being Thomas Obre who was still in office in 1829. The Obre family were landowners of a vast tract of land covering many of the existing townlands. Recently a descendent of the Obre family came from Canada to visit the Hall and to find out something about the family history. She presented to the Lodge a copy of a journal written by her Great, Great Grandfather who had been a member of 101 and had left this country for Canada in 1850.

There is a letter in the Lodge's possession dated April 3rd, 1885 and addressed to R. S. Obre, J.P. with the information:-

> *"We the Worshipful Master and Members of the above Lodge unanimously agree to use our utmost power in raising a Hall, as we have been badly accommodated for many years past. Brother Richard Matchett has already granted us his good will of the stand. We want to know if your honour would be so kind as to grant the request."*

In a poem entitled "The Opening of Clantilew Hall" there is a line which states:-

> *"It's site and part material he gave unto us free"*

which shows that the request was sympathetically received. The Hall was opened in 1885.

An old metal seal of the Lodge bears the inscription "King and Constitution - Breagh L.O.L. No.101". Breagh, Clantilew and Ballinary are adjoining townlands and it appears that before the Hall was built the Lodge met in various locations in that area. The oldest Minute Books state that the Lodge met in the Orange Hall Ballinary. The Hall is situated in the townland of Ballinary. Grand Lodge records show that in 1856 the Lodge was meeting in Ballinary, Tartaraghan in the District of Loughgall with Bro. William Matchett as W.M. and that remains so in the 1891 register.

The present warrant, being a replacement is in the name of Bro. William Matchett (1987) the previous one having been in the name of Bro. Thomas Aldridge (1902).

BALLYTYRONE L.O.L. No.104

This Lodge was formed in the late 1800's.

It meets in it's own Orange Hall, built in 1893. The Hall is situated between Richhill and Loughgall, just off the Creenagh Road.

The Lodge organises an annual Harvest service and their banner depicts the martyrdom of Bishops Latimer and Ridley (the famous Reformation event). The District Treasurer, Bro. Leslie McNeill, is a member of L.O.L. No.104.

Ballytyrone Accordion Band is associated with the Lodge and leads No.104 on the Twelfth.

DIAMOND-GRANGE L.O.L. No.118

"When the men who had gone to the village returned and found what had been done, nothing could exceed their disappointment, and finally they refused to take a Warrant. Others, more fortunate stepped in, and these poor fellows now rejoice in the possession of No.118." wrote the Orange Historian Edward Rogers about the events that followed the battle on the Diamond Hill, on the 21st September 1795.

In the Grand Lodge of Ireland's Returns for 1798, L.O.L. No.118 was clearly in existence but no information was returned by the Lodge, perhaps because the Diamond men were still smarting at having failed to obtain L.O.L. No.1. Legend has it that a Bernard Lamb of Castleraw obtained the first Warrant for L.O.L. No.118 and that Dan Winter was a member of this Lodge.

The Grand Lodge Returns of 1875 list W.Bro. Richard Jackson as Master. He is still the longest serving Master in the Lodge's history remaining in the Chair until 1904. L.O.L. No.118 has grown significantly from its 14 members in 1904 to just under 50 today.

Over the years L.O.L. No.118 has met in a variety of locations around the Diamond Grange area, many of which are now forgotten. In the townland of Tullymore near the site of the Battle; in the home of Moses Trouton beside where the Diamond-Grange Parish Church stands today, and in the home of a Mrs. Ruddock, further up the lane in which the Hall now stands. Mrs. Ruddock, a widow, obviously became so frustrated with the Orangemen using her parlour for meetings that she gave them the site on which to build their first and only Hall, which they completed just before the start of World War 1.

L.O.L. No.118 has never paraded behind a band, instead the traditional sound of the Lambeg Drum can be heard because L.O.L. No.118 remains a 'Drumming Number'. Brethren on parade wear the traditional Sash their fathers wore, except for the six officers who wear modern collarettes.

The Lodge's old banner, depicting Dan Winter's Cottage at the Diamond, was unfurled in June 1965 by the late Mrs. J. R. Winter, the wife of Diamond Dan's great-great grandson and her grandson W.Bro. Geoffrey Daniel Winter is L.O.L. No.118's current Worshipful Master. A new banner depicting Dan Winter's cottage was unfurled in 1997 in the farmyard in front of the cottage. In fact Diamond Dan has no less than six Great-great-great-great grandsons in L.O.L. No.118's ranks. Before obtaining this banner, the Lodge had an old-style flag and one other banner.

L.O.L. No.118 is proud of its heritage and organises an annual Battle of the Diamond memorial Service. The service is held every year in September at the Diamond and is organised in association with its neighbours in L.O.L. No.35 and L.O.L. No.85.

COLONEL VERNER'S TRUE BLUES L.O.L. No.162

The Lodge is named after Colonel Sir William Verner who fought at the Battle of Waterloo, in which Wellington defeated Napoleon. The Verners were a gentry family whose estate was at Churchill on the County Armagh side of Verner's Bridge over the Blackwater River dividing Counties Tyrone and Armagh.

The Verner family intervened in the Battle of the Diamond when they confiscated boats on the Blackwater, thus preventing more Defenders from Tyrone from joining those challenging the Winter family at the Diamond Crossroads in 1795.

The Verners did not join the Orange Order immediately after the Battle and the old Colonel James Verner M.P. never joined, but his five sons obtained Warrant No.162 early in October 1796 for a Lodge on the Estate. David Verner was the first W.M. and John Verner the first Secretary.

The Lodge has a portrait of Col. Sir William Verner on their banner. He was the youngest of the Brothers and he inherited the estate when the old Colonel died. He became the second County Grand Master and M.P. for County Armagh. His brother, Colonel Thomas Verner became the first Grand Master of Ireland to be elected by the newly-formed Grand Lodge of Ireland. He is recognised as the overall second Grand Master because Colonel William Blacker performed the duties of Grand Master until the Grand Lodge was formed.

The Lodge has it's own Orange Hall known as Verner's Inn Orange Hall. It was built in the early seventeenth century during the Plantation of Ulster about 1630. Sir William Verner's horse, "Constantia", which he had ridden at Waterloo was brought home after the Battle and lived in honoured retirement at Churchill until her death in 1835. Her tombstone is now built into the wall of Verner's Inn.

Colonel Verner died in 1885, serving as County Grand Master until the end.

DERRYCREW L.O.L. No.228

According to records received from Grand Lodge, the Minute Book states that L.O.L. No.228A was meeting in Loughgall District, and David Kilpatrick was Worshipful Master in the early 1820's.

They held their meetings at Gall in the Loughgall District and had ten members.

In 1824 the W.M. was a man by the name of George Fox who remained in the Chair until 1829.

Two other warrants were also working with the number 228, one in Londonderry County and one in Armagh County.

In 1856 Daniel Winter was listed as W.M. with the Lodge now meeting in Derrycrew Tartaraghan. John Jackson was also listed as W.M. in 1875 and 1891.

Derrycrew moved to new premises in the townland of Coragh, about two miles from Loughgall village in the year of 1923. These premises are still in use today and the Lodge meets regularly on a monthly basis for Lodge Meetings and Social events. Derrycrew L.O.L. No.228 has been noted down through many decades for its association with the Lambeg drum.

L.O.L. No.1287 CANARY

The Warrant for L.O.L. No.1287 was taken out in 1849 when the W.M. was Robert McKeown. The present Warrant is dated 13/2/1913.

The Lodge has met in it's own Orange Hall since 1849 on the Derrycaw Road in County Tyrone. This Lodge has had three banners, all with the same painting of the Burning of Bishops Latimer and Ridley during the English Reformation.

The present W.M. Bro. David Simpson is Deputy District Master.

Canary was known as a drumming Lodge and organised many drumming contests throughout the 1970's, 1980's and early 1990's. Bro. George Lutton was the main drummer, supported by Bros. Bertie and Sam Simpson who put up the drums. Bros. George, Herbie and the late William John Lutton drummed on the Twelfth for years. Now the Lodge is led by Hillharon Flute Band from Tullyroan (not associated with the Lodge).

Sadly the Lodge has not escaped the Terrorist Attack on Northern Ireland and in the recent "Troubles" three members of L.O.L. No.1287 have been murdered by the I.R.A..

Bro. George McCall
was murdered in 1975

Bro. Eric Lutton
was murdered in 1979

Bro. Melvin Simpson
was murdered in 1984.

THE DIAMOND WILL BE TRUMPS AGAIN

TUNE- "Burns's Farewell."

There was a time when 'twas no crime
To give the grateful thought its way-
When none need shrink who wished to drink
To the deeds of many a glorious day;
But popish power in evil hour
Has o'er us flung his galling chain
Yet bide a wee, and you shall see
How the Diamond will be trumps again.

The night is dark, no friendly spark
Is glim'ring through its cheerless gloom-
Nor moon nor star beams forth from far
The path of danger to illume
Yet still the ray of kindling day
Once more will brighten hill and plain
So bide a wee, and you shall see
How the Diamond will be trumps again.

Behold, before the billow's roar,
Yon shattered bark is borne away
The furious gale has rent each sail-
The yawning surges claim their prey
Yet there's power in that dread hour,
Will still the tempest, calm the main,
Then bide a wee, and you shall see
How the Diamond will be trumps again.

Thick flew the balls round Derry's walls,
Beleaguered by the ruthless foe,
And famine pale, bid stout hearts quail,
And death in every form of woe
Yet still she clung to hope and flung
Defiance forth-nor hoped in vain
Then bide a wee, and you shall see
How the Diamond will be trumps again.

But, away with care and dark despair-
Each thought of grief and suffering sore -
We'll put to flight this festive night
That celebrates the days of yore
The glorious day is on its way-
The brightest in Victoria's reign
The day of glee to the bold and free,
When the Diamond will be trumps again.

TANDRAGEE DISTRICT L.O.L. No.4

Tandragee District consists of 21 working Lodges, meeting in 20 Orange Halls plus a District Hall in the town of Tandragee. The District also covers the villages of Scarva, Poyntzpass and Laurelvale and the Hamlets of Acton, Clare and Ahorey. There are numerous townlands in the rural area. The District is noted for the formation of a "Ring" every Twelfth of July morning when all the Lodges gather their banners in order of numbers to form an outer circle and the Worshipful and Deputy Masters form an inner circle around the Open Bible. This ceremony is carried out at the head of the wide Main Street in front of the War Memorial beside the Castle Gates. The District Bannerette has a painting of Tandragee Castle, which was built by the Dukes of Manchester.

TANDRAGEE DISTRICT MASTERS

1893 JAMES HENRY
1894 JAMES HEAKE
1897 REV. WILLIAM J. JOHNSTON
1905 THOMAS McCOMB
1906 REV. ROBERT J. WHAN
1929 REV. CANON PERCY MARKS
1945 R. D. MEREDITH
1974 WILLIAM F. McCLELLAND
1986 HERBERT PLUNKETT
1989 THOMAS ASTON
1991 SIDNEY McILDOON
1994 LESLIE McTURK
1997 JOHN ADAIR
2000 RICHARD WHITTEN

The Minute Books of the District in the possession of the Officers go back to 1898, when coincidentally the Twelfth was held in Tandragee. The Demonstration in 1996 was the 15th Twelfth in Tandragee since 1898, not counting two Twelfths during the First World War at Ahorey in 1915 and Clare in 1917 for Tandragee District only. Tandragee District also hosted the Twelfth at Drumbanagher in 1932 and attended a Twelfth at Poyntzpass in 1948 organised by Loughbrickland District.

The major crisis for Ulster Protestants in the early years of the Century was, of course, the Home Rule Crisis leading to the Partition of Ireland. Some extracts from the District Minutes give an indication of the seriousness of those times: For Example: 1906 The Duke of Manchester was criticised for supporting the Liberals in Parliament at a District meeting. "In regard to his official connections with the Liberal Government, his Grace explained that the Prime Minister, Sir Henry Campbell-Bannerman, in giving the Duke an appointment, said that Home Rule would not come up for settlement until an appeal to the electors was made".

(Could this be an early example of Government being "economical with the truth"?)

2nd Sept 1912 Special District Meeting. Rev. Whan in the Chair. A letter was read from Bro. Crozier, Co. Grand Secretary, regarding a Demonstration in Portadown on 25th Sept when Sir Edward Carson, Lord Londonderry and other Unionist leaders will address the meeting. It was arranged that the whole District shall go in one body meeting in Tandragee on that day at 1 o'clock p.m. and walk to Shamrock Park. One pound to be given to the band. One shilling levy on each of the 22 Lodges. A committee was appointed to confer with representatives of Tandragee, Clare, and Mullavilly Unionist Clubs as to what steps we together will take in unison on 25th and also arrangements for Ulster Day. Special services for Ulster Day should be held by Bro. Rev. Whan in Clare Presbyterian Church; Bro. Rev McEndoo in Tandragee Parish Church; Mullavilly Parish Church by Rev. C. Dempsey; Ahorey Presbyterian Church or Orange Hall. (Ulster Day was the day the Covenant was signed)

The Minutes of 14th October 1912 indicate how the Orangemen intended to meet the crisis:-

> *"The Brethren of the neighbouring Lodges and any Unionist Clubs willing to come to meet for Drill in the Manchester Hall on Sat evening 19th inst under Command of His Grace the Duke of Manchester at 6-30 PM". (This marks the formation of the Ulster Volunteer Force in the Tandragee area.)*

The last Twelfth before the war was held at Tynan Abbey in 1914 for the entire County and the District travelled by train. There were no County parades during the First World War, but in 1915 the District met on Sunday 11th July in the grounds of Harrybrook House at Clare for an open air service and had a parade to Ahorey on the Twelfth with 2 bands, and only 2 flags. No banners were carried. Grand Lodge forbade any Parade in 1916 on account of the loss of life at the Somme. In 1917 the District walked to Clare and held it's own demonstration in the Manse grounds. The Minutes for 1917 record a resolution of sympathy to our County Grand Master, Sir James Stronge and Lady Stronge, on the instantaneous death on the Battlefield of Cambrai in Flanders of their only son, Bro. Matthew Stronge, Deputy County Grand Secretary of Armagh.

In 1923 the District went by train to Newry to take part in a two-County Twelfth Demonstration (Armagh and Down) as a mark of respect for Protestant families massacred by the I.R.A. at Altnaveigh the previous year.

During the Second World War from 1940 to 1944 no demonstrations were held. The Twelfth resumed again in 1945 when the District invited Gilford to join them in Tandragee.

The Twelfth returned to Tandragee in 1947 when Portadown, Lurgan, Markethill, Loughgall, and Richhill took part (Armagh and Newtownhamilton went to Keady).

In 1955 the District travelled by train for the last time when they went to Lurgan.

On 29th September 1962 the entire District went to Belfast for the Covenant Jubilee Parade to Balmoral Showgrounds.

In the recent troubled period of terrorist attack and political crisis several Orange Halls in the District have been damaged and several members of the Orange District wounded and murdered. The District attended the protest rallies in Belfast, Hillsborough, and Dungannon to show our continued opposition to the undemocratic imposition of a kind of Joint Authority on the Province by the Anglo-Irish Diktat.

Two members of the District have been elected to serve as Member of Parliament for County Armagh - Bro. J. R. E. Harden M.P. 1948 to 1954 and Bro. J. E. Maginnis M.P. 1959 to 1974.

In the present period of I.R.A. terrorist activity, universally known as "The Troubles", there have been four members of the District murdered by the Provos:-

Bro. Richard Alan Baird, L.O.L. No.116,
R.U.C. Constable, blown up in a landrover at Bessbrook in 1979.

Bro. Fred Morton, L.O.L. No.60,
R.U.C. Reserve, ambushed outside Newry while driving a breadvan in 1983.

Bro. Trevor George Elliott, L.O.L. No.116,
R.U.C. Reserve, murdered in a car-bomb incident at Belleek in 1984.

Bro. William Whitten, L.O.L. No.305,
died of 90% burns sustained in a firebomb attack
on the Marine Hotel in Ballycastle.

In addition 10 relatives of Orangemen have been killed,
and 5 Orangemen of this District have been wounded

Tannaghmore, Marlacoo and Tullymacann Orange Halls
have been attacked by terrorists in 1991 and 1992.

THE HILLS OF TANDRAGEE

O listen a while my countrymen and hear my latest news
Although my song is sorrowful I hope you'll me excuse
I left my peaceful residence a foreign land to see
I said goodbye to Ballylisk likewise to Tandragee.

Brave stalwart men around me stood, each comrade kind and true,
And as I clasped each well known hand, to bid my last adieu,
I says my fellow countrymen, I hope you'll soon be free
And raise the Orange Flag proudly o'er the Hills of Tandragee.

No more among the Sycamore I'll hear the blackbird sing
No more to me the brown Cuckoo will welcome back the Spring
No more I'll see your fertile fields and weeping willow tree
Nor raise the Orange Flag proudly o'er the Hills of Tandragee.

God bless you dear old County Armagh my own dear native land
In dreams I often see your hills and lovely orchards grand
And though three thousand miles do lie between yon hills and me,
You'll raise the Orange Flag proudly o'er the Hills of Tandragee.

May peace and plenty reign supreme upon Lough Erne's shore
May discord live forever in Ulster's homes no more
And may the time soon come around when I return to thee
To raise the Orange Flag proudly o'er the Hills of Tandragee.

THE BOYNE SOCIETY

The "History of The Royal Arch Purple Order" explains how the "Boyne Society" pre-dates the Orange Order. Other societies formed soon after the end of the Williamite wars in Ireland in 1691 were the Williamite Club in Dublin and the Apprentice Boys in Londonderry. However the Boyne Society which seems to have started in Enniskillen was different from the other two in that it allowed the setting-up of branches in other parts of the country. These societies were accustomed on their anniversaries, to march under arms, through Dublin city to College Green, where, with drums beating, colours flying and with green boughs and orange cockades in their hats, they drew up in military array around the statue of King William which had been unveiled on 1st July 1701 in the last year of the King's life. Having discharged a volley of small shot, they proceeded in regular order to hear a sermon in one of the parish churches, after which they retired to partake of a banquet provided for the occasion, where they toasted The Glorious, Pious and Immortal Memory of the Good King William.

According to one of the first Orange Historians, Ogle Gowan, writing in 1859, the Boyne Society after the 1795 Battle of the Diamond, was incorporated into the new Orange Society and the two became indistinguishable. It is interesting to note that the statue of King William was represented on all certificates and warrants of the Orange Order. In County Armagh there is evidence that the Boyne Society continued as a separate Organisation for another 50 years. There was a branch of the Boyne Society in Tandragee.

During the years 1825 -1828 the Orange Order was banned from parading and the Grand Lodge dissolved. The Lodges continued to meet and other societies were formed so that the parades could continue. One such society was "The Brunswick Constitutional Club" and The "Newry Telegraph" in 1828 reports in detail the formation of a Brunswick Club in Tandragee when the gentlemen of the Boyne Society were present.

The special correspondent of the Newry Telegraph writes:-

> *It has never before fallen to our lot to be present at a meeting so grand and imposing, as that which we witnessed on Friday 26th inst at Tandragee in the county Armagh, for the purpose of forming a Brunswick Constitutional Club for the town and neighbourhood.*
>
> *The morning was ushered in with appropriate and martial airs on drums and other instruments; and at an early hour crowds of well-dressed farmers, manufacturers, and active yeomen began to pour in from the surrounding country.*
>
> *The meeting was held in the large square of the Market Place, in which an elegant platform (about 50 feet square and richly carpeted) furnished with seats and accommodation for reporters, had been erected for the occasion. This platform was placed near the Castle gate, commanding a perfect view of the whole town and country, as far as the eye could reach.*
>
> *A flag waved in the rear just over the castle gate; and immediately behind the Chair was a handsome painting of King William, headed with the words "Tandragee Brunswick Constitutional Club", and underneath "No Surrender"! The windows of the adjoining houses were thronged with elegantly dressed females, who evinced their warm concurrence in the general feeling.*

At 12 o'clock the gentlemen of the Boyne Society walked in procession from their rooms, and ascended the platform.

Cecil Kilpatrick, co-writer of "the History of the Purple Order" poses an interesting question:-

"Presumably these few distinguished gentlemen were the Knights of the Order. Could they even have become the Black Knights of Tandragee R.B.P. No.1?"

THE FIRST TWELFTH IN TANDRAGEE JULY 12th 1796

In County Armagh the first Twelfth Demonstration after the formation of the Order in Sloan's house in Loughgall in September 1795, took place in Lurgan Park in 1796.

The Belfast Newsletter of July 15th 1796 stated:-

We understand that, on Tuesday last, being the anniversary of the Battle of Aughrim, a great body of Orange Men amounting to upwards of two thousand assembled in Lurgan, and spent the day with the utmost regularity and good order."

Lord Gosford's account of the Markethill Orangemen making their way home gives a good idea of how the Order paraded at it's first Twelfth:-

"One party consisting of 30 companies with banners and flags came towards this place about five o'clock in the evening marching in regular files by two by two with Orange cockades, unarmed, and by companies which were distinguished by numbers upon their flags. The party had one drum and each company had a fife and two men in front with painted wands in their hands who acted as commanders."

The Tandragee Orangemen paraded the town in the morning on their way to Lurgan. The following account is taken from the "Northern Star" newspaper of July 18th 1796. This newspaper supported the "United Irishmen"- a revolutionary Organisation which believed in the ideas of the French Revolution - and as such it gives a very hostile account of the first Twelfth in Tandragee:-

Happening to be yesterday in Tandragee, I saw with feeling and honest indignation, a grand division or party of Orange or Break-of-day men who, on pretence of celebrating the anniversary of the Battle of the Boyne, were, in reality, celebrating their own disgrace and degradation of their country.

The procession consisted of fourteen companies, each with ensigns and devices emblematical of the occasion, and formed a motley group of Turncoats, Methodists, Seceders, and High churchmen at least double all the rest, with a multitude of boys and country trolls cheering up the lagging heroes.

The pious Rector of the parish was seen bringing up the rear, conversing delightfully with the most ragamuffin of them, exulting in the happy sight, and praying for their success - as much as to say,' Go on my boys and prosper; fear not, I am with you, glorious defenders of the faith!'

How man can thus divest himself of all sense of shame, honour, religion, and humanity, or how such miscreants can be encouraged to show their faces in open day, is what I can't explain. I could not help observing that the Harp was thrown to some neglected corner of their standards, or trod on by a furious great man on horseback. Poor Ireland! said I, Thank God, in the other counties of Ireland they order things otherwise."

We can all laugh now at the obvious bias and hate in this account, especially at the description of King Billy as "a furious great man on horseback", but the account does give us one useful piece of information - that in 1796 there were 14 Lodges in Tandragee District.

TANDRAGEE DISTRICT AND THE LAMBEG TRADITION

"So let the drums rattle, the summons to battle,
The Protestant boys will carry the day."

This verse from a popular Orange ballad should remind Orangemen and their friends and supporters of an old tradition which is alive and well in Tandragee District. Lambeg drums are no longer a feature of the Belfast procession, because they slowed the pace, but anyone who attends the Twelfth in Tandragee will certainly remember them. You may love them or hate them, but you can't ignore them - and the same can be said of Tandragee folk themselves.

The forerunner of the Lambeg was a large war drum, used in battle in much the same way as the bugle or bagpipes: to put heart into the troops, fear into the enemy, and to transmit orders on a noisy battlefield. "Large drums" were brought to Ulster by the Dutch Blue Guards Regiment which accompanied King William on his way to the Boyne. These were probably stave drums, about the size of the present-day bass drum, but made of staves like a barrel, and they were heavier than the Lambeg as we know it. In any event they mightily impressed the local Ulstermen who turned out to cheer the Dutch Deliverer on his way, for after the Williamite Wars, the stave drum, in conjunction with the fife, was adopted by the Williamite Societies which were the forerunners of the Orange Order formed in 1795.

Thus the drums provided a link between the newly-founded Orange Order and the monarch who gave us "our freedom, religion, and laws". They were used not only in Orange processions, but also provided a rallying call to meetings at the Worshipful Master's house, and signalled to the surrounding populace that a Lodge was on the move.

However, few things are so good that they can't be improved upon, and by the mid nineteenth century larger, lighter drums were being tried out, although they were still being beaten with round-headed sticks similar to the tenor drumsticks of today. There is a story that these new drums were brought back by soldiers returning from the North-West Frontier of India. It is because these new drums were initially made at Lambeg, near Lisburn, that they have been called "Lambegs" ever since.

On 12th July 1870 the distinctive sound of the Lambeg as we know it was born, when the drums were beaten with canes for the first time. To quote Richard Hayward: "The noise is terrific and infectious as the measles!"

The drum consists of a round shell of oak (American oak is best), two goatskin "heads", and two wooden "hoops" which are placed over the goatskins and pulled tight across the shell with a rope lacing. So first catch your two adult goats- Richard Hayward might give you a hint here, with his cruelly witty song about the extremely hostile resident of Drumaness whose goat mysteriously disappeared a not inordinately long time before the local Lodge was fortunate enough to acquire a new drum head!

Don't expect to turn up on the twelfth morning, pick up your canes and start drumming. Preparations begin a few days in advance when drums are put-up in the Orange hall. These are slackened at the end of each night's drumming and next evening the ropes are pulled by hand again. Of course you must learn the rhythms that your Lodge uses. Each local area has it's own distinctive beat. Beginners often say little rhymes to keep the beat - these may or may not be for general consumption! After the Twelfth is over the drums are taken down by taking the hoops off the shell and removing the goatskin heads. Each drummer has his secret potion to rub down the head - some have even been rumoured to use peculiar concoctions containing white of egg, and even - dare we mention it - a drop of poteen! A word of warning, however - we don't advise an experimental lick!

You may ask what you receive in return for all the anguish involved. Well, there are drumming contests, organised by the five different Drumming Associations, the largest of which are the Down and Armagh Association, the Glenavy Association (which includes the Lisburn area), and the Moneymore Association (Cookstown area). These contests are a development of the last 30 years and some take place in village streets, while the majority are held in Orange Halls. There are cups and money prizes - but don't book your holiday in the Bahamas just yet! Really the rewards are more spiritual than material. There is simply nothing to compare with standing in the middle of a ring of drummers all in full wallop. You will still hear those drums long after you have wended your half-deafened way home. Do not laugh at the judges who bend so solemnly first to one side of the drum and then to the other. They are just checking that the tension of the drumheads is the same and the drum is level.

Whole families have been gripped by the lure of the Lambeg for generations, handing down the expertise from parent to child. In recent years there has been something of a revival of the drumming art and many young people have taken it up. The cost of hiring bands, or starting Lodge bands of their own, has persuaded many Lodges to maintain the Lambegs. One thing is certain - flute, pipe, accordion, and brass bands can be found in all the countries of the world. But the relentless, inspiring beat of the Lambeg is, uniquely, the voice of Ulster.

THE NAME TANDRAGEE

Tandragee comes from the Gaelic Toin re gaoith and means "backs to the wind" referring to the main street built on the side of a hill. It has had many spellings over the years such as:

TONERIGEE, TAWNTAGLEE, TON-LE-AGLEE, TONTLEGEE, AND TANDERAGEE.

The modern spelling is supposed to come from the English servants employed years ago at the Castle who spoke "posh" and "proper". Hence it is usually spelt "TANDRAGEE" nowadays.

A nineteenth century geography book described Portadown as "a small village near Tanderagee", giving us an idea of their relative sizes then.

Tandragee's motto is "Tandragee No Pinch". This is supposed to date back to the Eighteenth Century when, owing to the management of the landlords at that time-first the Sparrow family and then the Manchesters, there was full and plenty for all and no pinching or saving. Many years ago when the town had a flax fair and buyers came from all over, they found the cows in the district had all gone dry, and some wag enlarged the motto to read "Tandragee No Pinch, All Water, and No Milk"

LINES ON THE DEATH OF REV. BRO. WHAN.

Composed by Joseph Fowler, Mullahead, Tandragee

Cold death has taken the Rev. Whan, an Orangeman kind and true,
Who never was afraid to wear the Scarlet, Green, and Blue,
But God has taken his spirit back to the place from whence it came,
And what is Loyalty's greatest loss, we pray is his eternal gain.

And when the last trumpet sounds his body will arise,
Transformed, incorruptible, to meet the Saviour in the skies,
And when the sun and moon are changed, also the earth and sea,
He will live in Heaven with celestial joy to all eternity.

Over 46 years he was the Presbyterian Minister in Old Clare near Tandragee,
Also a sterling member of No. I Royal Black Preceptory;
For in Glasgow, on the Platform, he condemned Gladstone's Home Rule Bill,
And said that Ulster would oppose it to death, with all their power and skill.

He was Chaplain to the Grand Lodge of Ireland, and to the County also,
And District Master of Tandragee, and he feared no rebel foe,
For in the Pulpit he spoke the truth, on the Platform, and in the Hall,
And his Request was NO SURRENDER, and for GOD TO BLESS US ALL

On the day of his great funeral it was consolable for to see
The brethren who did attend the sad call that came from Tandragee
To come and pay their last respect to him, and what more could they do
To honour that sterling and radiant Pillar of Gideon's Chosen Few.

Our Sovereign Grand Master, Sir William Allen, did attend the sad call,
And so did the brethren of Armagh, Markethill and Loughgall.
Also brethren from Keady and Poyntzpass and Loyal Portadown,
With Scarva and Loughbrickland, Gilford and Newry Town.

May God bless his loyal Niece, who is left in sorrow to mourn,
And comfort her with his Holy Spirit, for her good Friend will not return;
Also to give us all power to cultivate Hope, Charity, Faith and Love,
Trusting we will all be members with him in the Great Grand Lodge above.

Sold in aid of Lord Enniskillen Memorial Orphan Fund

Price 2d

THE PRIVATE LODGES OF TANDRAGEE DISTRICT

BALLYMORE L.O.L. No.32

This Lodge meets in it's own hall on the Ballymore Road. The hall was built in 1906 and renovated in 1990. The Lodge was formed in 1828 and still has the original Warrant on vellum. The late Archdeacon Percy Marks held the office of District Master from 1929 to 1945 and the late Joseph Sterling Sen. was Town Clerk of Tandragee and District Secretary. Bro. John Maginnis J.P. was M.P. for County Armagh from 1959 to 1974 and William Gillespie J.P., O.B.E., is the present Chairman of the Southern Health and Education Boards.

Bro. William Gilbert was awarded the B.E.M. for Government service. The Walker family have a long military connection. The late George Walker served in the First World War, the late John Walker served in World War two, and the present John Walker is maintaining the tradition. The late R. Overend served with the R.A.F. and the late John Sinton, founder of John Sinton Ltd., was in the Territorials.

Ballymore hosts an annual drumming match and John Maginnis held the office of Chairman in the Armagh and Down Drumming Association. L.O.L. No.32's banner has portraits of King William and Britannia.

Past members include the late Duke of Manchester and the late Lord Mandeville.

CORDRAIN L.O.L. No.53B BIBLE AND CROWN DEFENDERS

Cordrain is a Townland situated on the outskirts of the Town towards Laurelvale direction. The Lodge was originally formed in a two-storey dwelling house still standing today in the Townland of Tamnavelton. The Orange hall at Cordrain was built by the members themselves in 1904. Major renovations were carried out in 1968 when the hall was re-opened by the late Brian Faulkner, later to become Prime Minister of Northern Ireland. Membership peaked in the 1960's with over 60 members. The present membership stands at 48, including Bro. Henry Diffin with 75 years service. Bros. H. Beattie, G. Black, W. Hazley and J. Neill have all 50 years service.

Cordrain has a long tradition of Drumming, both on the Twelfth and at competitions with drummers of the calibre of Bros. N. Beattie and W. Beattie. The Lodge had 6 Lambegs at one time but nowadays 3 drums are regularly used called "The Queen", the "Black Chief", and "The Horse". In 1996 major repairs were carried out to the hall.

Bro. N. Diffin was a P.O.W. during World War Two, having been shot down over Occupied Europe. The late Bro. G. Magee was also a War Veteran. The late Bro. Tom Black served as a Councillor on Armagh Council for many years. Wor. Bro. Mark Diffin is Deputy District Master.

SCARVA SONS OF WILLIAM L.O.L. No.60

With over 60 members, this Lodge is one of the largest in the District. L.O.L. No.60 has met at Scarva in County Down since 1896, meeting first in one of the weaver's cottages in the famous "Potstick Row", and moving to Scarva Orange Hall when it was built in 1908. A large, two-storey red brick hall, it features mock ramparts and tower to give the impression of a castle, and contains some fine examples of stained glass windows. The Lodge has carried out extensive renovations to the hall since 1990.

Scarva is best known for the Royal Black Institution Demonstration every Thirteenth of July and several members of L.O.L. No.60 play prominent roles in the Sham Fight. The present banner has a portrait of the late Bro. Ridley on the front and Carrickfergus on the back. Their old banner now hangs in Bro. W. Johnston's house in Canada. The Lodge organises the Scarva Festival in the second week of June each year and was led on parade by Scarva Accordion Band, formed in 1958, until 1996 when the band folded. For the last 3 years the Lodge has been headed by Lambegs.

Wor. Bro. John Adair, Past District Master, is Secretary of this Lodge.

TEEMORE GOLDEN SPRINGS L.O.L. No.61

This Lodge meets in it's own Hall on Teemore Lane just off the Tandragee-Hamiltonsbawn Road between Cabra School and Parkes' Corner and is named after natural springs nearby.

The warrant dates from the turn of the century and the hall was built in 1920. Wor. Bro. George Johnston is a Past Deputy District Master of Tandragee Royal Arch Purple District. Teemore is a Drumming Lodge and owns 6 Lambegs, 3 of which are drummed regularly. Two Drumming Matches are held each year and the Lodge drummers are Kyle, Joe, and Roy McFadden, Rodney Haire, and Tom Bell. The Lodge unfurled a new Banner in 1993.

AUGHLISH HEROES L.O.L. No.74

What heroic deeds, it might be asked, have the members of this Lodge on the outskirts of Scarva done to deserve such a grand title? The name "Aughlish heroes" derives from the 1872 clash with Home Rule protesters which later became known as the "Battle of Scarva". L.O.L. No.74's penchant for skirmishes extended to playing an important role in the "Sham Fight" before it came to be organised by the Royal Black Institution.

The Lodge was formed in the months following the "Battle of the Diamond" in 1795 and brethren have been meeting in the present Orange Hall in Aughlish Cottages for over 100 years. Otherwise known as "Potstick Row," the Cottages' eye-catching roofs, which sweep sharply downwards, owe much to the determination of the Duke of Manchester's wife. The Duchess fell in love with the design when on her travels in Switzerland and insisted on a reminder closer to home.

Bro. George Patton, the Executive Officer of the Grand Orange Lodge of Ireland, is instantly recognised in Orange circles. Other brethren from L.O.L. No.74 have also held prominent positions, including the late Herbert Plunkett, a Past District Master, who was also involved at County and Grand Lodge levels. The Lodge produces a monthly news-sheet to keep it's members informed as far away as Canada and USA. L.O.L. No.74 has also fraternal links with L.O.L. No.1053 in No.6 District, Belfast. The Lodge hosts an annual Drumming Match organised by Bro. Fred Mills. At the 1996 Twelfth the Lodge was led by the beat of a smaller model of Lambeg played by nine-year-old William Fleming, a member of Junior L.O.L. No.244. The Junior Lodge was formed 30 years ago at Aughlish and a Lodge for Junior girls was established in 1996.

LISAVAGUE L.O.L. No.76

Lisavague is situated on the outskirts of Laurelvale. The Lodge was formed at the side of the hedge by the Finns, Conns and Lynas families. The Orange Hall was built on land donated by the Finn family. Building started on July 1st 1908 and the members opened the Lodge on the Twelfth morning and had their dinner on the Twelfth evening although the hall was not finished and they had only a roof over their heads.

Lisavague was the first Lodge in Tandragee District to replace their Lodge flag with a Banner in 1919 and they have always had King William's portrait on the front and Britannia on the back. Often brethren would say "why not turn the banner back to front for a change?"

This Lodge has always had a good reputation as a Drumming Lodge and their most famous Lambeg Drum is called "Kitchener" and all good drumming men know that it is a one piece Herron shell. The members who drum on the Twelfth are William Lynas, Trevor Muldrew, Matthew Dillon, Walter Thompson, James Lynas, Stephen Lynas, Christopher Forde, and William Muldrew P.M.. They all learnt their art from deceased members, Joseph Irwin, George Thompson and Fred Lynas. These three men were renowned all over Ulster for their knowledge of the Lambegs.

CLARE CONQUERING HEROES L.O.L. No.102

The origins of this Lodge probably go back to the Volunteer Movement of the 1770's and 1780's, protecting Ireland from French invasion. There was a Volunteer Company established at Clare Castle (now a ruin). After the Diamond Battle many ex-Volunteers joined the Orange Order and a Lodge was formed in Clare meeting in a cottage near the entrance to the Castle on the Old Clare Road. After meeting in the homes of the Worshipful Masters, the Lodge built a hall in 1893 next to the Presbyterian Church on land donated by the Thompson family.

The most famous member of L.O.L. No.102 was the Rev. Robert James Whan, minister of that Church for 47 years and W.D.M. of Tandragee District, Deputy County Grand Master and County Grand Chaplain. Rev. Whan was only the second Presbyterian minister ever to hold the high office of Grand Chaplain of the Grand Orange Lodge of Ireland. He was also the local organiser of the U.V.F. during the Home Rule Crisis. A photo of the Clare Section of the U.V.F. is displayed in the hall with over 60 men included. During the First World War there were no large Twelfth Demonstrations, but in 1917 there was a mini-Twelfth in Clare to honour Rev. Whan, with Lodges attending from a wide area. L.O.L. No.102 is a drumming Lodge and still owns Rev. Whan's drum.

Major Richard Harden, who now lives in Wales, was a member of this Lodge and was elected as M.P. for County Armagh from 1948 to 1954.

The Lodge organises an annual Church Parade on the Sunday Evening before the Twelfth, and puts up an Orange Arch in the village. The Lodge unfurled a new banner in 1996, bearing a portrait of Rev. Whan on the front and The Battle of the Somme on the back.

Wor. Bro. Richard Whitten, District Master, and Wor. Bro. Douglas Cowan, District Treasurer, are members of this Lodge.

BEER'S TRUE BLUES L.O.L. No.105

Warrant No.105 was granted to Tandragee District in 1824 when 'the Master was William Foote. Between 1824 and 1894 the Lodge met at the homes of the Worshipful Masters and also for a time at Cloghoge Old School

The minute books of L.O.L. No.105 go back to the year 1891 when Thomas Greer was Master. This Lodge has a most unusual title which goes back to 1894 when Lieutenant-Colonel William Beers who was the landlord of Ballysheilmore Townland gave the cottage and surrounding ground to the Lodge to be converted into their Orange Hall. The cottage had previously been the rent-collector's house. William Beers lived at Ballyward near Castlewellan in County Down and his father was the famous County Master of County Down at the time of the Battle of Dolly's Brae in 1849. For his leadership of the County Down Orangemen at that time the Government stripped him of his J.P. title.

L.O.L. No.105 is usually simply called "Ballysheil". It is a Drumming Lodge and the Lambegs are called "Lord Nelson", "Queen Alexandra", and "Princess Mary". The Lodge organises an annual drumming match for the Ballysheil Perpetual Cup, Ballysheil Shield and the John Dodds Shield.

Bro. Leslie McTurk is Secretary of Ballysheil and Past District Master of Tandragee District. In this capacity he had the main burden of organising the 1996 Twelfth Demonstration. He has also carried out major alterations to the District Hall, including the installation of a new kitchen and central heating.

TYRONE'S DITCHES PURPLE GUARDS L.O.L. No.108

This Lodge sits in it's own Hall situated between Mossview Road and Tyrone's Ditches Road, approximately half-way between Poyntzpass and the Eleven Lane Ends. The name of the area comes from the Rebellion of 1641 which almost wiped out the Plantation of Ulster. Whilst the most famous event of that rebellion was the Drowning of the Protestants in the Bann at Portadown, it should not be forgotten that Mullabrack Parish church and Clare Presbyterian church were burned down by the rebels. In this part of the Province the rebels were led by the Earl of Tyrone and he established a series of defensive earthworks or "ditches" in this area to repulse Protestant counterattacks. Hence the name Tyrone's Ditches.

The Lodge was led for many years by Lambeg drums, but as they were no longer used some members took the courageous step of forming a new Pipe Band in March 1991. The Lodge ran many functions to raise the money to equip the band. Councillor Robert Turner is a member of this Lodge and their banner has a portrait of the late Bro. Sam Clegg. The Lodge organises an annual Church Parade and service on second Sunday in June.

TULLYMACAN RISING SONS OF WILLIAM L.O.L. No.110

This Lodge was first formed in 1796 soon after the Battle of the Diamond. It meets in it's own hall at Drumnaleg at the top of the Glebe Hill, just outside the town. The Hall is first mentioned in Griffith's valuation of 1863 as being Drumnaleg Parochial School, house and yard. It was exempted from rates and the lessor was Rev. Arthur Maloney. Even then, country schools were closing, and in 1912 Drumnaleg School became vacant. The Lodge bought the old school for £32. Prior to this the Lodge met in various farmhouses in the area such as the Finch, Cosgrove, Heak and Whitten farms. The hall suffered minor damage in a terrorist attack during the recent period of the "Troubles" and was re-opened by Bro. Jim Nicholson, M.E.P..

Tullymacan's banner has a painting of Queen Victoria and the Open Bible. With over 60 members, Tullymacan is one of the largest Lodges in the District. The late Bro. Douglas Meredith J.P. (a past District Master), the late Bro. John Black (Past County Committee-man), and the late Bro. Sam McCullough (District Lecturer) were all members of this Lodge.

The Lodge still holds an annual drumming match, and have burned a torch on 1st July every year since 1916 to commemorate the Battle of the Somme. The Tullymacan Lambeg Drums are called the King and the Horse Drum, but the Lodge is headed on parade by Tullymacan Accordion Band. The Lodge produced a book in 1996 to celebrate and record 200 years of Orangeism in Tullymacan.

TULLYHUE GUIDING STAR L.O.L. No.115.

This Lodge closed on 23rd September 1970 and the warrant was handed in to the District.

The last W.M. was Bro. T. A. Lockart and members (sixteen at the close) transferred to a Lodge of their choice.

Tullyhue minute books record the expenses for 12th July 1917 as follows:

2 Lambeg Drummers	£3-0-0.
1 Fifer	£1-0-0.
2 Small Drummers	5 Shillings (25p)
Flag Carrier	7 Shillings (35p)

The Fifer was William McCammick.

Between the Wars the Lodge met in a tin hut on the Armagh Road opposite the Church of Ireland graveyard. Then the late Walter Gracey sold the hut for a garage and the Lodge moved to the old Manchester Hall in Cornmarket Street. This large hall, originally built by the Duke, was also used as the District Hall, but it fell into bad repair, and after it was demolished and replaced by a row of houses the Lodge met in Cargans. For many years the Lodge walked with Mavemacullen and carried a Bannerette on parade.

TERRYHOOGAN BIBLE AND CROWN DEFENDERS L.O.L. No.116

This Lodge shares Scarva Orange Hall with L.O.L. No.60. The Banner of L.O.L. No.116 has a portrait of the late Bro. H. Thompson M.P. who gave the ground on which Scarva Orange Hall is built. The Foundation Stone was laid by Mrs. H. Thompson of Scarva House in 1906 and the Hall was completed in 1908.

The Lodge was formed in a barn on a farm at Terryhoogan Townland belonging to a man called Dawson Jones. The warrant dates from March 1849.

The Late Rev. Dr Michael Dewar, one of the more famous Orange Chaplains and always associated with Scarva Parish Church and the Sham Fight, was a member of this Lodge.

The Lodge organises an annual Church parade and service on the last Sunday in June and the parade starts at Aughlish Row.

CARGANS MEMORIAL L.O.L. No.122.

Cargans is Gaelic for "Little Rock" and "Memorial" was added to the title of the Lodge after the death of the then W.M. in the First World War. The present hall was built at the foot of the town in 1918, and is also used by No.1 R.B.P.

In the first minute book of Grand Lodge dated 1798 warrant No.122 is described as a Marching Warrant with the Armagh Militia, the then W.M. being a Thomas McCracken. The Armagh Militia played an active part in suppressing the 1798 Rebellion in Wexford. In the Register of Warrants of 1825 No.122 is listed as belonging to Loughgall District but by 1856 the Warrant had been transferred to Cargans. The earliest No.122 can be traced to a working Lodge in Tandragee is 8th March 1824.

Bro. Thomas Aston is a senior member of Cargans and a Past District Master. Bro. James Clayton is the Unionist Councillor for Tandragee in the Cusher Ward and is a Past District Secretary. Wor. Bro. Sidney McIldoon is a Past District Master and Grand Lecturer of the County Grand Lodge.

This Lodge has revived the art of Lambeg-drumming The Lodge is led on the Twelfth by the Horse Drum and the Carson Drum drummed by Bros. Keith Sinton, Colin Millar, and William Aston, assisted by Billy and Mark Ferguson.

POYNTZPASS BIBLE AND CROWN DEFENDERS L.O.L. No.139

L.O.L. No.139's warrant is dated June 1894 and the Lodge meets in it's own Hall situated right on the boundary between Counties Armagh and Down. The Hall was built in 1870 and re-roofed in 1981. Poyntzpass' Banner has a portrait of King William on the front and the Open Bible on the reverse.

Poyntzpass acted as hosts in 1948 when a Twelfth Demonstration was held in the village for part of County Armagh and part of Down. Tandragee District attended and most of the Districts arrived by train.

The Lodge organises an annual Church Parade to the local Presbyterian and Parish Churches in alternate years on the First Sunday in July. The late Bro. Edmund Loughlin served as a councillor on Newry Council until 1972. Until the 1940's the Lodge was led by Poyntzpass Flute Band. In the late 1940's Poyntzpass Silver Band was formed, which now has 30 members.

STAR OF BETHLEHEM L.O.L. No.203

This Lodge meets in it's own Hall near Laurelvale. However the Warrant for No.203 names Cabra as the place of meeting and for many years the Lodge met in a house in Cabra Townland. It moved to Tamnamore in 1929 when the Orange Hall was built. To this day it is better known as Cabra Lodge rather than Tamnamore.

L.O.L. No.203 is famous as a Drumming Lodge and organises two Drumming Matches each year. Their Drummers on the Twelfth Parade are Bros. Herbie Pierson, Robert Black, and Jarvis Pierson.

ARK OF SAFETY L.O.L. No.251

Known usually as just "Ahorey", this Lodge meets in Ahorey Orange Hall just outside the village of same name on the Portadown to Hamiltonsbawn Road. Prior to 1898 the Lodge met in a barn loft belonging to Samuel Patterson across the road from the present hall at a house now occupied by John Lewis. In 1898 their first hall was built and it was replaced by the large modern hall in 1954.

There is no record of when the Lodge was first formed, but Ahorey started with warrant No.1241. This no was registered to David Wisker W.M. in 1828 of Tandragee District. In 1856 it was renewed by the then W.M., Thomas Janfrey (which is the old form of "Jeffers"). In 1875 Number 251 was granted to Ahorey. This Warrant Number seems to have originated in Gilford, but was registered to Tandragee District. Apart from the Register of Warrants the No.1241 is remembered by the two hammers which have "Ahorey L.O.L. 1241" stamped on them. Recently the members found an old Orange Certificate in the name of John Pattison of L.O.L. No.1241 dated 5th Feb 1858.

A useful addition to the hall was the car park made a few years ago. The late Bro. Robert Woolsey J.P. put in a lot of work on this project. Two members of the Lodge served as District Chaplains, Rev. R. G. Fry and Rev. Dr. A. R. Scott. L.O.L. No.251 hosts an annual Church parade and service to Ahorey Presbyterian Church on the first Sunday in July.

This Lodge has four Lambegs, but these are no longer used and Rockmacraney Pipe Band leads the Lodge. During the First World War Ahorey hosted the Twelfth for Tandragee District in 1915.

GIDEON'S RISING STAR L.O.L. No.253.

This Lodge sits in Drumbanagher, a village near Poyntzpass. The Lodge organises an annual Church Parade on the third Sunday in June to Drumbanagher Parish Church. Their Banner has a portrait of the Protestant Martyrs Bishops Latimer and Ridley and the Lodge is led on parade by Drumbanagher Accordion Band, which was formed in 1958 and has 22 members.

The Lodge had declined in numbers in recent years but in the last 4 years there has been a great revival in interest and membership. In 1932 the Lodge hosted the County Twelfth Demonstration, in conjunction with the District Lodge, in Colonel Close's estate at Drumbanagher. Most Districts travelled by train.

ACTON TRUE BLUES L.O.L. No.254

"Acton is a place of fame and great renown,
It's not quite a city, but it's nobler than a town."

Records of meetings of the Lodge go back to 1822 but the earliest appear to have been little more than a roll-book of attendance on one page and a list of dues collected on the adjoining page. The small school-house on the East side of the village street became vacant in 1844 when the children were moved to a new larger building across the road with a large play-ground to the rear. The Brethren took over the old school and used it as their Orange Hall until 1988. Work started on a new Orange Hall in 1983 on a site generously donated by Bro. Floyd Ryan whose family has been associated with the Lodge for many years. The new building was opened in May of 1988 by Bro. Jim Nicholson M.E.P.. Dublin and Wicklow District sent a bus-load of members to the opening parade. The late W. C. Moody, a Deputy Grand Master of Ireland, was a lifelong member of No.254.

MOYROURKAN TRUE BLUES L.O.L. No.305

Grand Lodge records indicate that Warrant No.305 was issued in 1824 in the name of John Mulligan. In 1856 the W.M. was Jack Martin of Drumcarron, Gilford, with the Lodge a member of Tandragee District. The Warrant was transferred from Gilford to Drumnamether in 1873. The then W.M. was Robert Whitten of Drumnamether, who also served as Deputy District Master. Moyrourkan Orange Hall was built at Cabragh Road in 1913. The site was purchased from the late Bro. William Ferguson for £5. The hall has been renovated recently to provide central heating.

The Lodge first paraded with blue sashes in keeping with the title of the Lodge. It is believed that the District made a ruling that all sashes were to be Orange. The Lodge changed from sashes to collarettes in 1959. Since 1993 the Lodge has carried swords on parade. For many years a Lodge flag was carried and the first banner arrived in the early 1920's. The present banner was unfurled in 1968 by the late Mrs. George Whitten. It was purchased from Tutill's for £111-10-0. and has "No Cross, No Crown" on the front and "the Death of Schomberg" on the back

Throughout the Lodge's history Lambeg drums have featured prominently. Mosside Drumming Club meets in the hall and holds regular matches. Bro. Billy Ferguson is the Chairman of Armagh and Down Drumming Association, which holds monthly meetings in the hall and there is a weekly beginners class. In 1991 an Orange Ball was held, the first in Moyrourkan since 1946. From 1978 to 1982 the Lodge had it's own flute band. A Prayer Union has met in the hall every Wednesday night for many years.

Following the death of Wor. Bro. Jim Sinton, his wife Dorothy kindly donated a glassfronted display cabinet which houses Lodge memorabilia such as the old blue sashes.

MARLACOO RISING STAR L.O.L. No.306

Marlacoo is a townland situated on the Hamiltonsbawn Road. The Orange Hall was built in 1913 on the top of Marlacoo Hill overlooking the lake. The Warrant can be traced to 1824 when the W.M. was James Vance.

This Lodge is one of the largest in the District with over 60 members and was headed by it's own band, Marlacoo Pipe Band until numbers declined and the band folded in 1995. The Lodge is now headed by Tandragee Protestant Boys Flute Band. The Hall was attacked by terrorists and arsonists on 25th January 1992, but after a great effort the Lodge returned to a re-built Hall in May of that same year. The senior members of No.306 include one Past District Master - William McClelland.

TANAGHMORE PURPLE STAR L.O.L. No.312B

Tanaghmore Townland lies between the Markethill and Hamiltonsbawn Roads near Moyrourkan. The Lodge met first in a cottage at Tanaghmore Lough which is a continuation of the Brown Moss. It moved to Hugh McMahon's barn and then the members built a corrugated iron hall on McMahon's farm.

Between the Wars this Lodge was the largest in the District and it was decided to build a new hall on land at Manordogherty donated by the late Bro. Edward Quinn, a retired builder returned from America. Building started in 1945 and as the War was still raging materials were in short supply. Two large trees were "acquired" from Tandragee Castle Demesne by Harry Williamson and made into planks and slates came from an old mill owned by the late Christy McClelland. The Lodge opened the new hall and unfurled a new banner on the same day in June 1947. This large hall was damaged in a terrorist attack in 1991 and was re-opened by Bro. Jim Nicholson M.E.P. in May 1994.

The late Bro. Hugh McMahon was W.M. for 53 years and his son, the late Bro. Nath McMahon was W.M. for 33 years and also served as District Secretary. The late Bro. Norman Beattie was Deputy District Master. L.O.L.

No.312's banner has a painting of King William leaving Hillsborough Castle on the front and Queen Victoria on the back. The Lodge still owns lambeg drums and one has a portrait of Hugh McMahon on it. However the drums have not been used on parade for many years now and the Lodge is led by Battlehill Pipe Band.

THE CHOSEN FEW L.O.L. No.739

Otherwise known as Mavemacullen, this Lodge is the smallest in the District with under 20 members. It sits at it's own hall, built in 1923 near The Eleven Lane Ends. The hall was built with the voluntary assistance of Roman Catholic neighbours, and we should not forget that the 1920's were also troubled times. The Lodge was formed in 1845 when the warrant, which seems to have originated in Scotland, was granted to Frances Purdy.

Bro. Mervyn Adair, who as District Secretary had the main burden of the Organisation of the 1996 Demonstration in Tandragee, is a member of this Lodge. Bro. Harold Richardson is a past Foreman of the District Committee and is an expert at putting up the Orange Arch in Tandragee which must be one of the longest arches in the Province because it spans the very wide main Street. It was first erected in time for the tercentenary in 1990 at a cost of £5800.

The Lodge organises an annual Church Parade to Clare Parish Church on the second Sunday in June and supports Mavemacullen Accordion Band which was formed in 1953. Previously Mavemacullen Flute Band led the Lodge until the mid-1930's.

ARMAGH DISTRICT L.O.L. No.5

Armagh District covers the Primatial City of Armagh, surrounding villages like Milford and rural townlands. There are 13 Lodges in the District. Nine Lodges meet in their own halls and the remainder meet in the large Orange Hall on the Mall East.

TWELFTH DEMONSTRATIONS IN ARMAGH

1897 Armagh Orangemen assembled at the Gaol Square and marched with drums beating and colours flying to the Railway Station where they boarded for Lurgan. The morning and evening parades were headed by Bros. Irwin and Crozier. Newspaper reports detail how some of the returning Lodges were attacked by Nationalist protesters. Yes, in 1897!

1900 The principal meeting of the County was held in the Primatial City, although Tandragee, Bessbrook, Markethill, Lurgan and Loughgall Districts were absent. In the morning the local Brethren assembled in the Gaol Square and marched to the Railway Station to meet Killylea, Caledon, Portadown and other Brethren. The main Procession was then formed which marched through the City to the Palace Demesne, granted by Mr. George Beresford. The chair was taken by Sir James Stronge amid much applause. Many references were made to the events in China and the Boer War in South Africa which were major points of interest in British foreign policy. Bro. Henderson, ex-Mayor of Kimberley was present on the platform. There were no disturbances in the City and the weather was apparently 'fine'.

1911 As usual the Armagh Brethren assembled in the Gaol Square and marched to the Station to meet visiting Brethren. Despite new regulations stipulating that Brethren were to march four deep, the procession took two hours to reach the Field at Dobbin's Flowery Vale. Estimates put the crowd present at twenty to twenty-five thousand. Bro. James Matthew Stronge read his father's letter to those assembled,

> *"take every opportunity of showing that you will not submit to an Irish Parliament or to an Irish Executive responsible to it ...Prepare to defend yourselves and each other in the days of confusion which must follow a repeal of the Union. For you may feel sure that if separated from England, Ireland will return to the lawless condition which led to the formation of the Orange Society. Let us hope for the Union and good Government, but let us prepare for repeal and lawlessness if it must come".*

Bro. W. J. Allen also spoke on this subject bringing to the brethren's attention the depths of deceit to which the British Government had sunk in attempting to hand loyal Protestants over to their enemies.

1916 No Twelfth celebrations because of the War, but brethren paraded to St. Marks. The numbers on parade were the smallest on record. Many had fallen on the battlefields. The Rev. L'Estrange of Killylea, addressing the congregation, said of the July celebrations:-

"This is our Thanksgiving day and if the Lord had not been on our side in 1690 we should have lost the blessings which we now enjoy"

The theme of the service concentrated on the gallant efforts of the Sons of Ulster summed up in these poignant words:-

"The Ulster Division Force has won a name which equals any in history. This devotion deserves the gratitude of the British Empire."

1917 The Folly was the destination for the Armagh, Richhill, Grange and Keady brethren, having marched from the Gaol Square. All the speakers paid tribute to the sacrifices of Ulstermen and Orangemen in the War and as a result the atmosphere was extremely sombre.

1920 Because of Republican terrorism, the danger from Sinn Fein raids and the difficulty of train transport, District rather than County demonstrations were the order of the day. Despite heavy showers a large crowd gathered to the demesne. The City was also awash with colour, many houses bedecked with the Union Flag, and colourful arches were in position at Ballinahone, Lonsdale, and Callan Street. Armagh District headed the procession, W.L.O.L. No.36, a ladies Lodge were present, notable for their narrow Orange collarettes.

1924 A full County demonstration was held in Armagh. Modern motor transport and modern train services combined to bring many Lodges which formerly were unable to reach the City, so that practically every one of the 201 Lodges of Armagh County were present, in addition to two Districts, Newry and Loughbrickland from County Down, and a number of Lodges from the Free State. Estimates of the number of persons in the City varied between 30,000 and 40,000 and the procession took over 2 hours to pass a given point. It should be noted that the 2 County Down Districts were re-paying County Armagh for the two-County demonstration at Altnaveigh the previous year, 1923, when a massive Twelfth was held at Altnaveigh in protest at the murders of six protestants by the I.R.A..

1934 "Storm scatters procession"! The return procession was spread out between the field and the railway station when the heavens opened. On Barrack Hill the procession simply melted, banners were abandoned against walls, doors to all the houses opened and the brethren ran for shelter. In the Field Sir William Allen welcomed the Free State brethren but stated:-

> *"If we in the North had treated the other side as the Orangemen were treated in the South, what a hullubaloo there would have been about Orange bigotry."*

1945 The first Twelfth after 5 blank years during wartime. Only part of the County attended - Armagh, Killylea, Keady, Richhill and part of Loughgall Districts.

1946 All the above Districts paraded in Armagh again with the addition of Newtownhamilton District.

1949 Record weather - record crowds. 119 buses, 10 special trains and hundreds of private cars descended on the City. Armagh District marched to the station to meet the visiting brethren. Speakers made reference to De Valera pressing again to have the Union dissolved and advised him to mind his own business.

1958 181 lodges paraded. Sir Norman Stronge was the principal speaker.

1966 Television cameras were present for the first time and filmed the procession. At the Field speakers were heckled because of strong anti-Terence O'Neill feelings.

1975 Harold McCusker, Unionist M.P. for County Armagh, was the main speaker and he condemned some unionists for seeking independence for Ulster. He stated:-

> *" Our citizenship of the U.K. is not something bestowed on us by some benevolent politician or cabinet ministers. It was won and paid for by the blood of Ulstermen in every conflict since the seventeenth century and the declaration of being British and proud of it is signed by the tens of thousands of names cut in granite and marble on all the war memorials across the length and breadth of Ulster."*

1986 A feature of this Twelfth procession was the number of Lodges remembering their murdered Brethren on banners. There were memorials to Sir Norman Stronge and his son James and to Bro. C. Armstrong. Brethren marched under the new arch erected in memory of Bro. Herbie Burrows, also murdered by Republican terrorists.

1997 Another full County demonstration held amid the tensions surrounding Drumcree.

THE REV. E. A. FOY 1892 -1924

The Foy Memorial Orange Hall at Lisnadill is named after one of the most prominent Orangemen in the District. Although Rev. Edward Foy was rector of Lisnadill, he was for almost 40 years the Chaplain of Armagh Temperance L.O.L. No.94 which at that time met in the Abbey Street Hall. Before coming to Armagh, he had been a member of various Lodges in England, Scotland and different counties in Ireland.

During the Home rule crisis, Protestant church leaders were fully committed to the movement for the maintenance of the Union. When the Ulster Volunteer Force was formed in 1913, the Rev. Foy, together with Edward Wilson, were the heart and soul behind the Volunteers in the Armagh area. His own Company of 114 Lisnadill men attended a special service in the local church in January 1914. Much of the drilling took place in the Primate's Palace grounds.

At the outbreak of the Great War in 1914 Irish politics took second place and thousands of Volunteers went to France. Two of Rev. Foy's sons, both Orangemen, served as officers during the war. In November 1919 Rev. Foy was seriously injured when he was shot at point-blank range by a man with a revolver who called at the front door of the Rectory. This incident took place during the period of troubles which led to the setting-up of the Free State. There was strong suspicion of Sinn Fern involvement.

The Lisnadill Outrage, and others elsewhere, led to demands for a local defence force similar to the U.V.F., so when the "B" Specials were formed, Rev. Foy served for many years in this force, undeterred by the attempted murder. Shortly after his recovery in 1922 he hosted the Armagh District Twelfth demonstration in the Rectory grounds.

THE IMPACT OF THE "TROUBLES"

Since the present period of terrorist violence started in 1969 there have been seven Orangemen of this District murdered, which figure includes two District Masters.

Bro. David Stinson. L.O.L. No.174,
Killed in an attack by the I.R.A. on a policeman in 1979

Bro. Fred. Williamson, L.O.L. No.174.
Murdered along with two prison officers in 1982.

Wor. Bro. Charles Armstrong, L.O.L. No.174,
Worshipful District Master, and, Chairman, Armagh District Council.
Murdered by a bomb under his car at the Council Offices in 1983.

Bro. Trevor Elliott, L.O.L. No.540
Murdered at Keady in 1983

Wor. Bro. Robert Orr, L.O.L. No.109
Worshipful District Master,
Murdered by a bomb placed under his car in 1991

Bro. Herbert Burrows, L.O.L. No.368
Murdered by a bomb in his garage as he moved his car in 1994

Bro. Cyril Stewart, L.O.L. No.109
Shot dead outside a supermarket in Armagh in 1998

THE PRIVATE LODGES OF ARMAGH DISTRICT

TASSAGH TRUE BLUES L.O.L. No.49

This Lodge was formed in March 1798. L.O.L. No.49 meets in it's own hall on the Armagh-Keady Road, a short distance from the Hermitage.

In the late 19th century the Lodge met in a barn belonging to the W.M., George Adams, from Tullynamallogue, Keady, who died m 1893. His son, William James Adams was W.M. from 1896 to 1926.

In 1910 the Hall was built on land donated by Bro. G. Acheson. Slates and stones were taken from an old paper mill belonging to Dr. Acheson from Girvan's Bridge, Armagh.

The Lodge is privileged to have it's own Silver Band under the leadership of Bro. Thomas Shaw, whose late grandfather, Bro. James Shaw was one of many who built the Hall. The band originally met for practice in the Hermitage School room.

WESTMINSTER L.O.L. No.86

The earliest known record of L.O.L. No.86 is a Warrant dated 15th September 1828. The present Warrant is dated 1849. The first reference to the title "Westminster" is the title page of a minute book dated 28th June 1848.

The meeting place for the Lodge was Abbey Street Orange Hall until 1936 when they moved to the new Orange Hall on the Mall. It appears that sometime during the First World War the Lodge became dormant as the Warrant No.86 had to be re-issued in 1918. The Lodge had drums and fifes and carried a Lodge flag on parade up until shortly after the Second World War when their first banner was unfurled. The old flag went to a Lodge in the Free State where it was converted into a banner.

The current banner has a Painting of the Burning of Bishops Latimer and Ridley.

ARMAGH TEMPERANCE L.O.L. No.94

This Lodge was instituted in July 1872. The original Warrant bearing No.94 was sitting in Charlemont in 1834, probably a military Warrant for the Garrison at the Fort.

In light of recent events in the "Troubles", it is sobering to read in the minutes for 1908 when members discussed the Boycott of Protestant farmers and millers in the South and West of Ireland. L.O.L. No.94 were part of an Orange "Emergency Fund" set up at that time.

In the early days the Lodge was headed by two pipers and, after the Great War, the Boys Brigade band led the Lodge on the Twelfth.

The Lodge banner bears a portrait of the Late Dr. John Crozier, Church of Ireland Primate in the early part of the 20th Century. Crozier was a great supporter of the Loyalist cause. Their first banner was unfurled in 1923 by Rev. E. A. Foy, Chaplain of L.O.L. No.94 and a leader in both the U.V.F. and the B-Specials. Other prominent members were the Late J. A. (Sandy) Anderson, County Grand Master, and Capt. Michael Armstrong.

ARMAGH TRUE BLUES L.O.L. No.109

This Lodge was formed in 1845. At the inaugural meeting the Brethren decided to write the Obligations of an Orangeman on a parchment, to which they placed their signatures. From that date in 1846 every Brother either on initiation or transfer, was requested to add their signature to this unique parchment. The members of No.109 are very proud of this document and are unaware of any other Lodge being in possession of such a record.

At the outbreak of the 1914 War a large number of Brethren from this Lodge volunteered to serve in the various forces. The Roll of Honour hangs with pride in the dining room of the Orange Hall.

Several members served at District and County level. The Late Wor. Bro.. Robert Orr, District Master, was murdered by a bomb under his car in 1991. The terrorists were never caught. Bro. Orr's portrait is depicted on the Lodge's new banner.

Wor. Bro. George Proctor serves as the present District Master.

Wor. Bro. John Watson has been responsible for re-introducing a Lambeg-drumming contest to Armagh, which has attracted up to 50 drums in recent years.

LISNADILL GUIDING STAR L.O.L. No.174

Warrant No.174 was first issued in 1798 to Hugh Mathers of Edenderry, Co. Armagh. The number can be traced from 1814 to 1829 as a "marching warrant" for the Armagh Regiment of Militia. In 1887 the Warrant was brought to Lisnadill and a meeting there on 3rd June 1887 passed a resolution:-

"That this meeting desires to express it's gratification at the establishment of an Orange Lodge in immediate connection with the Parish of Lisnadill."

Bro. Rev. Stephen Radcliffe was Rector of Lisnadill at that time and the Warrant was issued in his name.

The first Orange Hall was built in 1887. The present Hall was built on a plot given by Mr. Havelock Foy, Toronto, Canada, from the estate of his late father, Bro. Rev E. A. Foy, Rector of Lisnadill. The new hall was named "The Foy Memorial Orange hall" and was opened on 4th July 1936 by Rt. Hon. Viscount Craigavon, Prime Minister of Northern Ireland. Improvements have been made to the Hall in 1950, 1975 and 1997.

In 1985/86 Bro. Rev E. D. Smyth, minister at Redrock, gave a series of talks on the Order and the Lodge published these in a book entitled "Heigh O The Lily O".

Three members of this Lodge were murdered during the "Troubles". A memorial plaque was erected in the hall to Wor. Bro. Charles Armstrong, Bro. David Stinson and Bro. Freddie Williamson.

The Lodge has had 4 banners, unfurled in 1918, 1938, 1959 and 1989. The present banner has a painting of Lisnadill Parish Church.

Lisnadill was a drumming Lodge until 1916 when a flute band was formed which is still an integral part of the Lodge today.

ARMAGH CITY GRAND L.O.L. No.184

The Lodge was founded in Armagh City with the Warrant being issued on 17th September 1847 to W.M. Bro. Edward Rodgers.

Bro. Rodgers resided at 4 College Street, Armagh and was only twenty-six years old when he received the Warrant. He was to become a well known and deeply respected Historian and deputy Librarian. He produced several political lectures of value. Chief of these was one entitled the 'Conquest of Ireland and its results', which was delivered to the Armagh Young Men's Mutual Improvement Society in the Protestant Hall on the 9th November 1877. Contained in the lecture is the historic fact that Pope Adrian IV authorised Henry II , King of England to invade Ireland in 1157, on condition that the Pope received an annual contribution of one penny per household, thus the ancient Irish were betrayed by the Roman Church. Another lecture of note, 'The Revolution of 1688' was delivered in 1880. We recommend these readings to our readers and some of his lectures can be consulted at the Irish Studies Library situated at Library Headquarters, Woodford, Armagh.

Under the leadership of Bro. Rodgers, Orangeism in Armagh and district began to re-emerge among the Protestant population and he with several others who we think came from the Portadown area were the founder members of the Grand Lodge of Ulster and the catalyst behind the re-emergence of the Grand Lodge of Ireland in 1849.

The Lodge was reorganised in 1905 and many of the old Armagh names appear decade after decade. Peel, Webster, Bounes, Bennett, McCullough, Stinson, Proctor and Elliott to mention just a few.

Many members gave unstinted service during World War One and World War Two.

KILLYCOPPLE L.O.L. No.345

Early Orange records show that in 1798 Warrant No.345 was meeting in Co. Fermanagh. In November 1823 the warrant was working in Armagh District, the W.M. being Robert Johnston of Lisnadill.

The earliest record in possession is a warrant dated 1st May 1849, issued to James Laing, with the place of meeting being Outlack. Bro. James Laing was still W.M. in 1857 when the roll showed a membership of 22. The next dated record is a roll for 1864 which shows Benjamin Black as W.M. At this time the Lodge was known as the Outlack, Coran L.O.L. No.345.

A house at Trodders Crossroads in the townland of Coran has been identified as the place where 345 had their Lodge room.

There was no mention of an Orange Hall until 1868 when there was an agreement with John Balfour of Killycopple to rent premises for the yearly sum of 1 shilling. From that time onwards the Lodge was known as Killycopple. At a meeting on 4th May, 1870, the Lodge agreed upon bye laws. Printed copies, dated 6th July, 1870 are still in existence. In 1995 there were suggestions that they be rewritten and updated. After examination it was decided that they were in perfect condition and should be left alone.

In June 1927 an ante-room was built at the back of the hall, costing £25. However, the hall was unsuitable for social functions and in the 1930's dances in support of a new banner were held in the nearby Drumgar School. In 1946, by which time Drumgar School had closed, the Lodge bought the premises for £100.

This is now the present Killycopple Orange Hall as it was opened as such by Sir Norman Stronge on 2nd July 1947. Various repairs and extensions have been carried out over the years and both the Hall and Lodge are presently in excellent condition, with 63 members on the roll.

The Past District Master of Armagh, Bro. Gordon Frazer is a member of L.O.L. No.345.

ROYAL STANDARD L.O.L. No.347

The early history of this Lodge is only recorded in the G.O.L.I. Registers of Warrants beginning in 1823. In November 1823, the Warrant was granted to Alex Dickson in the District of Armagh.

In the register of 1828, two No.347's appear, one in Fermanagh and the other in Armagh and at that time the Master in Armagh was Gerald Tyrell. No locations of where the Lodge resided at this time are known. The current Lodge Warrant is dated 1849 and the Master at that time was John Nimmo. In the 1856 Register of Warrants, John Nimmo is still Master of the Lodge but also recorded is the location of Ballymartrim off the Battleford Road, Armagh. While the Lodge sat at "Nevilles' Hill", Ballymartrim, it shared premises with Edenderry L.O.L. No.150 (now Mullintur Lodge, Killylea District). On each 12th July morning, both Lodges would set off from their meeting place along the narrow laneway to the main road and there L.O.L. No.150 would head towards Killylea and L.O.L. No.347 would walk into Armagh.

In the 1891 Register of Warrants the Master of the Lodge was James Neville of Ballymartrim.

By 1894, the Lodge had moved to Oulart on the Portadown side of Armagh and the roll book of that year indicated that the Lodge was called Royal Standard and over fifty per cent of the membership still resided at Ballymartrim. The Master at this time was John George of Cloughfin who remained in the chair until 1915. During this time (Nov. 1913), the address of the Lodge changed to "Killooney" which coincided with the Secretary's address. Even today people refer to both the Lodge and the band as "Killooney".

A number of Lodge members served in the Great War and after the war the Lodge acquired land at Ballinahonemore on the Hamiltonsbawn Road to build a new Orange Hall in memory of the Brethren who died in the 1914-1918 war. The hall was opened on the 1st July 1927. A number of Lodge members took up the call again in 1939 and on the 1st July 1947 the Lodge paraded to the Cenotaph on the Mall to lay a wreath in memory of all their fallen Brethren in the two Wars. The Lodge has continued with this tradition ever since.

Up until 1913, the Lodge paraded with flag and drums, but they then decided to form a First Flute band which was called Royal Standard and to purchase a banner. In 1950 the band was renamed "Clarke Memorial", after their conductor Brother James Clarke and in the early Fifties it became a part flute band and remains so today.

More recently the Lodge decided to make available a special commemorative certificate to those Sisters and Brethren who paraded in Loughgall on 23rd September 1995, to mark the Bicentenary of the Orange Institution. Applications were received from the jurisdictions of Ireland, Scotland, England, Australia, New Zealand and Canada.

MILFORD TEMPERANCE AND BENEFIT L.O.L. No.353

Warrant No.353 dated from the earliest days of the Orange Institution in Ireland. It was in existence before the foundation of the Grand Orange Lodge of Ireland in April, 1798 and most probably was issued early in 1797.

The first definite records of its location and Master appears at the re-issue of warrants in 1823 when the Lodge was sitting in Aughavilly with Bro. John Bothwell in the Chair. This was still the case in 1829.

The Lodge in its present form dates from 1903, when Bro. David Couser was Master, although the membership was very small. At that time Milford was a growing village and a number of men from there either transferred or were initiated into No.353. Within a few months the place of meeting was moved to Ballyrea Orange Hall which continued to be the Lodge's home until 1911, when the present Milford Orange Hall was opened at a County Black Demonstration on the last Saturday of August.

The first banner had been unfurled on 1st July, 1905 and a flute band was quickly formed, which continued with one or two short breaks for about 80 years. A subsequent banner was unusual in that it portrayed King William III seated on a black horse, rather than the traditional white horse, and the present banner has been in use since 23rd June 1973 when it was unfurled by W. Bro. Rev W. Martin Smyth, then Grand Master of Ireland.

Over the years many Brethren have given long and dedicated service to the Orange Institution through L.O.L. No.353. Perhaps the best known was Bro. R. Cyril Hyde, for many years District Secretary of Armagh and subsequently Deputy District Master and Worshipful District Master.

Bro. Alfred Briggs was the guiding hand of the improvement and furnishing of the Lodge Room during the 1950's and 1960's. He was also closely associated with the renovation and extension of Armagh Orange Hall and became Chairman of the former Armagh Urban District Council.

Bro. David Scott was initiated in 1914 and served the Lodge at various times as Secretary and Bandmaster. He was able to take part in the Tercentenary Celebrations in 1990, passing away in 1993 at the age of 97 - 79 years an Orangeman.

Today L.O.L. No.353 draws most of its membership from men who either live in or have family links with the village of Milford.

NELSON'S CONQUERING HEROES ALLISTRAGH L.O.L. No.368

Little is known of the origins of the Lodge, other than that it was working in Killylea District No.7, meeting in various locations under Warrant No.1282. In 1911, a corrugated iron hall was built at Allistragh by the late Bro. John Thompson at a cost of £90, where the Lodge has remained ever since.

In 1947, the Lodge transferred from Killylea District No.7 to Armagh District No.5, taking out the Warrant No.368. The name of the W.M. on the Warrant was that of the Late Bro. William J. George.

During the early years of the Lodge it was accompanied to various Twelfth demonstrations by two Lambeg drums, one of which still remains the property of the Lodge. In the Autumn of 1947 a flute band was started and this remains active to the present day. Its first outing was to Caledon on the Twelfth in 1948.

Like so many other Lodges in Ulster we have suffered as a result of terrorist action. A highly esteemed member, Bro. Herbert Burrows was murdered by a bomb explosion in Armagh on the third of March 1984. The hall itself has been the target of arsonists on two occasions, fortunately both attacks failed. Numerous Union Jacks have been taken off the hall and on Sunday morning, 14th July 1996, an Irish Tricolour was flying on the flagpole, needless to say this was speedily removed.

Every year on the second Sunday in June the Lodge hosts an Orange Service and Parade with Brethren attending from Lodges in Co. Tyrone as well as Brethren from Loughgall, Armagh, Keady, Killylea and Newtownhamilton Districts.

In April 1989, the Lodge decided to purchase a Marquee, which is hired out to various Lodges, vintage rallies, festivals and show jumping events during the summer season.

In February 1990, a small cottage standing on one acre of land adjacent to the hall came up for sale. The Lodge purchased the property at a cost of £26,000. With help from our Brethren throughout Northern Ireland and other fund raising events the debt was cleared in four and a half years. The cottage and land are presently rented out to a nurseryman who is carrying on a successful business.

KILDARTON TEMPERANCE L.O.L. No.540

This Lodge was formed following a disagreement in L.O.L. No.114 when some members left to form a Lodge of their own. They met and decided to erect a hall and elect their officers. However, since they had no warrant it was really a hall building Committee.

A site was obtained and a hall erected in 1911 which was named Kildarton Protestant Hall. The members then transferred to L.O.L. No.184 in Armagh where they remained until 1912 when Wor. Bro. James Irwin, Worshipful District Master and several other District Officers came to Kildarton Protestant Hall along with all the brethren who wished to form a new Lodge.

The District was opened and a warrant bearing the number 540 was issued to Bro. Thomas Henry Irwin as Worshipful Master of the new Lodge and the election of officers was duly carried out.

It was agreed to start a flute band in 1913 which continued until 1937 when it changed to a part accordion band which, due to a shortage of players, has now closed down.

Since the Lodge was formed it has had four banners all bearing the same portrait, that of the burning of Latimer and Ridley. What a glorious testimony for all to follow!

Each year a Divine Service is held two Sundays prior to the Twelfth Demonstration when brethren walk the short distance from Lough Lane to Kildarton Parish Church.

Through its history the Lodge has had many esteemed members who have given long service; some having served in high office at District level. The present Deputy District Master, Wor Bro. Roy Pillow, is a member of L.O.L. No.540.

RISING SONS OF AGHAVILLY L.O.L. No.619

Grand Lodge records indicate that the Lodge was formed sometime between the months of May and September 1798. However, there is little information available on its early years. On 11th November 1823 the Warrant was renewed and issued to Bro. James Keys. It was later renewed in 1856 in the name of Bro. Robert Keys and again in 1891 to Bro. Hugh J. Robinson.

It is interesting to note that at one time there was another Lodge which met in Markethill District bearing the same Lodge number.

Brethren originally met in the home of Bro. Bertie McCarragher. The Orange Hall where the Lodge now meets is situated four miles outside Armagh in the Parish of Aghavilly and is a one-storey building built of red brick with cut stone facings. Over the porch there is a stone arch on which is inscribed in well-cut letters, "Pert Protestant Hall 1888".

The name Pert was thought to have derived from the seven townlands meeting there. The place Aghavilly means the field of the old tree - perhaps some tree under which chieftains were inaugurated.

The official opening took place on Monday 5th November 1888 at 3p.m., when Orangemen with their bands, assembled from Killeen, Lisnadill, Keady, Killylea and Ballymartrim, together with the Victoria Flute Band.

1888 was a memorable year for the Brethren of the District as well as being the Tercentenary of the defeat of the Spanish Armada and the Bi-centenary of the Landing of William III.

The hall celebrated its 100th anniversary with the unfurling and dedication of a new banner, held on Saturday 18th June 1988 when the then Grand Master, Most Wor. Bro. Rev. Martin Smyth, B.A., B.D., M.P., was present.

The Lodge, along with Milford Temperance and Benefit L.O.L. No.353, hold a Divine service each year on the fourth Sunday in June. At one time Brethren walked to this service from Milford Orange Hall to St. Mary's Parish Church, Aghavilly a total of six miles, there and back.

Through its history the Lodge has had many esteemed members who have given long service. Two members have served in high office at District level. The late Bro. Albert Agnew served as Deputy District Master of Armagh District Royal Arch Purple Chapter No.5 for ten years and was installed as Worshipful District Master, a number of months before his death in 1994.

Another member, Bro. Harold Price, held the position of Deputy District Master of Armagh District L.O.L. No.5 for five years. He was Superintendent of Primatial Junior L.O.L. No.27 and served the Junior movement at District and County level.

Aghavilly Accordion Band also use the hall and head the Brethren each year to their Church service and on the Twelfth. The band have been successful at various Accordion Band Championship contests.

KILLEEN STAR OF FREEDOM L.O.L. No.124

Although hard to document, this Lodge is believed to have received its No.1249 from a dormant Canadian Lodge, exactly when is not certain but the original Warrant was issued on 12th May 1847.

The Lodge formerly held its meetings in what we call the "old hall" which is situated at Killycopple Road and has now been incorporated, after being derelict for some years, into a garden centre. Our new much larger hall was opened in 1962 and after a lot of deliberation and soul searching this enormous task was commenced. Built mostly by voluntary labour and private funds, the hall now commands the high ground of the Newry Road. Looking down into Armagh City it remains a monument to the Brethren of that era, for their foresight and dedication in preserving the Orange Order in this often troublesome area.

While our records show that in the early years of the Lodge, Office bearers seemed happy to hold Office for unusually long periods of time. In some instances the Worshipful Master and Deputy Master being unchanged for ten or twenty years. However this situation was to change and around 1950 a new system of re-election every two years was adopted. This system sought to bring new life and ideas to the meetings, much needed to contend with modern business brought before the Lodge. Worshipful Bro. James Mcgarity P.M. who was responsible for this change still keeps regular contact with the Brethren and is now in his sixty-fifth year of service to this Lodge.

1996 proved to be an unusually busy year for the Lodge and along with numerous events the main occasion was the unfurling of a new banner in June which replaced the previous banner which had seen thirty-nine years of service. The guest speaker on this occasion was Worshipful Bro. Sir James Molyneaux, M.P.

The Lodge is also very proud to have leading them the only Pipe Band in Armagh District, namely Killeen Pipe Band. Under the supervision of P.M. Brian Megarity and D.M. Graham Megarity, the band is registered with the Royal Scottish Pipe Band Association. They have competed successfully in the local competition scene and also in the World Pipe Band Championships at grade 2 level.

LURGAN DISTRICT L.O.L. No.6

The early history of Lurgan has been associated with the Brownlow family since the plantation of Ulster. Lurgan is derived from the name Lurganballyvacken or Ballylurgan. John Brownlow and his son, William, came from Basford near Nottingham when they were granted 2500 acres of land in the barony of O'Neilland East by James 1 in 1610.

Carew in his Report of 1611 records that John and William Brownlow were both resident and dwelling in an "Irish House". They had brought over six carpenters, one mason, one tailor and six workmen and had placed one freeholder and six tenants upon their lands. Preparations were being made to build two bawns (walled enclosures) and they had some muskets and other arms in readiness for defence of the properties.

By 1619 John Brownlow was dead and William came into possession of the two manors. Pynnar's "Survey" of that year states that there was "upon Ballynemony a strong stone house within a good island and at Doughcoron a fair house of stone and brick with a bawn of timber and earth with a pallazado about it and in readiness lime and stone to make a bawn thereof in the summer". There was then a very fair town consisting of forty-two houses, all inhabited by English families, with streets paved clean through. There were also two water-mills and a wind mill, all for corn, and a store of arms in the manor.

In 1629 William had a re-grant of the two manors by which they became united as the Manor of Brownlow's Derry. At the same time a patent was issued for a market every Friday at Ballylurgan and two fairs on the Feast of St. James and Feast of St. Martin. By this time the town had become a place of importance in the social life of the area and gives Lurgan's markets and fairs an ancestry of over three hundred and twenty years.

In 1641 the Civil War broke out and Lurgan was taken by a force of native soldiers said to have numbered 1,000 men. From Carte's "Life of Ormonde" the outbreak was not entirely unexpected for Sir William Brownlow had been supplied with powder for the defence of his Castle. The attack took place on the 23rd October, 1641 (in his later account he changed the date to 1st November) and the raiding parties under the Macans, Magennises and the O'Hanlons burnt the town and murdered several inhabitants. The Castle surrendered and Brownlow was taken prisoner with his wife and children, first to Armagh, later to Dungannon and finally to Charlemont where he was eventually freed by the English. According to O'Mellan's Journal there was a second burning of Lurgan in May 1642.

The town seems to have suffered little inconvenience during the Williamite Wars. Some of Schomberg's troops were stationed in the town and neighbourhood and the General made them responsible for the repair of the highway, with, of course, an ulterior object in view - the facility of his troops when the occasion should arise. Tradition says that during this work the General once used the Blue Stone at Lylo as a luncheon table. The famous landmark is now buried.

In the closing years of the 17th century Lurgan began to develop as a linen manufacturing centre and Dr. Thomas Molyneaux (of Castledillon) in his book "Journey to ye north" written in 1708 describes the town:-

> *"at present the greatest mart of linen manufacturers in the north being almost entirely peopled with linen weavers, and all by the care and cost of Mr. Brownlow, who on his first establishing the trade here, bought up everything brought to the market of cloth (linen) and lost at first considerably, but at length the thing fixing itself, he is now by the same methods a considerable gainer. This gentleman is more curious than ordinary and has by him several old Irish manuscripts which he can read and understand very well. He shewed me one in parchment of the Bible (as I remember) pretended to be written by St. Patrick's own hand but this must be a fable. This gentleman is not satisfied about the petrifying qualities of Lough Neagh waters. Having supped with him we lay at an Inn."*

In 1712 James Quin of Carlow was induced by William Brownlow to take up his abode in Lurgan and begin the manufacture of damask and by 1714 fine cambric was being produced in the district.

At that time the making of linen was an essentially domestic affair. Farmers grew the flax on their own lands and it was scutched at home. The families then combined to spin the thread effected by the same hands. From Young's Tour of Ireland published in 1780, the writer mentions the great improvements Mr. Brownlow had made in his demesne. Although mainly concerned with agriculture but being in the town on a Market Day he walked to the mart to see the way in which linens and cambrics were sold and gives an excellent account of the proceedings. Weavers were able to earn by coarse linens 1/- per day and by fine linen 1/4d, and the same applied to the spinners - they received more for the fine yarns.

A parcel of linen woven in 1809 was of such excellence that it was presented to Princess Charlotte; and later on Lurgan cambrics were sent to Queen Victoria.

The town then boasted a handsome Market House situated in the old Middle Row, and a Linen Hall built in 1825.

Lurgan was the second town in the County in importance in 1819 and it contained 379 houses and 2207 inhabitants. The weekly trade in linen then averaging from £2,500 to £3,000 per week.

The first power loom factory was built in 1855 by the Malcolms who, in the days of handloom weaving, had been engaged in the manufacture of cambric. The new venture was unpopular with the hand-loom weavers who gathered together on one occasion to wreck the plant.

The Mechanics Institute was opened in 1858 and in 1865 the Linen Hall was abolished. Owing to industrial changes it had outlived its usefulness. In 1866 the Malcolms also established the first hem-stitching factory in the town.

Johnston, Allen & Co. was set up in 1867 for the manufacture of linen and cambric by handloom but transferred to power-loom weaving in 1888. In an account of Lurgan written in 1751 by the Rev. Richard Barton, there is a vivid representation of the Lurgan linen market. While the linens were sold in the open market they were measured under cover in the public houses and custom had made it a rule that the sellers of webs should expend at least three-pence in liquor for the good of the house.

In 1793 the Irish Militia was re-organised and county units raised. Lurgan, possibly due to its geographical position, sent very few men into the Armagh Militia. Three years later Yeomanry Corps formed and Lurgan acquired a Cavalry and Infantry Corps - the latter in the next century became involved in certain squabbles of a political nature, whereby its loyalty to authority became suspect. Part of the trouble was due to the then agent who was very anti-Orange in his views. A coat of the Lurgan Corps survives in the National Museum, Dublin, and very full records presented by the late Sir William Allen are preserved in Armagh Museum.

In 1795 when the Orange Order was formed, its principles were quickly adopted in Lurgan. In 1797 the town was the place of meeting for the second demonstration since the Order's formation. Great preparations had been made. From sunrise that morning crowds of people were on their way. Districts west of the Bann joined together at Portadown where they were inspected by Major Acheson (later Lord Gosford) then a candidate for the county.

About that time William Blacker of Carrickblacker received a present form his grand-uncle, Col. Carey, of some horse furniture used by King William at the battle of the Boyne, and the meeting was deemed a most fitting occasion for its exhibition. Blacker, accordingly, placed it upon a magnificent black hunter and escorted by twelve of the finest looking men in the country, all above six feet high and dressed alike, two of whom led the horse whilst the others tried to keep off the crowds who strove to touch the valued relics as they passed along. They were accompanied by several hundred well-mounted horse-men, many of whom had come from Killyman and other parts of Tyrone, followed by the districts in their order with all manner of music. The story from this point had best be told in William Blacker's own words.

> *" At Lurgan we were met by two other processions from Down and Antrim and there we found General Lake, the Commander-in-Chief of the Northern district, waiting to receive us, attended by one or two other General officers and their entire staff in full rig. We defiled past these grandees near the head of the Castle Lane, down which we proceeded into Mr. Brownlow's demesne and round the lake which was completely surrounded and more, the head of the procession having reached the street of Lurgan again ere the last had entirely quitted it. I do not recollect having ever since seen a sight so beautiful as the lake surrounded as it was upon that occasion by a slow moving processional mass. The day was extremely fine. The women gaily dressed were as numerous as the men. There was a marked sparkling of scarlet, the Yeomanry wearing their uniforms, the Banners, the music coming softened across the water, the general appearance of cheerful exultation, all conspired to form a scene which can never be obliterated from my memory. In less than two hours afterwards the town was cleared. My father and I dined there with a large party of gentlemen and on going home on horseback about ten at night I do not think we saw four people on the road between Lurgan and Carrick. One of these was old Frank Baird, a fiddle playing school-master from Drumlyn Hill, whom we came up with near the "Red Cow" fiddling and dancing a pass seul along the road which he actually kept up with unabated spirit until we reached the turn to Carrick and no doubt continued it the entire way to his domicile. It has frequently happened to me to traverse many miles of the country on the night of the 12th of July and I can safely assert that I invariably found the roads more quiet on that night than on any other. It seemed a point of honour among the Protestants to keep that night from becoming marked by an impropriety. Men whose conduct might be loose enough 364 nights in the year were on their guard on that one."*

In September 1912 the Ulster Covenant was signed at Brownlow House by thousands of Lurgan people and not a few were called to make the supreme sacrifice between 1914 and 1918. Many of them were Orange Brethren and their names are all recorded on the roll of honour at the town's war memorial.

At the outbreak of the first World War, Brownlow House was the headquarters of the 16th Battalion Royal Irish Rifles and the 10th Battalion Royal Irish Fusiliers. The flag of the Old Comrades Association of the former Battalion and the Kings Colour of the 2nd Battalion of the Royal Irish Fusiliers are laid up in Shankill Parish Church.

In the Second World War that readiness to serve King and Country was again demonstrated and indeed more recently many have been serving in the defence of freedom and for the right to remain British.

Various contingents of British and American troops were stationed in Lurgan between 1939 and 1945 and when the United States forces were billeted in Brownlow House, General Dwight D. Eisenhower, the Supreme Allied Commander is said to have spent at least one night there with his men. The corridor to the room in the House where he slept is still called the Officer's Corridor. One of the stained glass heraldic panes on the grand staircase was removed then reputedly by the Yanks as a memento of their stay. It has however been replaced by a replica.

Brownlow House, or Lurgan Castle, so named presumably after the Rt. Hon. Charles Brownlow, who built it in 1833, was created Baron Lurgan in 1839, was owned by the Brownlow family until the turn of the century. Changing fortunes resulted in the property being sold to the Lurgan Real Property Company Ltd. and subsequently the House and surrounding grounds were purchased on behalf of Lurgan Loyal Orange District Lodge. The legal document of conveyance is dated 11 July 1904. In appreciation of the effort of the late Sir William Allen, K.B.E., D.S.O., D.L., M.P. in obtaining the House, an illuminated address was presented to him by District Lodge and now hangs in the Dining Room beside the portrait of Sir William painted by Frank McKelvey. He together with Messrs. Hugh Hayes, John Mehaffey, George Lunn Jun. and James Malcolm Jun. were the first Trustees.

Not only does Brownlow House claim to be the largest Orange Hall in the world but as the headquarters of the Imperial Grand Black Chapter of the British Commonwealth, it is in fact well known throughout the world.

Brownlow House, built in an age of grandeur and cultured tastes, is an imposing building. It has retained much of the atmosphere of bygone days and one can readily pause and still imagine what life was like when it was occupied as a dwelling. While the echo of successive Brownlow Households along its corridors has long since died away, the building has however remained alive ever since it became the home of Orangeism in Lurgan almost one hundred years ago.

Situated within a few minutes walk from the centre of the town, the House is a prominent landmark with its lantern-shaped tower and forest of tall chimneys dominating the skyline. It commands a fine view across the park and lake, which were once part of Lord Lurgan's estate and are now owned by Craigavon Borough Council. The building which is of Scottish sandstone was designed in the Elizabethan style by the famous Edinburgh Architect,

William Henry Playfair and it was recently listed by the Department of Environment (N.I.) as being of special architectural and historical interest. (The collection of Playfair's 383 drawings of the House are in Edinburgh University Library) The elegant wrought iron entrance gates are also listed. Originally the entrance to the avenue started at Market Street where there was a stone-arched gateway and Lodge house, but no trace of either remains today. Likewise Castle Lane, where the previous Lurgan Orange Hall Building had stood has also been demolished with other houses once occupied by many of the tradesmen employed by the Brownlows.

A few years before the re-organisation of local government took place in 1973 in Northern Ireland, the Trustees of Brownlow House were pleased to put part of the House at the disposal of Lurgan Borough Council, The R.U.C. had requisitioned the Town Hall after the barracks in Church Place had been bombed by the I.R.A.. The dining room of the House was used as the Council Chamber. The Brownlow family motto "Esse quam videri" surrounds the cipher letters WAB (William Arthur Brownlow) above the archway in this room. The Latin can be freely translated "To be, rather than to seem" and the sentiment is not unlike that of Lurgan Borough Council motto, which was "Be just and fear not", (Craigavon Borough Council's motto is "Together we progress")

The first Lord Lurgan was one of the fourteen members elected to the newly formed Town Commissioners in 1843, the predecessors of Lurgan Urban and Borough Councils. The 4th Lord Lurgan in fact presented Lurgan Borough Council with the Mayoral chain of office. It incorporates the Brownlow armorial bearings. The link with the new Borough is perpetuated as the same chain is still is use and worn by the Mayor of Craigavon Borough Council.

Further evidence of the Brownlow link with Lurgan is seen in Shankill Parish Church. The stained glass window on the south side of the chancel, representing Faith, Hope and Charity was erected by the second Lord Lurgan in memory of his father. Shankill meaning the "old church" is a very ancient parish as the name implies. Documentary evidence traces its history back to 1411, when the parish of Kilwilke was subsequently changed to "Kilymlcon" and later to "St. Finton alias Caillmore". The church originally stood in the townland of Annaloiste on the shores of Lough Neagh to the north of Lurgan. When Lurgan developed, a site in the town for the Church of Shankill was found in what is now the old Shankill graveyard. This site is now occupied by the Brownlow family vault. In the intervening years with the increasing population a new site for the Church had to be obtained and with permission from the Irish parliament, it was built on the "Fair Green of Lurgan"

The present Church was erected and consecrated on 8 August 1725. The spire, which had been added, was burned by a fire in 1792 and the wooden one that replaced it was blown down by the wind one stormy evening in 1839. Enlarged in 1832 at a cost of £1,000 it was subsequently taken down to allow the present building to be erected in 1863. The new Church cost £8,000 and is reputed to be the largest Parish Church in Ireland, capable of seating almost 2,000 people. The only relics from the old Church in Shankill graveyard transferred were the stone baptismal font, dated 1684, and the silver communion vessels made in 1696.

Lurgan like other towns of Northern Ireland has had its share of sectarian violence and vandalism. The murder of the young Soldier, Private Paul Genge by the I.R.A. on 7th November 1971 near the hospital was the first of many tragic deaths in and around the town. Good men and women, as they endeavoured to maintain law and order have been severely tried and tested in the cause of Civil and Religious liberty. The destruction of property which has been widespread has included Brownlow House. There have been at least three serious attempts to burn it. The wing occupied by the Imperial Grand Black Chapter was destroyed by a petrol bomb on the night of 28 November 1979 and a similar attack on a previous occasion damaged another part of the building occupied by Lurgan Purple Star Orange Lodge.

Major repairs and renovations were carried out with the assistance of a government grant aided ACE scheme and the House was restored somewhat to its former glory. The building was re-opened after the first phase of restoration by the Most Wor. Bro. Rev. Martin Smyth B.A., B.D., M.P., Grand Master of the Grand Lodge of Ireland on 3 July 1982 and it was followed by a mini-twelfth parade through the town. This parade has now become an annual event and is an important part of the twelfth celebrations in the town.

The furnishing of the room by the Imperial Grand Black Chapter in memory of the late Brother and Sir Kt. H. A. Cushnie M.B.E., J.P., has been a fitting tribute not only to his long service as Grand Registrar but also to the fact that he was 45 years Secretary to the House Management Committee.

Brownlow House was opened as an Orange Hall on 4 July 1903 and the ceremony was performed by Brother Colonel Wallace. Brother Sir James Stronge, County Grand Master of Armagh presided and the brethren present were not only from County Armagh but special trains to Lurgan conveyed some 1200 from Belfast and 400 from Dublin.

During 1996 several attempts were made to burn the building but on 30th August an arson attack destroyed almost 50% of the building. The magnificent oak carved staircase and stained glass window bearing the

Brownlow family crest were completely destroyed as were many other priceless artifacts. At the height of the fire nine fire crews including crews from Armagh and Belfast were in attendance. As a result of their actions in arduous conditions a considerable amount of valuable memorabilia, documentation and relics were saved, including a famous painting of Sir William Allen by Frank McKelvey and the mounted hares used in the Waterloo Cup won by Master McGrath were saved.

As the firemen damped down the blaze members of Lodges and Preceptories formed a human chain and worked tirelessly to salvage drums, banners and paintings.

Ignoring warnings by the fire crew the Worshipful District Master Samuel Gardiner and Bro. Clive Higginson entered the building and through the smoke and burning embers made their hazardous journey to the tower where they proudly hoisted the Union Flag.

Initial work to secure and protect the building from the elements was immediately carried out, and only hours after the destruction architects were already on the site to commence the enormous task of restoring the House to its former glory at an estimated cost of around five million pounds, of which the Brethren of Lurgan District will have to raise one and a half million, has already commenced.

Lurgan District has had four members murdered by terrorists in the recent "troubles".

Bro. Tom Taylor, L.O.L. No.44
R.U.C. Member

Bro. Ivan Vennard, L.O.L. No.91
Part-time U.D.R.

Bro. Noel Webb, L.O.L. No.91
R.U.C. Member

Bro. Keith Dowey, L.O.L. No.82

MASTER McGRATH

Master McGrath is probably the best-known greyhound of all time. He was small, black with a long white streak on his chest and a small white patch over one of his shoulders. Over his back he was ticked with white, as if a shower of hail had fallen on him. He had two white toes on all his feet. Master McGrath achieved acclamation and fame by winning that great event in the coursing world - the Waterloo cup - in 1868, 1869 and 1871.

He was called after a young boy who walked him when he was a pup and bred by the Galway family from Colligan, near Dungarvan.

He was owned by Charles second Baron Lurgan (1831-1882). The second Lord Lurgan was a leading figure in the coursing world. He held an annual coursing meeting at Raughlin, in which the visitors' cup was the main attraction. It was at this meeting in October, 1867, that having been little more than a week in training, Master McGrath won the visitors' cup (32 dogs) and was nominated to contend the Waterloo cup. He is remembered by the well-known ballad and there are also two monuments to honour him -one at the residence of his owner Lord Lurgan at Bury St. Edmunds, and the other at the junction of the Clonmel and Cappowuin Road near Dungarvan.

Stories about Master McGrath are still told particularly at a wake in the countryside.

"Did you hear about them and Master McGrath ("them" being the great-uncles of the deceased). It's a wonder they're still in the place (the "place" being a wee farm on the banks of the Lagan)

I suppose Lord Lurgan thought the Lagan air would do him good or maybe the hares were that bit bigger and faster out there.

The two ould fools (the great-uncles again) had so much faith in him they took the boat to Liverpool in 1868 with all the money they could raise, and put it on Master McGrath. In 1869 they took the boat again to Liverpool and placed the last year's winnings on him. They say that's how they were able to buy the other place in.

Now, you all know what happened in 1870. Master McGrath lost the Waterloo cup and the ould fools lost all their money with him. He was doped of course and nearly drowned in a half-frozen drain. The English just couldn't stand the thought of 'Paddy' winning a third time.

In 1871 the great-uncles went across to Liverpool with no money this time but they brought as many livestock as they could muster on the boat with them. February is no month to be crossing the Irish sea and a terrible storm blew up. The ship was tossed from side to side. I believe ould Charlie was in a fearful state in case his prize bullock would have to be cast overboard. As luck would have it, they arrived safe enough and sold their animals in Liverpool. The proceeds all went on Master McGrath. This time he was not doped and won the Waterloo cup magnificently for the third time. The people in Lurgan nearly went mad. They had bonfires and singing, and the celebrations went on into the wee small hours of the morning.

Master McGrath was presented at the court of Queen Victoria after royalty had expressed a wish to see this fabulous coursing dog. Lord Lurgan was Lord in waiting to the Queen at the time.

I wonder will we ever see another Master McGrath? Maybe better not; they say the fella who has inherited 'the place' is a chip of the ould block."

Early in December, 1871 the news emanating from Brownlow House that 'The Master' (Master McGrath) was poorly with a bad cold saddened the populace of Lurgan and district. The Waterloo cup was looming up again; February 1872 didn't seem that far away and Master McGrath would need to be fit. Sadly, however, he died of pneumonia just a short time before Christmas. A press account of his burial states:-

> *"The funeral was a most touching scene. In front of Brownlow Castle at Lurgan is a large green sward, at the left of which is a small wicket gate. When the dog was to be buried the tenants and retainers of the Brownlow estate gathered together, each man with a greyhound in leash. Slowly each one passed in through the little wicket gate, across the main hall entrance, where Lord Lurgan stood, circled round the lawn and round the little oaken coffin, placed in the middle of it, pausing for a moment at the coffin. So out again by the same little gate, while the trainer carried the coffin away to be buried in the laurels some few yards away in the shrubbery."*

Not only Lurgan mourned his passing but the whole of Ireland. His gallantry and courage had won their hearts.

Master McGrath will be remembered in song and story long after the rest of us are forgotten. The borough of Craigavon have given him pride of place in their armorial bearings, a well deserved token of remembrance to a truly great little greyhound.

MASTER McGRATH

Eighteen sixty nine being the date of the year,
Those waterloo sportsmen and more did appear;
For to gain the great prizes and bear them awa',
Never counting on Ireland and Master McGrath.

On the twelfth of December, that day of renown,
McGrath and his keeper they left Lurgan town;
A gale in the channel, it soon drove them o'er,
On the thirteenth they landed on fair England's shore.

And when they arrived there in big London town,
Those great English sportsmen they all gathered round
And some of the gentlemen gave a 'Ha! Ha!'
Saying, 'Is that the great dog you call Master McGrath?'

And one of those gentlemen standing around
Says, 'I don't care a damn for your Irish greyhound';
And another he laughs with a scornful 'Ha! Ha!
We'll soon humble the pride of your Master McGrath."

Then Lord Lurgan came forward and said, 'Gentlemen,
If there's any among you has money to spend
For your nobles of England I don't care a straw
Here's five thousand to one upon Master McGrath."

Then McGrath he looked up and he wagged his old tail,
Informing his lordship, 'I know what you mane,
Don't fear, noble Brownlow, don't fear them, Agra,
For I'll tarnish their laurels,' says Master McGrath.

And Rose stood uncovered, the great English pride,
Her master and keeper were close by her side;
They have let her away and the crowd cried 'hurrah!'
For the pride of all England -and Master McGrath.

As Rose and the Master they both ran along,
'Now I wonder,' says Rose, 'what took you from your home;
You should have stopped there in your Irish demesne,
And not come to gain laurels on Albion's plain."

'Well, I know,' says McGrath, 'We have wild heather bogs
But you'll find in old Ireland there's good men and dogs.
Lead on, bold Britannia, give none of your jaw,
Snuff that up your nostrils,' says Master McGrath.

Then the hare she went on just as swift as the wind
He was sometimes before her and sometimes behind,
Rose gave the first turn according to law;
But the second was given by Master McGrath.

The hare she led on with a wonderful view.
And swift as the wind o'er the green field she flew,
But he jumped on her back and he held up his paw
'Three cheers for old Ireland,' says Master McGrath.

Lt.-Col. Sir William Allen, K.B.E., D.S.O., D.L., M.P.

December 1997 marked the fiftieth anniversary of the death of Sir William Allen. Linen manufacturer, Orangeman, Blackman, Unionist politician, soldier and Member of Parliament; his life spanned nine decades.

While not of the same prominence in national terms as Edward Saunderson, Edward Carson or James Craig, William Allen was an important figure locally who commanded respect in County Armagh and represented the county at Westminster for thirty years.

During the Great War he had served with the 36th (Ulster) Division, ending the war as a battalion commander. As well as being a leading Orangeman, for twenty-three years he was Sovereign Grand Master of the Imperial Grand Black Chapter of the British Commonwealth. William James Allen was born on 15 October 1866. He was the son of Joseph Allen, one of the founders of Johnston, Allen & Co., linen manufacturers. Educated at Lurgan College, he followed his father into the linen business but launched out on his own in 1906 and built the Windsor factory.

Most businessmen in that era believed that Ulster's continued prosperity and the economic well being of her people depended on the maintenance of the Union between Great Britain and Ireland. A staunch supporter of the Unionist cause, Allen had thrown himself wholeheartedly into Unionist politics, Orangeism and the Black. He cut his teeth in politics in local government.

The extent of his commitment to politics is evidenced by perusal of the Ulster Unionist Council's Yearbook for 1907 and the years which follow. In 1907 he was Secretary of Lurgan Polling District of North Armagh Constitutional Association, one of the two North Armagh delegates to the Ulster Unionist Council from the County Armagh Grand Orange Lodge, a member of the U.U.C.s Watch Committee, and one of the U.U.C.s three Honorary Secretaries.

In 1908, in addition to the above, he had become one of the U.U.C.s six representatives on the Unionist Associations of Ireland Joint Committee. By 1910 he was a member of the Standing Committee of the U.U.C.. However, in that year he only attended one meeting out of eleven. In 1911 his attendance significantly improved as he was present at five of the Standing Committee's eleven meetings during the year.

As the third Home Rule crisis unfolded, the frequency with which the standing committee met increased. In 1912 the committee met no less than seventeen times and Allen was present on ten occasions. In 1913 Allen was present for seven out of the eleven meetings of the Standing Committee. By 1914 he was no longer a member of the Standing Committee; other commitments, as will become evident, prevented him from being so. Nevertheless, he continued to be one of the U.U.C.s then three Honorary Secretaries.

During these years before the Great War Allen liaised with Southern Unionists, served on delegations to meet leading mainland politicians, such as A. J. Balfour in March 1907, and undertook speaking engagements, some of which were on the mainland as part of the U.U.C.s efforts to explain the Unionist case to the wider British public. For example, he addressed a meeting in Glasgow on 13 April 1908 and the annual conference of the National Conservative Union at Leeds in November 1911.

He was also prominently associated with the formation and training of the Ulster Volunteer Force in County Armagh and in Lurgan in particular. His activism in the campaign against the Third Home Rule Bill almost certainly laid the foundations for his subsequent political career, allied to his war record.

In November 1914 he obtained a commission. By 1916 he was a major and by 1918 he commanded the battalion which he had raised. Mentioned in despatches four times, he was awarded the Croix de Chevalier of the Legion of Honour and the D.S.O. (1918). In 1921 during King George V's visit to Ulster to open the first Parliament of Northern Ireland he was knighted, probably in recognition of both military and political service. However, that is to anticipate developments a little.

In 1917 William Moore K.C., the M.P. for North Armagh and, along with Charles Curtis Craig, joint founder of the Unionist Council, was appointed a High Court judge. Allen was prevailed upon to fill the vacancy but he made it a condition of his candidature that he should continue his military service to the conclusion of hostilities before taking his seat. On 22 November 1917 Major W. J. Allen was returned unopposed as M.P. for North Armagh.

With the establishment of Northern Ireland's devolved legislature, Northern Ireland's parliamentary representation at Westminster was reduced to thirteen. County Armagh's representation was reduced from three seats to a single seat for the entire county. At the General Election in 1922 Allen was returned unopposed to represent the county. On six subsequent occasions Allen placed his name before the electors of County Armagh.

On three occasions 1923, 1931 and 1945 he was returned unopposed. In 1924, 1929 and 1935 respectively Allen was opposed by Sinn Fein, a Liberal and a Republican. On each occasion he secured an overwhelming majority. In 1945 he was one of only three M.P.s in the whole of the United Kingdom to be returned without a contest and the only Conservative and Unionist, the other two being Labour members. He regarded this as a very signal honour.

Douglas Savory, the Unionist M.P. for the Queens University seat, provides a vignette of Allen, the parliamentarian:-

> *His judgment was sound. His experience was great and to the end he was assiduous in attending to his parliamentary duties. He could be seen in the library of the House of Commons at 10 a.m. writing letters in his clear, beautiful handwriting. He never employed a secretary. Sir William was always attentive to the debates. At 10 a.m. he was as fresh as paint, though he had been up all night and was on his feet demanding to know if the bill under consideration applied to Ulster. Sir William was recognised by his fellow MPs, irrespective of party, as a man perfectly straight and honest, firm in his convictions and staunch in his beliefs. As such, he was well regarded at Westminster. Of him it was said, No man enjoyed greater affection and respect and trust in the House of Commons.*

Sir William was also held in very high esteem by his constituents. In December 1938 at a meeting held to mark the completion of twenty-one years service in parliament, he was presented by the Loyalists of the county with a motor car and a cheque, a measure of the great affection in which he was held.

Lord Craigavon, Northern Ireland's first Prime Minister, in a debate in April 1934 told the Northern Ireland House of Commons that he was an Orangeman first and a politician and a member of this House afterwards. Sir William Allen seems to have viewed his membership of the Mother of Parliaments in a similar light.

He had a long and active association with the Orange Order and the Black. He was the County Grand Master of Armagh for forty years and Grand Secretary of the Grand Orange Lodge of Ireland.

In 1924 he succeeded W. H. H. Lyons as Sovereign Grand Master of the Imperial Grand Black Chapter of the British Commonwealth. This position, which he valued above all others, he retained until his death. He travelled widely and extensively on behalf of the Black, believing it to have a special role in preserving the Union.

At the beginning of the century he was instrumental in acquiring Brownlow House in Lurgan for the Orange Order. As the largest Orange Hall in the world and the headquarters of the Black, Brownlow House is his most obvious legacy to the loyal orders.

On one occasion a political opponent, responding to Allen's oratory, described him as Roaring Meg, It was an allusion which he greatly relished, and regarded as a compliment. It is also indicative of his close identification with the vibrant Loyalist heritage and culture of the people he represented.

Sir William was married twice. His first wife was Maria, daughter of John Ross of Lurgan. Like her husband she was a staunch Loyalist.

She founded the first Women's Orange Lodge in County Armagh and was Worshipful Mistress of her own private Lodge of Armagh. She was also vice-chair of the Ulster Women's Unionist Council. The first Lady Allen died in November 1937.

The second Lady Allen was Lillah Irene, daughter of R. Hill Forsythe, also of Lurgan. She played a prominent role in the musical life of the town and performed much useful work on behalf of the Unionist cause.

On 5 December 1947 Sir William was knocked down by a lorry as he was getting off a tram on the Lisburn Road in Belfast. He sustained severe chest and head injuries and a fractured leg. Although he showed some signs of recovery, he died a fortnight later on 20 December in the Royal Victoria Hospital. He was buried in Lurgan New Cemetery after a service in Shankill Parish Church in the town. At the time of his death at 81, Sir William was the second oldest member of the House of Commons. Sir Murdoch McDonald, the National Liberal M.P. for Inverness, beat him by five months for the distinction of being the oldest member. On the occasion of his 80th birthday in October 1946 Sir William had promised to go on batting for a century. The sporting analogy was appropriate. As a young man he had played cricket for Waringstown. (He had also captained Lurgan at rugby.) Nevertheless, he had a good innings, even if the century eluded him.

R.W. Bro. Norman. R. S. Hood, D.G.M.I., C.G.M., Armagh

The late County Grand Master's name was synonymous with Orangeism in County Armagh for many years. Moving from his native town of Bessbrook to Lurgan, he soon became deeply involved in Church activities as well as the Institution.

In 1977, he was installed as Deputy District Master of Lurgan District L.O.L. No.6 and in 1980, assumed the office of Worshipful District Master, an office he held with great distinction for 5 years.

His leadership qualities were soon recognised at County level, when he was installed as Deputy County Grand Master of Armagh in 1982 and then County Grand Master in 1984, an office he carried with pride and distinction up to his sudden demise.

As a Deputy Grand Master of the Grand Orange Lodge of Ireland, he was a faithful and diligent member of Grand Lodge, taking part in constructive debate and sharing ideas. When the idea of starting a Credit Union for the Orangemen and their families was suggested in 1989 he was enthusiastic at adding a new support, in this case financial, for the Orange Family.

He was very active, promoting the cause of Orangeism right up to his death in New Zealand attending a meeting of the Orange Council (representing Ireland) and spearheading plans for the Bicentenary celebrations in County Armagh.

Rising to the highest levels of leadership in the Institution, he never forgot his roots and up to his death, served diligently as Chaplain of Elizabethan Temperance L.O.L. No.278, Worshipful Master of Sir William Allen Memorial Temperance R.B.P. 19, Foreman of Committee Lurgan District L.O.L. No.6, as well as Chairman of the Trustees of Brownlow House.

THE PRIVATE LODGES OF LURGAN DISTRICT

BLEARY CRIMSON STAR L.O.L. No.12

This Lodge meets in it's own Hall at Dean's Road, in the hamlet of Bleary, between Lurgan and Portadown.

William Blacker, of Carrickblacker, was one of the founder members of L.O.L. No.12 in 1795. He was present, along with other Bleary men at the Battle of the Diamond on 21st September 1795 and he intervened as the Battle neared an end, bringing supplies of lead shot which he and estate workers had made by melting lead from the roof of Carrickblacker House. Blacker obtained Warrant No.12 from James Sloan of Loughgall, who acted as the first Secretary.

The first meeting of the Lodge was in October 1795 in a half-built house owned by Patton in the Long Lane, just off the Gilford Road and opposite the gates of Carrickblacker House (now Portadown Golf Course). Blacker became the first County Grand Master of County Armagh and he organized the first Twelfth Demonstration in Lurgan Park, which was attended by 20,000 people. For the first two years, until the formation of a Grand Lodge in Dublin, the County Grand Lodge of Armagh served as a Grand Lodge for all of Ireland and so William Blacker is recognized as the first Grand Master of the Institution.

In April 1798 the newly formed Grand Lodge of Ireland held it's first meeting. An inventory of Lodges was drawn-up and L.O.L. No.12 is listed as having 103 members with it's first W.M. being Edward Calvert.

When the Rebellion broke-out in 1798 the Chief Secretary for Ireland asked William Blacker to raise a company of Yeomanry in the area. Known as the Seagoe Yeomanry, they saw service in the Lisburn and Wexford areas.

The Lodge has a roll-book dating back to 1876 which shows the Calverts still active in the Lodge.

The present Orange Hall was opened in 1896. The Lodge formed an accordion band in 1985 but it began to struggle in 1987 and it folded in 1991.

Wor. Bro. Melvin Hamilton served as a Deputy Grand Secretary of the Grand Lodge of Ireland and Wor. Bro. David Coffey has served as District Lecturer.

The present Banner of L.O.L. No.12 bears the legend "Dieu et Mon Droit", or God and my Birthright and displays symbols intended to convey the message:-

"Here we are, the British of Ulster, here we are and here we stay."

BOYNE STAR L.O.L. No.16

This Lodge was formed shortly after the Diamond Battle in 1795 and is first recorded in the papers in the Grand Lodge Archive in the House of Orange for the year 1798.

It meets in Brownlow House and unfortunately it's original Warrant was destroyed in the fire in 1996, along with the Lodge Banner. Their new banner has a portrait of Brownlow House.

The Lodge intends to attend the Scottish Demonstration at Falkirk in 2000.

Bro. David Martin is the District Lay Chaplain and Bro. Clive Higginson is Foreman of the District Committee.

BANNFOOT GOLDEN STAR L.O.L. No.27

This Lodge was formed after the Battle of the Diamond in 1795. The Lodge meets in it's own Orange Hall in Hill Lane, Bannfoot, near Lough Neagh. The Hall was built in 1910.

Their present banner has a painting of Britannia. The Lodge carries lambegs on parade. Three of the drums belong to the Lodge and two more are privately owned. The drummers are John Murphy, Lawrence Turkington, David Murphy and Charles Parks.

The Lodge organizes an annual church parade to the Methodist Church.

The report in the Armagh Guardian of 21st July 1846 contains an interesting reference to Bannfoot on the Twelfth in the year 1846:

> *"A riot occurred at the Bannfoot owing to a party of Roman Catholics attacking Orangemen, with the result that Lancers were sent from Portadown to prevent a further breach of the peace. At Derrytagh, however, the Orangemen were again attacked on going home, shots being fired at them and their sashes torn off. The Orangemen seem to have retaliated, as six Roman Catholics were wounded; two of the Orange party, a girl and a boy, were also wounded and had to be sent to the County Infirmary."*

CARRICKBLACKER L.O.L. No.41

This Lodge meets in it's own Orange Hall at Levaghery, built in 1912.

The Warrant is dated 1825. The Lodge is now one of the smallest, in terms of members, in the District.

L.O.L. No.41 has a painting of King William riding into the camp of the army on their banner.

LOYAL SONS OF ULSTER L.O.L. No.44

This Lodge was formed soon after the Diamond Battle and now meets in Brownlow House, reputed to be the largest Orange Hall in the World. At present it is being re-built after a terrorist arson attack in 1996.

The Lodge formerly had Lambeg drums but these are no longer used. Their present banner has a portrait of the Late Bro. Tom Taylor, a member of the R.U.C. murdered by terrorists and the previous banner had a portrait of the Late Bro. W. G. Best.

The Late Bro. Joseph Twyble, County Grand Master 1969-1972 was a member of this Lodge, as was the Late Bro. Fred Rusk J.P.. Over the years many councillors have been members of this Lodge, including the late Bro. R. J. Mitchell, the late Bro. A. F. Black, the late Bro. W. G. Best who was Town Clerk and the late Bro. Thomas Ross. Councillor Phillip Black is a member of the Lodge.

GIDEON TEMPERANCE L.O.L. No.48

This Lodge meets in Brownlow house and it's banner was burnt in the fire which destroyed the greater part of the building in 1996.

LURGAN PURPLE STAR L.O.L. No.63

This Lodge has the largest membership in the District and meets in Brownlow House.

It's banner has a painting of Lurgan War Memorial on one side and the Open Bible on the reverse. It is led on parade by Craigavon Protestant Boys Flute Band, Bro. Samuel Parks is District Lecturer and Bro. Richard Monteith is Deputy District Master. The Late Bro. George Matthews was caretaker of Brownlow House for many years.

GIBSON'S HILL TRUE BLUES L.O.L. No.91

This Lodge was formed soon after the Diamond Battle. It met first in the townland of Levaghery. By 1829 it was listed as meeting in Lurgan District and the Lodge met in Dukestown School. It moved to it's present location at Corcreaney in 1913 when the Orange hall was built.

Wor. Bro. John Crozier, District Master, is a member of this Lodge, as are the present District Lecturers, Bros. Kenneth Dawson and Jonathan Flavell.

Bro. Eric Crozier served as a councillor in Lurgan and Craigavon Councils.

The banner of L.O.L. No.91 depicts King William leaving Hillsborough Castle and also "the Secret of England's Greatness." All their previous banners had the same scenes.

Sadly L.O.L. No.91 has suffered in the present "Troubles". Bro. Noel Webb, R.U.C., was killed by a landmine explosion at Bessbrook in 1979 and Bro. Ivan Vennard, U.D.R., was murdered by the I.R.A. at Killwilkey Post Office in 1973.

BOCONNELL L.O.L. No.123

This Lodge was named after the Townland and the lane where their Orange Hall was sited.

The Lodge used to meet in Gracey's barn at Boconnell, near Silverwood, and built the Hall in 1920. The Hall was vested by Craigavon Council and the Lodge now meets in Brownlow House.

A new banner was unfurled and dedicated in 1998. It depicts Brownlow House Orange Hall and was painted by John Jordan.

The late Bro. Harold McCusker, M.P. for County Armagh from 1973 to 1983 and M.P. for Upper Bann from 1983 until his untimely death in 1990, was a member of this Lodge and a keen Lambeg drummer. Bro. McCusker will be remembered in Ulster Unionist circles for his hard-hitting speech on the Anglo-Irish Agreement, or Dictat, signed by Margaret Thatcher. He said in the House of Commons:

> *"I will carry to my grave with ignominy the sense of the injustice that I have done to my constituents down the years when in their darkest hours I exhorted them to put their trust in this British House of Commons which one day would honour the fundamental obligations to treat them as equal British citizens."*

Boconnell is a drumming Lodge and organized a special Drumming Gala in 1971 and other drumming contests over the years. Their current drummers are Bros. Charles, David and Joe Allen, Brian Winton, Alvin and Phillip McNally, James and Colin McCusker.

The Lodge Drums are called The Kitchener, The Challenger and the Sir Henry Wilson.

ABRAHAM'S CHOSEN FEW L.O.L. No.230

This Lodge meets in it's own Orange Hall at Derryadd on the shores of Lough Neagh.

The title of the Lodge probably comes from the biblical Abraham and Isaac, although The Abraham family have been prominent in the Lodge for many years.

The Lodge is recorded as sitting at Glenavy in 1823 and moved to Derrytrasna in 1825 and Derryadd in 1901. The first reference to the Lodge working in Lurgan District is 1829.

Their Hall was built in 1894 and was damaged by a terrorist arson attack in the recent "Troubles". The banner has a painting of Abraham and Isaac and the Lodge takes part in an annual church parade on the first Sunday in July. L.O.L. No.230 shares Derryadd Orange Hall with L.O.L. No.15.

ELIZABETHAN TEMPERANCE L.O.L. No.278

L.O.L. No.278 meets in Brownlow House. It was always known in the District as the Businessman's Lodge.

Their original banner had a painting of the Northern Ireland Parliament building at Stormont. In recent years the Lodge has had a bannerette, but it was destroyed in the fire at Brownlow House.

Wor. Bro. Samuel Gardiner, Past District Master and Past County Master of the Royal Black Institution and Member of the Northern Ireland Assembly for Upper Bann, is a member of this Lodge.

L.O.L. No.278 has the distinction, unique among County Armagh Lodges, of having produced two County Masters, namely the Late Wor. Bro. Norman Hood and Wor. Bro. Denis Watson. A member of the Salvation Army, Bro. Watson is a Past District Secretary and County Grand Master since 1996. He has also been elected to the Northern Ireland Assembly for Upper Bann. He also serves the Institution as Grand Secretary of the Grand Lodge of Ireland, replacing Wor. Bro. John McCrea who retired from this post after many years.

ANNALOISTE TEMPERANCE L.O.L. No.372

This Lodge was formed at Annaloist (old spelling) townland on the shores of Lough Neagh in 1899. The Warrant, dated 1830, seems to have come originally from a Lodge in Corcreaney at a time when Lodges tried to hand in their Warrants and take out lower numbers. The Lodge celebrated it's centenary in 1999.

The Lodge now meets in Brownlow House and the banner was destroyed in the fire and the Warrant damaged. Their new banner depicts the Open Bible and Crown and the Warrant has been restored. The Lodge had Lambegs on the Twelfth parade up until 1955.

Two members of this Lodge hold office in the District Lodge, namely Bro. Geoffrey Morrison, District Secretary and Bro. David Wylie, District Treasurer.

CHRISTIAN VOLUNTEERS TOTAL ABSTINENCE L.O.L. No.388

The original Warrant for this Lodge is dated 1867 and met at Ballygargan, Portadown.

The Lodge meets in Bro.wnlow House Orange Hall. Their banner has a painting of Samson slaying the lion.

All members of No.388 must have a personal faith in our Lord Jesus Christ, and the Lodge organises Gospel musical evenings, attends all church parades in the area and holds open-air meetings in the demonstration Field each Twelfth.

Past members include the Late Bro. George Matthews, a County Lecturer, and Bro. S. Gardiner, a Past District Master, and Rev, P. J. Synott, Rector of Shankill Parish church.

MUCKERY HEROES L.O.L. No.1685

This Lodge meets in it's own Orange Hall at Lower Muckery, about 1.5 miles from the old Bannfoot ferry near Lough Neagh.

The Orange Hall was built in 1911 and was completely destroyed in an arson attack by terrorists in October 1996. It was re-built and opened in May 1999.

The present banner is 44 years old and depicts the Bible and Crown and the All-seeing Eye. Their previous banner is over 100 years old and so must be one of the oldest banners in existence. It had been lent as part of an exhibition in Brownlow House and fortunately was returned just before the terrible fire. This Lodge used to have five Lambeg drums but all were destroyed in the fire in the Hall, except one which only survived because it had been loaned to the Bannfoot Lodge. There is a portrait of Rev. Cordner on the drum.

KILLYLEA DISTRICT L.O.L. No.7

There are 12 Lodges in the District, meeting in 11 Orange Halls, plus a District Hall in the village of Killylea. The District includes the village of Caledon.

Extract from the minutes 1892 records that the Worshipful Master was James H. Stronge. It was proposed by the Reverend Sandford to send a strong protest to the local newspapers against Home Rule. In 1894 the District agreed to pay for a framework to be erected for a flag on Killylea Church on condition that the Lodges provide a proper flag which was subsequently provided by Col. S. Blacker.

In 1896 there were eighteen Lodges in the District. It was not unusual for the members to walk all the way from Killylea to Loughgall for their annual demonstration. These were often held in the Palace Grounds, Armagh, at Darton, Tynan Abbey, and Elm Park. In 1916 no Annual Demonstration was held on the 12th July due to the troubles in the country, and members were advised that no colours be worn at Church Services until the brethren were inside the Church premises.

In 1918 a number of Military brethren of the 10th Battalion Royal Irish Fusiliers stationed at Annagh took out Warrant No.318 which had been working in the 9th Battalion previous to their going to France. In 1931 the County Demonstration in Killylea on the 12th was held in Armstrong's field. In the same year they procured a pole to erect a flag on Killylea Church.

In the year 1896 the first subscriptions were made to the Lord Enniskillen Memorial Orphan Fund. In 1897 the Rev. G. W. L'Estrange rector of St. Marks Killylea, Church of Ireland, became the District Chaplain. He followed in the footsteps of the Rev. Ellis a well-known churchman and loyalist. Many other prominent ministers of Religion were keen members of the District, Rev. H. M. Harpur, Rev. C. A. B. Millington, Rev. C. Bloomer, Rev. A. Crooks, to mention but a few. In 1919 Women's L.O.L No.24 was formed at Caledon when more than 50 ladies were initiated.

Flags and bunting have been removed from Orange Halls in the District many times and there have been repeated graffiti and arson attacks. The worst attacks on property have been at Mullintur Orange Hall, which was attacked several times, the worst being in 1993.

Ballyrea Orange Hall suffered minor arson attacks in 1997 and 1998.

Protestant Churches in the District have been attacked.

Caledon Presbyterian Church was severely damaged in 1994 by an I.R.A. mortar attack and an attempt was made to burn Drumnacanlier Gospel Hall.

Killylea District had completed arrangements to host the County Demonstration in 1999 but supported the proposal to switch the venue at short notice to Portadown as part of the protest at the decision of the Parades Commission in relation to the Drumcree Church Parade. Killylea will therefore host the first Twelfth in the 21st Century.

The Provos have been responsible for the murders of 7 Orangemen from this District during the recent "Troubles".

Bro. William Morrison, L.O.L. No.311,
murdered while working at his milking parlour.
Bro. Morrison had no links with the security forces,
so his murder was purely sectarian.

Bro. William Johnston, L.O.L. No.768,
Murdered in 1972 at the Border.

Bro. Thomas Armstrong, L.O.L. No.297,
Part-time U.D.R. member living on the border,
murdered at his home in 1976.

Bro. Harry Livingstone, L.O.L. No.630,
murdered in 1980 while feeding his livestock.

Bro. Sir Norman Stronge,
and his son Bro. James Stronge, L.O.L. No.768,
both murdered at their home, Tynan Abbey, on 21st January 1981.
Sir Norman was the former Speaker of the Northern Ireland Parliament.
Tynan Abbey was set on fire after the murders and reduced to a ruin.

Bro. Charles Neville, L.O.L. No.150,
ex-U.D.R. Sergeant. Killed in 1981 in Armagh as he returned from work.
Murdered by a grenade and gun attack.

A further 7 Orangemen have been wounded
and 2 have been intimidated out of their homes.

In addition 11 relatives of Orangemen in this District
have been murdered.

YOU'RE ALL WELCOME TO KILLYLEA

12th July, 1931
Composed by Alex Reaney. Milford, Armagh

Another twelfth has come around with another sweet July,
Like days of old may the sun now shine from a blue cloudless sky;
Let our hearts feel light while the day is bright and the bands
sweet music play,
We'll join hand in hand at the old command -
'You're all welcome to Killylea'.

Every blade of grass like each hour we pass will re-echo the refrain,
Like a heavenly dove come from above to remind us once again,
Come and join us all both great and small upon this glorious day,
Our invite we give and while we live -
"You're all welcome to Killylea."

Men like the late Sir James who have still great names will be there
to greet you all,
E'en Rev. Millington our good D.M. in such accents sweet does call,
To Caledon and to Tynan too, with Portadown and Ballyrea,
Our best wishes sound through the County round -
"You're all welcome to Killylea."

Kindly Brother Peel who's as true as steel and whose fame
is near and far,
In the hour of need he'll be there indeed, he's the pride of old Armagh.
Like true men then come with your fife and drum and your bands
that sweetly play,
Let your hearts be light while you know its right -
"You're all welcome to Killylea."

Your Lodges one by one would take too much room for me
them all to name,
Likewise other things as my mind now rings so I hope I'm not to blame,
Extend we to all now this faithful call to join us this glorious day,
And you'll not regret nor will you forget -
"You're all welcome to Killylea."

THE PRIVATE LODGES OF KILLYLEA DISTRICT

L.O.L. No.6 TANNAGH - HILL

The Lodge was formed in 1795 being one of the first warrants granted after the founding of the Orange Institution. Initially the Lodge sat in the townland of Cullentraugh, but moved to the neighbouring townland of Tonnagh in the 19th century where it has remained ever since. The site is near Tannagh-Hill a local landmark and the well-known ancient Navan Fort.

Little is known of the Lodge in its formative years, but the earliest recorded Master was William Turner who held office in 1823. The local Church Of Ireland Rector of Killylea, the Rev. Thomas Ellis is believed to have been a member of L.O.L. No.6. He was a great Loyalist and the District Hall is named in his honour.

In 1897 a new hall was built. Over the years it was enlarged and modified. As well as the regular meetings, the hall is a centre point for socials and dances and other relevant meetings connected with the social, political and religious life of the Protestant community.

1901 saw the formation of a Flute Band which is still in existence. Every Twelfth it faithfully leads the Lodge in its annual walk. During the Second World War it was the only band in the District that was on parade. The band is always noted for its good appearance and regularly updates its uniform as well as its flutes and drums.

Since its formation, Tannagh-Hill Lodge has gone from strength to strength. In celebrating its 200th anniversary it unfurled a new Banner in 1995. Wor. Bro. Stephen McLoughlin, District and County Secretary, is a member of this Lodge.

L.O.L. No.29 CORMEEN RISING SONS OF WILLIAM.

Cormeen Lodge was formed shortly after the Battle of the Diamond. We know that it sat in Killylea village in 1825 and moved to Cormeen shortly afterwards where the members held their meetings in farm houses in the area. In 1895 a hall was built at a cost of five pounds sterling. This hall served the Lodge and its Flute Band for nearly 100 years. In 1994 the old hall was demolished and a spacious new hall built on the site.

The Lambeg Drum is a familiar sound in and around Cormeen. There is a keen interest within the Lodge and as well as participation in area contests, competitions are run each year for which there is great enthusiasm. At present there are fifty members in the Lodge as well as the long-established Flute Band.

In the year 1875 an Orange Ball was held in the house of James Steele of which we have notice:-

CORMEEN ORANGE LODGE No.29
AN ORANGE BALL

Will be held in the House of James Steele, Cormeen
On Thursday 14th October, 1875,
Where the favour of your company is requested by the STEWARDS
Clark Ewart, Robert Hall, Robert Lowery, Robert Clougher
Thomas Steele, Alex McCelvey

You bonny lassies, all so fair, We do you here invite
And with the boys of 29, You'll spend a pleasant night.
All you that know the system true, Adorn yourselves with orange and blue;
And every young man that does find a true lover,
Will see her safe home when the Ball does be over.

Dancing to commence at 6 o'clock — Ladies 6d Gentlemen Is 6d

L.O.L. No.150 MULLINTUR

This Lodge has its hall situated at Maydown Road between Killylea and Benburb. Earliest records show that it met in Blackwaterstown (Englishtown) as far back as 1823 when the Lodge was then part of Charlemont District. Afterwards it held its meetings in several farm houses at Cavanbellaghy, Ballymartrim and Edenderry. The hall on Maydown Road was erected in the 1890's by the Garret Brothers from Lisdown. Records show that the hall was extensively used for many social functions. A ticket for one of the socials held in 1907 contained the verse:

You noble sons of William, who rally round our Throne,
Who would support King William's laws and popery disown
And like a gallant hero that would now with us join,
In support of our country, and keep Home Rulers down.
And when we assemble all round in the ring,
We will all join hand in hand, and with one voice we'll sing,
To the memory of William, that true and gallant King.
You ladies fair and beautiful, once more on you we call,
To spend a night with the boys in Mullintur Orange Hall,
With the Orange all around you, and banners bright and glee,
As your forefathers wore in the days of yore, and gained the victory

Down the years the hall has suffered at the 'hands of local I.R.A. sympathisers, having been burned on a number of occasions. Many members have suffered at the hands of Roman Catholic terrorists. The Lodge banner carries a portrait of our late Brother Charles Neville, brutally murdered while at work in Armagh City

During the Centenary celebrations in 1997 at least six members received their 50 year long service medals. The oldest serving member Herbert Lee, now in his 94th year received a 75th decoration some years ago. Although surrounded by unfriendly elements, the Lodge is determined to maintain a Christian and Protestant witness in the area.

L.O.L. No.177 CALEDON

The Lodge was formed on the 13th October 1969 as a result of the amalgamation of Caledon True Blues L.O.L. No.1268 and Limnagore L.O.L. No.299. This union was agreed by the brethren of both Lodges because of decreasing membership.

The Warrant for L.O.L. No.177 had originally been issued by the Grand Orange Lodge of Ireland to Cavan Militia as a 'Marching Warrant' in 1798. Bro. W. R. McEleavey was elected as the first W.M. of the New Lodge, and Bro. Harry McCoy as the first D.M.

The Killylea District minutes of 27th October 1900 record that L.O.L No.299 had handed in their old Warrant for renewal, and asked that it be not defaced but handed back to them. This request was granted.

L.O.L. No.289 COOEY DINGERS

This Lodge was formed in 1798. Although the early minutes books have been lost, the Lodge was known to have sat at Killylea. It moved to Tynan Village in 1820 where it held its meetings in a private house.

The name Cooey comes from the townland between Killylea and Tynan in which the Lodge is domiciled. It is believed that the word Dingers, often wrongly pronounced, originates from the sound of the bell "ding" associated with the chime from the Lambeg Drums. The sound was known to be an aboriginal war cry.

The Cooey Lodge is the only Lodge in the District that proudly walks behind Lambeg Drums at every demonstration. In the early 1890's the Lodge had a Flute Band and paraded behind a Standard depicting a portrait of King William Ill mounted on his horse. This Standard is still extant along with other drums and memorabilia depicting well-known personalities.

The Lodge was in existence long before the present Hall was built in 1900. It was built on what was known as "Gordons Land", and the present W.M. Bro. Noel Gordon is a direct descendant of the original landowners. The hall had a Mr. Blake as a live-in caretaker. During the years the faithful members of 289 refurbished and maintained the hall in good repair, and have recently purchased a piece of land for a car park.

The Lodge still holds an Annual Drumming Match and is a member of the Mid Ulster Drumming Association. Some of the members still display the skills of drum making, skin curing, and of course 'beating the drum' at competitions all over the North of Ireland and in Europe.

The current Banner shows a painting of Tynan Parish Church on the obverse and King William III on the reverse. This banner was unfurled in Tynan village in 1978

L.O.L. No.297 CAVANAPOLE PURPLE STAR

The first record of this Lodge states that it sat in Killylea in 1825. William Brimmigan was the W.M. and George Lemon the Secretary. Little is known of the working of the Lodge between the years 1829-1888 when it is believed to have held its meetings in various houses in the Cavanapole townland, and at Woodpark. The Lodge has notice of a Ball that was held in the year 1888. It reads as *follows:*

An Orange Ball will be held in Killylea Orange Hall under the auspices of Cavanapole Purple Star L.O.L. 297 on Friday 20th January 1888 at 8 o'clock PM.

Come all you Brethren to our Orange Ball,
In Memory of William of Immortal fame.
Come and his valiant deeds recall,
And Celebrate his glorious name
Come fairest sisters and dance by our side,
for a true Orangeman will make you his bride.
He will greet you with kisses and deck you with blue,
For an Orangeman's heart is both loyal and true.

Often it has been stated that the original site for the hall in Cavanapole was too boggy and an alternative was obtained on 27th June 1898 from Fellowshall Estate. (20 perches).

The present Orange Hall which is still in good repair was built in 1898. The W.M. was Alex Ritchie who retained his office until he died in 1947. He was also the Killylea District Master. His funeral was the last Orange one remembered when the Orangemen who attended wore full regalia.

The first Banner was purchased in 1912 and during these early years the Lodge was headed by Lambeg Drums, one of which bore the words 'The Conqueror of Cavanapole'. Later a Flute Band replaced these and by 1947 this was replaced by a Pipe Band named The Crozier Memorial Pipe Band in memory of Bro. Thomas Crozier who made the supreme sacrifice on the Battlefield of Sicily in 1943.

The Revd. C. A. B. Millington, Rector of Tynan was a member of this Lodge and also District Master of Killylea No.7

On the 5th November 1998 the Brethren of L.O.L. No.297 held a service of thanksgiving to mark the 100th Anniversary of the opening of Cavanapole Hall. The Lodge Chaplain the Rev. T. R. B. Taylor conducted the service. Bro. Rev. William Bingham, County Grand Chaplain, was guest speaker. Wor. Bro. David Scott, Deputy District Master, is a member of this Lodge.

L.O.L. No.309 BALLYREA

L.O.L. No.309 received a seal from the County Grand Lodge on 2 December 1895 and on 12 December the foundation members were Robert John Leeman, Roesbrook (W.M.); William Richardson, Navan; William, David, James and Pooler Leeman, Navan.

In 1898 an Orange Hall was built by James Bell and this was declared open on 1 July 1898 by Bro. Sir James Stronge, District Master. In 1903 band instruments were bought and a band started. In 1909 a Banner was unfurled by Miss Magee, daughter of the Rector of Killylea.

On 10 April 1921 Bro. John Fluke of Ballydoo was murdered in an ambush at Craggan Crossroads in Crossmaglen. Bros. Hans Leeman, Archie Murray and Knipe were severely wounded. On 29 April of the same year the Orange Hall was damaged by malicious fire when the door and woodwork was destroyed.

A new Banner was unfurled on 25 June 1932 by Mrs Leeman of Navan. In 1935 the Orange Hall was again damaged by fire - the door had been forced open using gelignite and fuse. Drums, collarettes, delph and pictures were destroyed. The trustees were awarded £16.00 at County Court. On 8 July 1940 the Orange Hall was lent for the use of the local Defence Force

Home Guard and in the same year also to Lieutenant Colonel Coyna, 5 Battalion, Welsh Guards Regiment for manoeuvres.

In June 1974 the old banner was given to Bro. J Rowntree and a new banner was unfurled in Killylea by Rev. Martin Smyth.

Wor. Bro. William Lee, District Master, is a member of this Lodge.

L.O.L. No.311 BREAGHEY

This Lodge holds its meetings in the hall situated in the town land of Breaghey on the south side of Monaghan. The existing Warrant is dated 1896. In April 1895 the District Lodge called in Warrants 311 and 630 in order that fresh Warrants be issued. In its earlier days the Lodge was known to have sat at Naul before coming to Breaghey in 1896.

The Lodge is accompanied on its parades by the Breaghey Silver Band which was formed in 1906 and has acquired a good reputation for its smart turnout and music.

The present Orange Banner has the portrait of William Morrison who had been a lifelong member of the Lodge. The previous banner depicted a portrait of Queen Victoria.

L.O.L. No.318 STRONGE MEMORIAL, LISNAFEEDY DEFENDERS OF THE NATION FROM COUNTY ARMAGH

This Lodge held Warrant No.1411 and was known as the Wilsontown. Towards the end of the last century the W.M. was a William Wilson of Wilsonstown. William was no doubt related to John Wilson of the Dyan Boyne Society, now Dyan L.O.L. No.1, who was present at the formation of the Orange Society in Sloan's Inn at Loughgall on 21st September 1795.

Warrant No.318 was known as the Military Warrant. At the request of Bro. George Posnett, an ex-serviceman of the First World War, this was granted to Lisnafeedy. Bro. James Matthew Stronge, son of the County Grand Master, J. H. Stronge of Tynan Abbey, took this Warrant with him to France during the Great War of 1914-18. This Lodge had a membership of 450 loyal Ulstermen, many of whom were initiated in the trenches in France. Sadly, with many other gallant men, on the 17th August 1917 Bro. James Stronge was killed in action at Ypres leading his men into a dangerous battle.

At the end of the hostilities the Warrant was returned to the Killylea District, and remained there until it was given to Lisnafeedy. The Warrant was aptly titled 'Defenders of the Nation from County Armagh'.

In 1906 the Lodge built a new Orange Hall at Lisnafeedy townland. This was opened on the 3rd of November of that year by the late Bro. Earl of Caledon, assisted by the late County Grand Master, Bro. Sir James Stronge, when all of the District Lodges were present. It was like a mini-Twelfth, so great were the crowds who came in support of their brethren.

In 1969 the Hall was renovated and extended and has more recently been brought up to date and modernised as it is greatly used by the Orange fraternity. In 1969 a new Accordion Band was formed and is reputed to be the best dressed Band in the District.

L.O.L. No.390 KILLYLEA GUIDING STAR

The origins of this Lodge can be traced back to 1825 as a Warrant bearing the name of the W.M. Bro. W. Huston is still extant. The usual meeting nights were the third Friday and Saturday of the month in the townland of Mullan, Tynan. They were known to have sat in the home of Bro. John McAnea in the College Hall- Kennedys area. The membership of the Lodge had a catchment of Brethren from these local areas. In 1886 no returns were submitted to the District Lodge. At this time the Lodge was sitting in a hall at Killylea and eventually in the new Ellis Hall which was built in 1879. On the 20th June 1900 L.O.L No.390 applied to the Killylea District for permission to use the title Killylea Guiding Star.

The Killylea Orange Hall was renovated and reopened on Friday 8th July 1988. In the years prior to the troubles the local U.S.C. had their drill hut in the same grounds. Bro. Jack Martin was the tenant-caretaker of the hall. As a well-decorated ex-serviceman, Jack took great delight in decorating the hall for the 12th July Celebrations.

The Banner was dedicated and unfurled on 24th May 1974 by Bro. Revd. Martin Smyth G.M.O.I. On one side King William III is displayed on his white horse, and on the other, there is a painting of the Good Samaritan helping the victim of assault. It bears the title "Bear ye one anothers burdens". It is a copy of the previous banner which was unfurled on Saturday 2nd July 1932. This old banner was bought from Bro. William Bridgett for £27:15:00

Membership of the Lodge extends to England; Canada and Australia when members return annually for the 12th demonstrations. Bro. Robert Murray our oldest member and a native of Tynan has celebrated seventy Twelfths. Richard and Alex Patton members of the Lodge paid the supreme sacrifice in the Second World War. In their memory, the Patton Memorial Band was formed and was very successful down the years. Seven members of the Patton family belonged to the band at one time. The Lodge now has an Accordion Band with about 18 members.

L.O.L. No.630A KILLYLEA TRUE BLUES

The records of the Grand Lodge indicate that the Lodge was formed sometime in 1798, however, there is little information available of its early years. On the 9th June 1811 the Warrant was renewed and issued to Bro. Thomas Scroggie of Middletown.

There are two Lodges numbered 630. In order to avoid confusion the Killylea Lodge was renumbered 630A.

In 1860 there was at least one Band in Killylea playing an assortment of instruments. They were without uniform, but we do know that some members wore tall hats which was the fashion in those early days. The Killylea Brass Band was formed after the First World War when members of the local 'B Specials' used their earnings to buy an assortment of brass instruments. This Band led the Lodge while on parade, and it was in great demand for many local functions. During the Second World War the band was in abeyance, some members answering the call of their country. It was re-started after the war in 1946 by the late Bro. Joseph Linton.

Killylea True Blues L.O.L. meet for their monthly meeting in the Ellis Memorial Hall in Killylea village. This is the District Hall, named after the Rev. Thomas Ellis, Rector of St Mark's Church in the 1880s. In the Lodge room there is a Memorial Plaque erected by the brethren to the memory of fellow brethren murdered by the republican I.R.A. over the years.

L.O.L. No.768 BOYNE DEFENDERS

The Warrant of this Lodge was issued in 1824 to Bro. Samuel Johnston of Killylea. The Lodge held their meeting in the loft of the old barn that used to be in the yard beside the Huntsman Inn at the top of the Main Street in the Killylea village.

In 1856 Bro. Thomas Marshall was installed Worshipful Master with the Lodge meeting in his home at Drumgulliph until 1875 when with the new W.M. Thomas Donaldson, the Lodge returned to Killylea.

On 29th October 1902 the Lodge applied to the District for the title 'Boyne Defenders'. This was granted. In 1907 members of Breaghey L.O.L. No.311 decided to reform L.O.L. No.768. As most of the members lived in the townland of Derryhaw the members adopted the name 'Derryhaw Boyne Defenders'. The following year permission was granted by the District for the Lodge to collect money to help build a new Hall at Derryhaw.

Over the years the Lodge has had some very distinguished brethren in its ranks. Bro. Capt. Rt. Hon. Sir Norman Stronge, retired speaker of the Northern Ireland Parliament and his son Bro. James Stronge, J.P. were brutally murdered in their home in Tynan Abbey in 1981 by the scurrilous Irish Republican Army. Another valued member Bro. W. J. Johnston J.P. was also murdered in 1972 by the I.R.A.

In 1986 the Lodge unfurled a new Banner at Tynan Abbey in memory of their murdered brethren. The banner shows a picture of Tynan Abbey along with the names of the deceased.

KEADY DISTRICT L.O.L. No.8

Keady District covers a mainly rural area, and is a Border District. The area forms a part of the County Armagh which has been described as "Bandit Country" where there has been a high level of terrorist activity. Consequently there has been a drift of Protestant families away from the area in recent years.

There are seven active Lodges in the District, six meeting in their own Halls and one Lodge, No.298, sharing the District Hall in Keady. In 1900 there were 9 active Lodges in the District, the present seven plus L.O.L. No.1152 and L.O.L. No.1428 (both no longer working).

Wor. Bro. Robert Maxwell, District Master in 1820, led the opposition to the plans of the Grand Lodge to eliminate the old degrees of the original Orange order such as the old degree of "Purple Marksman".

Maxwell was a signatory to a circular letter sent to all Lodges throughout Ireland as follows:-

> *"Sir and Brother*
>
> *Whereas the Grand Orange Lodge of the County of Armagh, having assembled in Portadown on Monday 5th June 1820 and having differed in opinion with respect to the reception of the new Regulation Book, which we disapprove of.*
>
> *Now we the undersigned, request all Masters and Officers of Lodges throughout Ireland, who are determined to support and maintain the Original Orange Institution, as formed in 1795, to meet in Armagh on Monday the 10th July at 12 o'clock, at the house of Mr. John Brown, Scotch Street, then to enter into such Regulations as may be deemed necessary for the further support of our glorious Institution."*

This meeting seems to have ensured that as much as possible of the old degrees would continue in the Royal Arch Purple Order. This Order was to "shadow" the Orange as every Orange Lodge would operate a Royal Arch Purple Chapter for the purpose of giving the Arch Purple Degree.

The Armagh Guardian of 21st July 1846 contains an interesting report on the Twelfth in Keady:-

> *"At Keady a force of police, with a company of the 44th Regiment, guarded the Orangemen in their parade, but left rather early in the day. Two Lodges returning by Campbell's Crossroads were attacked by 20 entrenched musketeers, but whose fire was so bad that none of the Orangemen was seriously hurt. The Orangemen quickly separated into two sections and made a flank attack, routing their adversaries, wounding some, and securing a hundred and sixty rounds of ball cartridge.*

On the 14th July Mr. Singleton R.M. met an armed party near the Armagh turnpike on the Keady road. He asked them why they were armed and they told him to mind his own business. The R.M. sent out a party of police who searched some men they found on the road, but did not find any arms on their persons. A large cavalry pistol was, however, discovered, hid in the ditch, and when the police waited a man came for it. He was arrested and on him were found a large number of bullets."

Keady Orange Hall was built in 1869. In 1936 Bro. Thomas Kirkwood, the last surviving member of the committee who built the Hall, passed away. The Armagh Guardian reported:-

"Mr. Thomas Kirkwood, Tullyglush, who died at his home on Saturday morning, in his 85th year, was known throughout Keady District for his staunch loyalty. He was a member of Corkley L.O.L. No.219, and until a few years ago took a principal part in it's activities; he was one of the few survivors of the select body who carried out the building of Keady Orange Hall in 1869."

In the Keady area Protestants have always been in a minority and have often felt the need for protection from violent elements. On 22nd June 1921 King George V opened the Parliament of Northern Ireland and Partition came into effect. Soon after this the new Parliament had to take powers to dissolve any local council which refused to carry out their functions because they would not recognise the Parliament.

One Unionist M.P. complained about Nationalist-dominated Councils:-

"We had to sit there and listen to our King being insulted, to our Government being derided. We have been told that killing was no murder unless committed by the foreign invader."

Keady Rural District Council was one of the local authorities which was dissolved in 1921 and it's powers were exercised by Government-appointed commissioners.

Keady District has hosted the full County Twelfth Demonstration in 1933, 1964, 1978, and 1989.

Of course there had been Twelfth Demonstrations in Keady before 1933, but these were local affairs, either for Keady District only or else for the neighbouring Districts as well. 1933 was the first time all Districts in the County paraded in Keady.

To quote the Armagh Guardian, dated 14th July 1933:-

THE TWELFTH
WONDERFUL GATHERING IN KEADY
COUNTY GRAND MASTER STATES ORANGE POSITION
WHAT WE HAVE WE HOLD

"We are going to hold the position we have gained," said Bro. Lieut-Col. Sir Wm. Allen, K.B.E., D.S.O., Grand Master of County Armagh, when he addressed the Keady meeting on Wednesday last, July 12th. "That is the message we are sending out to all whom it may concern, whether it be the Roman Catholic hierarchy, who think that some time or other they may have control of all Ireland, whether it be the Government now in power in the Free State, or the Republicans who are drilling openly in Southern Ireland and secretly in the North. We are going to hold what we have here."

It was the first time a county demonstration had been held in Keady and the border town provided a right royal welcome for the twenty thousand visitors who from nine o' clock began to pour in from all over the county. Eight special trains brought the brethren from North Armagh and from Bessbrook and Markethill Districts. The trains were packed, even the guards' vans being used for passengers; bitter complaints were made in some districts that they could not get their banners into the vans provided."

In 1947 four Districts (Keady, Newtownhamilton, Bessbrook and Armagh) held a Twelfth Demonstration in Keady. The other seven Districts went to Tandragee. As the Armagh Guardian stated:-

"At Keady the brethren assembled in the town and marched through the gaily decorated streets to the field close to the Annvale factory. Here the District Master, Bro. W. J. Watson, J.P. took the chair and welcomed the brethren, particularly those from Eire. "They have come to see how we are living," he said. "They are supposed to be living in the Promised Land, but I think we have a little bit of a garden here ourselves."

In 1964 the full County returned to Keady. The Armagh Guardian stated:-

ORANGEMEN APPRECIATE R.C. HELP IN KEADY

"Keady, the Border outpost where 85% of the population is Roman Catholic, rolled out the red carpet in welcome for the men of the Diamond when after a gap of 30 years the Orangemen of County Armagh celebrated the Twelfth of July in the town on Monday.

The unity and co-operation of the people of Keady in preparing for the Orangemen was praised by the county officers and the District Master of Keady on Monday. Bunting flew from building to building without interruption along the route and the Town Hall was given a face-lift for the Orangemen's visit by the Roman Catholic council. Many traders too, brightened up their premises for the occasion.

Throughout the day of pomp and pageantry with the colourful banners flying and drums beating, the Roman Catholics of Keady stretched out the hand of friendship to their Orange countrymen and it was noticeable how many lined the route to watch the procession – something very new."

Sadly this spirit of co-operation did not last, but such a newspaper report does give the lie to recent Sinn Fein propaganda that the parades were never welcome in Nationalist areas.

In 1996 the District Church Parade on the Sunday before the Twelfth had to be cancelled because Republicans blocked the road. The service was held in the Orange Hall car-park in the open-air.

The same Church parade had to be cancelled in 1997.

There was no District parade in Keady on the Twelfth in 1996 and again in 1997 because of blocked roads. This was obviously an attempt by Republicans to retaliate over Drumcree.

In 1998 the Parades Commission ruled that the District Church Parade was lawful and should go ahead, and a crowd of Republicans had given assurances to the police that they would stand aside and let the parade pass. However when most of the Brethren had passed the hostile crowd, the Republicans attacked the rear of the parade with bricks in their hands covered with handkerchiefs. One of the Orange marshals was severely injured to the face and had to have an operation in the Ulster Hospital, Dundonald, which specialises in facial injuries. Several cars were seen in the area with Republic of Ireland numberplates and the actions of a Sinn Fein Councillor from Co. Monaghan only helped to increase tension.

In 1999 the Parades Commission again ruled in favour of the Church Parade taking place and this time the police were ready for any trouble. The parade passed through two lines of R.U.C. Constables wearing full riot gear and only two bottles were thrown. For the brethren present it was a sad comment on the times we are living in.

Two Orangemen from this District have been murdered since the start of the present period of terrorist activity.

Bro. Norman Watson, L.O.L. No.88

was shot dead by mistake by the army when returning from work in 1971. The I.R.A. ambushed an army patrol and he was shot in the crossfire. His wife was wounded in the same incident.

Bro. Joseph Reid, L.O.L. 88
a member of the Ulster Defence Regiment,
was shot dead on his own doorstep in 1975.

Drumderg Orange Hall suffered an arson attack with minor damage.
The Lodge flag has been removed several times.

Crosskeys Orange Hall suffered an arson attack
and their banner was destroyed.

Keady Orange Hall has suffered minor damage.

Keady Primary School had windows broken in 1997,
as had Keady Parish Church.

Tassagh Presbyterian Church had windows broken in 1996
and Mountain Lodge Pentecostal Church was burned in 1995.

THE PRIVATE LODGES OF KEADY DISTRICT

DERRYHENNETT TRUE BLUES L.O.L. No.37

This Lodge meets in it's own Orange Hall built in 1912. The Hall has been renovated in 2000 and a new floor and central heating installed.

The banner has a painting of the Burning of Bishops Latimer and Ridley and previous banners have had the same design. The Lodge has it's own accordion band which won an all-Ireland championship in the 1980's, tutored by Mr. Winters. However with the decline in the population of young Protestants in recent years with many studying many miles away, it has proved difficult to keep the band going. Wor. Bro. John Carson, Past District Master, is a member of this Lodge.

CROSSKEYS L.O.L. No.88

L.O.L. No.88 meets in it's own Hall on Crosskeys Road in the townland of Moneyquin, about 3 miles from Keady off the Armagh Road. In terms of membership it is the largest Lodge in the District.

Crosskeys Lodge was once called "the Buffs." The Lodge was formed about 1900 and is headed on the Twelfth by Crosskeys Victoria Flute Band. Their banner has a painting of the Battle of the Somme.

The Armagh Guardian contains an article on the opening of the hall on July 11th 1924:-

> *"Though no 88 is a strong Lodge, they have never had a hall of their own, and the amalgamation of Cross Keys National School with the Temple School, a short distance away, was an opportunity too good to be lost. They purchased the vacant school building and have converted it into a neat and commodious hall. Bro. Rev. Canon M.B. Hogg presided at Saturday's ceremony and Bro. Samuel Acheson, of L.O.L. 49, performed the actual opening with a silver key presented to him by Wor. Bro. David Faloon. W.M. Bro. Acheson was chosen, the Lodge explains, because he had proved a true friend to the Lodge and because he is everything a loyal man should be. Bro. Acheson is S.D.C. of the "B Special" Force of police."*

The Late William James Watson was District Master for 25 years and his son Albert Watson who is still an active member of the Lodge was District Secretary for 25 years.

The Lodge attends First Keady Presbyterian Church yearly in July.

Two members of L.O.L. No.88 have been killed in the recent period of "Troubles":

Bro. Norman Watson
was shot by mistake by the army

Bro. Joe. Reid
was murdered by the I.R.A.

CORKLEY L.O.L. No.219

This Lodge was formed in the late 1800's and first met at Orange Hill, Dundrum.

It now meets at Corkley Mountain between Keady and Newtownhamilton in a Hall built in 1960 and renovated in 1991. The present banner, unfurled in 1991 has a painting of the Bible and Crown – the main symbols of the Order. The previous banner, unfurled in 1948 had a portrait of the late Cpl. Sandy Shilliday.

William Shilliday, Thomas Shilliday and George Fleming served as District Masters.

Bro. George Bingham also served as District Chaplain. Bro. Thomas Shilliday served as a councillor on Armagh District Council.

The Lodge organises a church parade on 3rd Sunday in June and is headed on parade by a pipe band. Wor. Bro. Noel Jenkins, Deputy District Master, is a member of this Lodge.

DRUMHILLERY FRONTIER GUARDS L.O.L. No.229

This Lodge was formed in the early 1900's and meets in it's own Orange Hall sited at Drumhillery midway between Keady and Middletown. It's close proximity to the Border with the Irish Republic explains the unusual title of the Lodge. Their banner has a painting of the main symbols of the Orange Institution, the Bible and Crown.

The present District Secretary, Bro. T. Ross is a member of this Lodge and the Lodge is headed on the Twelfth by Drumhillery Pride of the Frontier Flute Band.

The Lodge organises an annual Church parade and service alternating between Drumhillery Presbyterian Church and Madden Parish Church.

KEADY TRUE BLUES L.O.L. No.298

The Warrant for this Lodge is dated 1st Jan. 1825 and was signed by Col. Verner, Grand Master. The Lodge met first at Orange Hill near Tassagh Bridge and then moved to Chapel St. in Keady. L.O.L. No.298 now shares the District Hall in Keady.

Wor. Bro. Cecil Kinnear, District Master, and Bro. Gordon Boyd, District Treasurer, are members of this Lodge. The banner has a painting of the Open Bible and Crown with the legend: "Fear God, Honour the Queen."

The Lodge had it's own Pipe Band, formed in 1918. The first band uniforms belonged to the Black Watch Regiment and were delivered on a Sunday. Some members refused to wear the uniform as a result and took a deal of persuasion! In the 1950's numbers declined but the band was reformed for the Coronation in 1953 and continued until 1997 when numbers declined again. The Lodge still has the instruments, but a decision to sell will have to be made if there is little hope of starting the band again.

MADDEN L.O.L. No.972

The official title of this Lodge is Drumacanver, after the Townland in which the Orange Hall is sited, but the Lodge is universally known as "Madden". Their new Orange Hall was built in the 1980's to replace a very small Orange Hall beside Madden Parish Church.

The Lodge has it's own accordion band, still going strong after many years and it is a fixture in the local community.

DRUMDERG L.O.L. No.1236

This Lodge is headed on parade by it's own band, Drumderg Loyalist Flute Band, formed in 1923 and still going strong. Drumderg Orange Hall was built in 1954 and is being renovated in 2000. The Hall has been attacked during the "Troubles."

The Lodge banner depicts the Black Chief receiving the Bible and the legend: "The secret of England's Greatness."

NEWTOWNHAMILTON DISTRICT L.O.L. No.9

Newtownhamilton District covers a wide rural area centred on the market town of Newtownhamilton.

A large part of the District runs alongside the Border with the Republic of Ireland and many minor roads provide crossing points.

Although no register exists detailing the issue of District Warrants, the earliest knowledge of Newtownhamilton working as a District Lodge comes from the 'Memorials of Orangeism' by Edward Rodgers. On the 5 June 1820 John Simpson, District Master of Newtownhamilton had added his name to a proclamation supporting the original Orange Institution Regulations as formed in 1795 and disapproved of the new regulation book of 5 June 1820.

John Simpson was supported in his disapproval by the addition of signatures from Thomas Seaver, D.M., Camlough, Henry Sling, D.M., Armagh, Robert Maxwell, D.M., Keady and Richard Warmington, D.D.M., Newtownhamilton. Incidentally, Edward Rodgers informs us that a warrant first issued in 1795 by James Sloan cost £1-2s-9d. Another issued in 1799 by J. Verner, Grand Secretary, cost 5s 5d.

The next information is from the 1823 register where the following private Lodges were listed under Newtownhamilton District, Co Armagh.

Lodge No.	Date of Issue	To whom Issued
117	10 November 1823	Robert Cornett, Newtownhamilton
153	10 November 1823	James Crozier, Lisceenan, Newtownhamilton
305	10 November 1823	Robert Hunter, Newtownhamilton
363	10 November 1823	Nevin McConnell, Tullyvallen
687	10 November 1823	Richard Warmington, Cavemakill, Newtownhamilton
1157	10 November 1823	Tommy Heaslip, Corkley, Newtownhamilton
1437	8 March 1824	John Boyce, Tullyvalin
1703	10 November 1823	John Jackson, Newtownhamilton
1710	12 February 1824	James Jackson, Lurganearly, Newtownhamilton.

It is noted that Lodge numbers 153 and 305 were at this time issued to two different Counties at the same time although the 1798 minute book does give the earlier credence of 153 being issued to Co. Down but does not state where.

The next information on the District may be gained from W. H. Wolsey's (Editor of the Portadown Times), booklet published in 1919, entitled ' Story of the Battle of the Diamond' .This booklet also contains a list of Orange Lodges in Co. Armagh in 1825 at the time the Order was 'proscribed'.

From Newtownhamilton we are told that Henry Barker Esq. was District Master (perhaps he that gave his name to Barkers Road), Robert Hunter was Secretary, Robert Cornett, Treasurer and Thomas McCosh, Deputy Master.

In 1834 a Select Committee was appointed to report to the House of Commons for enquiring into the state of Ireland so as to develop the true nature of the Orange Institution.

Marcus Synnot of Ballymoyre Lodge represented Newtownhamilton District on this Select Committee. In the appendix to the Report he confirmed that Nevin McConnell was then District Master and that Warrant numbers 117, 153, 363, 687, 1157, 1158, 1159 and 1160 were held by the Newtownhamilton District but the Master's name and place of meeting were not disclosed.

The next register of 1856 begins by giving some detail on two distinguished gentlemen from Newtownhamilton District who held office.

John R. Irwin of Carnagh House, Keady, W.M. of Carnagh L.O.L. No.898 was a Deputy Grand Master of the Grand Orange Lodge of Ireland and Deputy Grand Master of Co. Armagh. He also sat on the General Central Committee representing Co. Armagh.

Parker George Synnot of Ballymoyer, Newtownhamilton was Grand Treasurer for Co. Armagh. Newtownhamilton District at this time was comprised of the following private Lodges: 117, 153, 305, 363, 630, 670, 687, 898,1033,1151, 1157,1158,1159, 1160, 1162,1206,1212 and 1650 for whom the W.D.M. was still Nevin McConnell.

Parker George Synnot (sometimes spelt Sinnot) was to become County Grand Master in 1885, following the death in office of Colonel Sir William Verner. P. G. Synnot was to serve as C.G.M. until his own death in 1901. He was also the District Master of Newtownhamilton and W.M. of his private Lodge of Ballymoyer.

DISTRICT MASTERS OF NEWTOWNHAMILTON DIST No.9

1820 John Simpson
1825 Henry Barker
1828 Nevin McConnell
1867 Parker George Synnot
1902 James McKee
1908 P. G. Shaw
1913 Andrew Bailie
1924 Rev. R. B. White
1941 John Cooke
1956 James Hughes
1962 Joseph Hawthorne
1979 John Ardis
1981 Samuel Shanks
1984 Hamilton Mills
1993 James Copeland

Over the years the Protestant population of the area has declined. There are now 10 active Lodges in the District, as compared to 18 Lodges in 1856. Rural de-population has had a part to play, but the role of terrorist activity should not be under-estimated, since the District is part of the South Armagh so-called "Bandit Country."

Since the present period of terrorist violence started in 1969, there have been 9 members of this District murdered, 7 members wounded and there have been 14 separate attacks on Orange Halls.

The Brethren of the District who were murdered are listed below:

Bro. Sidney Watt, L.O.L. No.106,
member of the U.D.R., shot outside his house in 1973.

Bro. Robert McConnell. L.O.L. No.305,
member of the U.D.R., shot in his own yard in 1976.

In September 1975 the I.R.A. carried out an attack
on Orangemen during a Lodge meeting in their own hall,
5 members of Tullyvallen, L.O.L. No.630, were shot dead.

Wor. Bro. James McKee, the then W.M.
Bro. Ronnie McKee
Bro. William Herron
Bro. John Johnston
Bro. Nevin McConnell

5 members of Tullyvallen Lodge were also injured
and hospitalised in the attack

Also in 1975
Bro. William Meeklim, L.O.L. No.630,
was kidnapped, tortured and killed by the I.R.A.

Bro. Joseph McCullough. L.O.L. No.630
was killed by terrorists (never claimed by the I.R.A.)

There have been 14 separate attacks on Orange Halls in this District. The first record of cars having to be guarded when parked at the District meetings was in 1971. This was a precaution against the planting of bombs and booby-traps.

Carrickawilkin Orange Hall was destroyed in 1972.

Carnagh Orange Hall has suffered 4 attacks, damaged by a bomb in 1971 and another bomb in 1972; an arson attack in July 1991 and a second arson attack in Sept 1995.

Ballymoyer Orange Hall, Outlacken, was destroyed in 1973 by a pipe-bomb and their new Hall damaged by petrol-bomb in 1994

Cladybeg Orange Hall has had 4 arson attacks, one in 1996 and three in 1997.

Tullyvallen Orange Hall suffered an arson attack in 1995

Aughnagurgan Orange Hall was partly destroyed by fire in 1995.

Knockavannin Orange Hall had an arson attack in 1995.

Carnagh L.O.L. No.898 was forced to hold it's annual Divine service in a car park at Keady Orange Hall in 1997 because Republicans had blocked the Main street in Keady and refused to let the parade pass.

Also in 1997 the District parade on the Twelfth evening in Newtownhamilton had to be called off because of the threat of a rocket attack and an actual attack the night previous.

In recent years Newtownhamilton District has hosted the full County Demonstration on the Twelfth in 1960, 1970, 1979 and in 1990.

The following extract from the Armagh Guardian of July 14th 1960 gives a flavour of the occasion:-

NEWTOWN BULGED WITH 20,000 VISITORS

"I cannot understand why members and sympathisers of the I.R.A. continue to live in Northern Ireland", said Bro. J. A. Anderson, County Grand Treasurer, speaking at the Twelfth Demonstration in Newtownhamilton.

It is estimated that 20,000 people packed the narrow streets of Newtownhamilton on Tuesday for the town's first ever County Twelfth Demonstration. The thousands of visitors to the town were mainly transported by the Ulster Transport Authority and it was the first time that double-decker buses had been seen in the town.

Visiting brethren included Bro. T. Finlay, Past Supreme Grand Master of Chicago, and late of Drumhillery, and Bro. Robert McCarten, a member of Enniskillen L.O.L., Toronto, and late of Crosskeys. Both men emigrated 49 years ago.

THE PRIVATE LODGES OF NEWTOWNHAMILTON DISTRICT

L.O.L. No.106 BALLYMOYER

formerly holders of warrant No.670

Synnots True Blues owe their name to a distinguished Pastmaster, District Master and Co. Grand Master - Parker G. Synnot. The first confirmation of warrant 670 being in the Newtownhamilton District was from the 1834 Select Committee Report to The House of Commons. Although Marcus Synott of Ballymoyer Lodge had represented Newtownhamilton District on the Select Committee, it was also confirmed that a 670 number existed in the Loughgall District.

The 1856 register confirmed that Parker J. Sinnott was master of Ballymoyer in the Newtownhamilton District. Parker G. Synnot [spelling had changed] continued as master of Ballymoyer in 1875 and indeed was still master in 1891.

During his distinguished career, Parker G. Synnot not only loyally served his private and district Lodge but also the County Grand Lodge of Armagh. He was District Master from at least 1867 to 1896. He was County Grand Treasurer from 1853 and County Grand Master from 1886 to 1901 until his death on the 20 March 1901.

In 1875 he was also named as Master of L.O.L. No.812 and he was still holder of the 812 warrant in the 1891 register. P. G. Synnot was reported as W.M. of L.O.L. No.670 in the Armagh Guardian of 18 July 1884 and John Hamilton W.M. in 1902 and also in 1905 when Colin Patterson then assisted him as Secretary. William R. Hamilton of Outlacken, Belleek was still Master in 1909. William R. Hamilton of Outlacken continued as W.M. to the end of the 1920's when he was then still assisted by Isaac McIlwain of Cavankill. Both men were still in office in 1924 when the Ballymoyer Lodge attended the 12th July celebrations in Armagh, although the reporter did not say what number they walked under.

Some of Ballymoyer's events were recorded in the Armagh Guardian as follows:-

July 17, 1868

Ballymoyer Loyal Orange Lodge, No.670. The members of this very much esteemed praiseworthy Loyal Orange Lodge, met on the 14th to commemorate the glorious anniversary of the 12th. Parker G. Synnot, Esq., J.P., occupied the chair, and amongst those present were Mr. Black, D.M., Markethill; Rev. James Meek, Presbyterian Minister of Kingsmills; John Donaldson, Esq.; Lady Synnot, Miss Richmond, &c. The proceedings were of a very enthusiastic character. The cloth being removed, Mr. Synnot in very appropriate terms stated the reason why they were there assembled, and amongst other things, referred to Mr. Gladstone's attack upon the Church. The health of Marcus Synnot, Esq., D.L., J.P., was proposed, and it was stated that he could not attend on account of his having been in bad health. Great credit is due to Misses Synnot, and Richmond for the excellent style of the entertainment. The room was beautifully decorated with orange lilies. After dinner dancing was resumed in the barn loft, and carried on till an early hour the next morning, when all passed off in a very quiet and peaceable manner.

(Descriptions of the room and loft makes Bro. Joe Watt believe that this event took place at Synnot's big house Lurgana.)

Following Parker G. Synnot's death on the 20 March 1901 the Lodge continued to meet in the parish hall and various brethren's barns until they acquired the old Knockavannon school in the early 1920's. This was located on the Newtownhamilton to Ballymoyer road just below Frazer's. They remained here until after the Second World War when they then moved to the old school in Outlacken townland in the late 1940's. It was originally known as Laven's School. Three or four rooms were then knocked together in the early 1960's to make one large hall. It was blown up by the I.R.A. in June 1973 when a pipe bomb was placed at the door in the northern gable. In the ruins one can still see the cut stone reveals which formed the large school windows.

On the 2 June 1922 for the sum of 10/6, warrant No.106 was granted to Isaac McIlwaine of Newtownhamilton District. Isaac McIlwaine was also D.D.M. in 1924. Prior to this 106 had a significant history. In the 1798 to 1819 Minute Book it sat in Loughgall with 20 members for whom the W.M. was John Brownlee.

July 4, 1941 Big Ballymoyer Gathering (Armagh Guardian)

The ancient and historic church of Ballymoyer was filled to overflowing on Sunday last when a July anniversary service was held. The following Lodges were represented: - Newtownhamilton District – Ballymoyer 106; Armaghbreague 153; Newtownhamilton 117; Cladybeg 305; Tullyvallen 630; Outlacken 670; Aughnagurgan 687; Knockavannon 1157. Markethill District –Tullyhappy 59, Glenanne 132; Markethill 222; Mountnorris 346; Belleeks 528; Lurgaross 620. Bessbrook District – Divernagh 77; Bessbrook 294.

Following the bombing of Ballymoyer's hall in June 1973 the Lodge met in Harold Patterson's house formerly owned by Minnie Stinson and which had been Outlacken school between the 1920's and the 1960's. The Lodge moved about for their meetings in the 1970's, also using Newtownhamilton

Orange hall, until they eventually acquired land on the Ballymoyer Road for the building of a new hall which was opened on the 15 June 1984 by Bro. Jim Nicholson M.P.

L.O.L. No.117 NEWTOWNHAMILTON, WHITE WATER TEMPERANCE

May attribute their name to the White Water river which flows just to the west of Newtownhamilton. It is reported that the Lodge originally sat in the 'hollow' near John McKee's house and only moved into the town in the late 1920's.

The first mention of 117 appears to have been an Armagh warrant in 1798 but no masters name was given. On the 10 November 1823 it was renewed to Robert Cornett of Newtownhamilton. Later that year on 29 September 1823 it was also issued to James Buchannon of Mullaglass but then reconfirmed to Robert Cornett on 8 March 1824 and again on the 2 February 1829 as detailed in the 1828 register. On the 24 December 1828 it had been granted to Adam Rankin of Newry but a note in the register says it was 'Not Returned'.

Marcus Synnot confirmed its existence in the Newtownhamilton District in the Select Committee's Report of 1834. By 1856 John Graham had become Master of L.O.L. No.117 sitting at Mullaglass, Newry District and Robert Wigham was their Master in 1856.

July 17, 1931 Newtown Banner unfurled (as reported in the Armagh Guardian)
Three Generations of Orangeism

On Friday night at Newtownhamilton a new banner was unfurled for Whitewater L.O.L. 117, the ceremony being performed by Miss Eileen White, the 7 year old daughter of Bro. Rev. R. B. White M.A., W.M. of the Lodge and District Master, who presided over the function.

The Chairman congratulated the Lodge on their enterprise in purchasing a new banner in these days of stress and thanked all who had assisted.

Bro. John Cooke, Secretary of No.117, presented Miss White with a handsome pair of scissors with which she cut the ribbons binding the banner, which was then unfurled amid great enthusiasm.

On one side the banner shows King William III, the other depicting the Relief of Derry.

Proposing a vote of thanks to Miss White, Bro. Cooke said that she had three generations of Orange ancestry behind her on both sides, and he hoped that she would be spared to represent the fourth.

Bro. David Campbell seconded and the resolution passed.

Bro. William Hawthorne, J.P., W.M. of Newtownhamilton Border Volunteers L.O.L., brought greetings from his Lodge and congratulations on the prosperity of No.117.

The Chairman, replying for his daughter; spoke of the lessons to be learned from the pictures on the banner.

The proceedings were closed by the singing of the national Anthem, after which the new banner was carried in triumph through the town, the Newtownhamilton Pipe Band heading the cortege.

In 1937 the Lodge started a band, tutored by Mr. F. Malone and in 1954 built a new Orange Hall.

In 1940 there was no Twelfth parade because of the War, so the Lodge agreed to hold a religious service on the Twelfth followed by a dance that same night.

In 1947 the band was asked to lead the District when it attended the Carrickfergus Pageant to re-enact the landing of King William.

In 1950 a new banner was purchased. Wor. Bro. Samuel Courtney, District Secretary, is a member of this Lodge.

L.O.L. No.153 ARMAGHBREAGUE TRUE BLUES

From the mountainous Fews area, the locality attributes its name to - Pseudo or False Armagh

The warrant number 153 is first mentioned in the 1823 register as being granted to William Bell of Drumbaugh, Rathfriland District on the 24 September 1823. It was then also issued to James Crozier of Lisceenan in the Newtownhamilton District on the 10 November 1823.

By 1909 153 was confirmed as sitting at Armaghbreague under Thomas Harvey W.M. assisted by Jonathan Harvey, secretary.

Robert Deanes of Armaghbreague was W.M. and Jonathan Harvey was still secretary in 1913 when the Lodge consisted of 23 members.

The Deanes farm was up the lane just to the right of the entrance of Grouse Lodge and the Harvey farms were further up the mountain to the rear of Grouse Lodge.

Up to 1931 the Lodge was sitting in a stone built small house adjacent to Armaghbreague School, now G. Dougans. The pipe band continued to use this house for practice for many years after the new hall was opened.

On July 15, 1910 an article appeared in the Armagh Guardian describing when L.O.L. No.153 were the host Lodge to the 12th held by Newtownhamilton District:-

Armaghbrague – An enjoyable re-union.

Temperance was the key note of the Newtownhamilton district meeting at Armaghbrague Church, where the Lodges of Newtownhamilton district – except Ballymoyer, which went to Bessbrook – together with every Protestant man, woman and child in the district, gathered to make holiday and celebrate the Battle of the Boyne. The weather could not have been better, the dead heat being lessened by a cooling breeze, while everyone's enjoyment was heightened by the fact that alcohol was absent and unobtainable. Everyone enjoyed themselves, and the speeches were brief and pointed, so that the listeners might have the more time to devote to merry-making.

Following the speeches which were chaired by Rev. Bewick, Rector of Armaghbrague, Mr. P. G. Shaw, D.M., proposed a hearty vote of thanks to Mr. Andrew Kelly who had lent the field and built the platform and who had always been a good friend to the brethren in the district.

July 10, 1931 The New Hall (Armagh Guardian)

Armaghbrague L.O.L. No.153 have for years met in a little hall which was once a school, small and inconvenient, only a few yards from the new building. Now in a field beside Armaghbrague Church, and on the side of the road, a little building of neatly painted iron work has been erected on a site given by Mr. Andrew Kelly. It is forty feet long and just half as wide, consisting of one great panelled room. From each end a Union Jack fluttered in the wind. A little platform was erected in the adjoining field for the meeting, and here Rev. R. B. White, W.M. of Newtownhamilton District, took the chair.

A sports evening has been traditional for many years and was originally held in the field behind the hall i.e. Church Hill. Prior to 1948 the Lodge was led by a flute band but in 1948 a new pipe band was formed.

L.O.L. No.305 CLADYBEG FAITH DEFENDERS

L.O.L. No.305 had its first mention in the 1823 register as being issued to Robert Hunter of Newtownhamilton District but it was then deleted. Within 4 months it was then issued to John Mulligan of Gilford in the Tandragee District.

The 1828 register records another double issue, firstly to John Boyce of Newtownhamilton District on the 2 February 1829 and John Gilmore of Tandragee on the same date – 2 February 1829. Neven McConnell, District

Master of Newtownhamilton stated in a letter dated 22 January 1835 that 305 was still in his district, meeting in Cladybeg and that Peter Pillar who lived on the Pole Hill Road was W.M.. Another note states that the warrant was taken to America by a Bro. Boyce.

Marcus Synnot did not mention 305 in his report to House of Commons Select Committee in 1834 but the representative reporting on the Tandragee District confirmed it was held there in 1834.

The 1856 register confirmed the existence of two 305 warrants – that sitting at Drumcorran, Gilford and that sitting at Cladybeg, Newtownhamilton under Peter Pillow W.M. – the same Peter mentioned in Neven McConnell's letter.

The brethren of Newtownhamilton District met on Monday 13 July 1891 in a field of Mr. Thomas Kernahans, Armaghbreague, (i.e. off the Slaterock Road almost opposite the Slaterock quarry now belonging to David Crozier), to give him 'a day' he being an honoured member for 48 years. The District Master and County Grand Master Mr. Parker G. Synnot spent the day with the brethren and everything passed off in quietness and order:-

Armagh Guardian Feb 3, 1911:

Armaghbrague L.O.L. No.305 - Annual Ball

The members of above Lodge held their annual re-union and ball in the hall kindly lent for the occasion by Wm. Morris. There was a very large attendance and the hall was very tastefully decorated for the occasion. Supper was served in good style by Mrs. Cornet, Miss Bella Morris, and Miss M. J. Leeman, assisted by Bros. Hugh and Joseph Cornet. After the good things had been disposed of the ball was opened by the brethren filling into the ball room in processional order to the air of the Boyne Water. The W.M., of the Lodge, Bro. John Kernaghan was called to the chair and gave a hearty welcome to all, and said as all the Lodges in the North were making their voices heard in favour of the Union, the boys of Armaghbrague were not behind. They were loyal and true to the cause and by God's help would remain so; they feared neither John Redmond of the priests of Rome; they were sons of their fathers who were not afraid to die for their country, and the brethren of loyal 305 were prepared to do the same before they would bow their knees to the Nationalists of Ireland. (Applause). This was not a night for speechmaking, so he would declare the ball open. Dancing then commenced and was kept up with enthusiasm for several hours, the music being rendered by Bro. John Graham (L.O.L. No.687) and the duties of M.C. were supplied by Bro. John Kernaghan. At intervals during the night, songs were rendered by Bros. Abraham Cornet, William Dixon, Joseph Cornet, James Kernaghan, Hugh Cornet and Thomas Cornet. The singing of God Save the King concluded a most enjoyable night.

In 1909 L.O.L. No.305 was meeting at Armaghbreague under the Mastership of Jonathan Kernaghan of Armaghbreague on the last Friday of the month, with William Dixon of Corran, Secretary. Jonathan Kernaghan was still Master in 1913 assisted by James Kernaghan of Ballintemple as Secretary and although the meeting night had changed to the first Friday of the month there was a membership of 20.

Since the building of Cladybeg Orange Hall in 1910 both L.O.L. No.305 and L.O.L. No.1181 were meeting there and on the 2 June 1922 the 305 warrant was reissued to Jonathan Kernaghan for the sum of 10/6 and has since remained at Cladybeg.

In 1931 the hall was extended. Having suffered an arson attack in 1997 the hall was then extensively refurbished and re-roofed and the Lodge continues to loyally defend its title "Cladybeg Faith Defenders" which it had sought permission to obtain from the County on the 20th October 1954

Wor. Bro. James Copeland, District Master and County Grand Treasurer, is a member of this Lodge.

L.O.L. No.630 TULLYVALLEN GUIDING STAR TEMPERANCE

The first mention of warrant 630 is in the 1834 Select Committee's Report to the House of Commons when it was simply stated to be operating in Co. Armagh.

By 1856 the register contained two listings for 630 – one being at Killylea under the mastership of John Gillespie and the others at Armaghbrague, Newtownhamilton District under the mastership of Thomas Kernaghan. Another duplicate (or rather triplicate of) 630 was working in Fermanagh in 1849.

Thomas Kernaghan was still W.M. of Newtownhamilton's 630 in 1875 and a note entered on this register states that the warrant was renewed in 1874. In the 1884 Armagh Guardian he was again reported as W.M.. In the 1891 register of warrants, 630 Newtownhamilton was still under the mastership of Thomas Kernaghan and a note in this register states it was renewed on the 21 January 1972 to James McKee J.P. as W.M..

The current register from 1891 informs us that John Henry renewed the warrant on the 1 January 1920 for the sum of 2/6. However prior to this we learn from the Armagh Guardian of 1902 that David McKeernan was W.M. and retained the chair through 1905 and 1907 with William J. McKeeman, Secretary. The 1909 County Report states that the Lodge met on the first Monday of each month still under the mastership of David T. McKeeman of Altnamackin, Castleblayney, the secretary now being James A. Stevenson also of Altnamackin.

In the 1913 County Report, Tullyvallen was still meeting on the first Monday with a membership of 30 men now under the mastership of John Henry of Tullyvallen and James McBride of Aughnagurgan, Secretary.

We know at this time that they enjoyed the comforts of a new hall, which had been opened in 1907.

L.O.L. No.630 suffered terribly at the hands of I.R.A. terrorism in the mid 1970's. Five members of the Lodge were murdered by I.R.A. terrorists when they broke into a Lodge meeting and sprayed the Hall with bullets. Also another Brother of this Lodge was tortured and murdered in a separate incident. The details are mentioned in the County Grand Lodge section of this Millennium Book and also in the Newtownhamilton District section.

L.O.L. No.687 AUGHNAGURGAN (formerly Cavemakill and Corclea)

Has no Lodge title but it is first mentioned in the 1823 register as being issued on the 10 November 1823 to Richard Warmington of Cavemakill, Newtownhamilton. It was then reissued to John McIlroy of Cavemakill on 8 March 1824 and in Woolsey's Report of Orange Lodges in Co. Armagh 1825 it was stated to be under the Mastership again of Richard Warmington now of Mulladuff.

Following proscription in 1825 it was reissued to James McClarney of Newtownhamilton on 2 February 1829. Marcus Synnot on his report to the Select Committee reporting to the House of Commons in 1834 confirms its existence in the Newtownhamilton District.

By 1856 in the register of this period L.O.L. No.687 had moved to Corclea under the mastership of Jonathan Hill. It is now known that its place of meeting before the opening of the present hall, in 1911, was in a barn on the Black Hill now belonging to Wilsons. This is located in the townland of Corkley. It is remembered that a large ribbon was painted on the inside of one gable of this barn depicting the name of L.O.L. No.687 but sadly this has since been eradicated by the storage of hay etc.

By 1875 the register still records Jonathan Hill as W.M. and this was still the case in 1891. A note in this register states 687 Newtownhamilton District was renewed in 1896 but the current register does not confirm to whom this was, except to say that on July 17 of this year the Armagh

Guardian reported W. Monaghan as W.M.. By 1902 the W.M. was John Gwyne and he still occupied the chair in 1905 and 1907. The 1909 County Report informs us that 687 Corclea was meeting on the first Monday of each month still under the mastership of John Gwynne of Armaghbreague, with the Secretary being Joseph Gwyne of Tullyvallen.

Enjoying the facilities of a new hall built in the townland of Aughnagurgan on land donated by Alexander McKee, 25 brethren met on the first Monday of the month in 1913 under the mastership of Joseph Blackstock of Aughnagurgan.

Following an arson attack on the hall in July 1995 it was severely damaged and completely lost its roof but was quickly re-roofed and repaired. A new floor was laid by David Gibson shortly before he and his daughter met their untimely deaths in a tragic motor accident. Central heating has since been installed and a new concrete forecourt has just been laid at the end of 1999.

L.O.L. No.898 CARNAGH

As the first minute book of Grand Lodge dated March 1798 showed that warrant numbers at that time had not exceeded 740. Carnagh's 898 warrant gets its first mention in the 1828 register with the note 'see new book'. Woolsey had no mention of 898 in his list of Lodges for 1825.

The new book referred to above is the 1856 register which states that warrant No.898 is operating at Carnagh, Keady in the Newtownhamilton District of Co Armagh with the W.M. being John Robert Irwin. We also learn from this register that the warrant had been renewed on the 26 November 1834 and again on the 8 September 1854. But to whom the warrant was issued at these dates is not stated nor indeed did Marcus Synnot include any reference to warrant 898 in his report to the Select Committee reporting to the House of Commons for enquiring into the state of Ireland so as to develop the true nature of the Orange Institution in 1834. It may however be fair to assume that L.O.L. No.898 began its workings at Carnagh mid 1834.

In the early 1900's the Lodge met in Argue's barn now at the home of Harry Boyd but around the period 1918 to 1920 when Fred Nesbitt was W.M. a piece of land at the side of the former coachmans house, i.e. coachman to the Irwin estate, was acquired from the Irwin sisters by James Strahan for the building of an Orange Hall. He was their Bog Bailiff, and was the present secretary's grandfather. The ground was given free of rent so long as the building remained an Orange Hall.

When looking at the front door of the present Carnagh Hall, the original Orange Hall was the half of the building to the left hand side, i.e. toward the southern gable. The right hand side being the home of Johnstone Dundas and was known as the 'Coachman's House'. Herbert Allen drew the stones for the new hall by horse and cart.

The Coachman's House was lived in by Walter Mayse up to 1963 or 1964. After his death renovations were carried out to knock out the middle wall and join the two buildings into one. A stage was provided at this time.

Repairs and the provision of a kitchen and toilets at the rear were carried out following a pipe bomb attack on Friday 10 September 1971.

1960 saw the demise of the flute band and the formation of a new accordion band which is still led by James Strahan one of the founder members. James Curry another of the founding members still occasionally plays in the band. Fredy Mills, played the big drum until recently.

New uniforms were obtained for the band in time for the 12th in Newtownhamilton in 1969 and a new banner for Carnagh was also unfurled on Friday 13 June 1969.

L.O.L. No.1157 KNOCKAVANNON

Gets an early recording in the 1823 register as having been issued on the 10 November 1823 to Tommy Heaslip of Corkley in the Newtownhamilton District. It was again reissued to Tommy Heaslip on 10 March 1824.

Woolsey's list of Orange Lodges in Co. Armagh 1825 records 1157's W.M. as John Boys with the number held at Dungorimony (Dungormley House still stands off the Keady Road in the townland of Tullyvallen).

Marcus Synnot reporting to the House of Commons enquiry in 1834 confirms its operation in the Newtownhamilton District.

The 1856 register confirms 1157 as having its place of meeting in Newtownhamilton in the Newtownhamilton District, Co. Armagh and the W.M. was now William Thompson. But a note adds to the history by informing us that 1157 was issued on the 7 July 1802 to Co. Wicklow with Ralph Stone of Carnew W.M.. In 1805 it was a marching warrant in the 82nd Regiment and although I haven't researched which regiments were actually stationed in Newtownhamilton it is known that Militia were stationed here in the 1800's. This may explain the continuation of the note which goes on to say "Renewed to Co. Armagh 10 November 1823 and in 1822 and 10 July 1829".

Andy Hawthorne, grandfather of the present W.M. Jim Hawthorne was instrumental in seeing the building and opening of a new orange hall at Knockavannon in 1909 and indeed it is still colloquially known at "Andy's Hall" to this day.

A prominent member of the community who gave many years loyal attendance to the Lodge was Dr. T. D. Carson G.P. for the Newtownhamilton area.

Situated a mile and a half from Newtownhamilton on the Markethill road the hall suffered an arson attack in May 1995 but repairs were quickly carried out by the members.

Traditionally the Lodge was led by the Big Drums, the 'slashers' or Andy's drums which were there in Jim Hawthorne's life time. But when a new accordion band was formed in Aug 1980 the big drums fell silent. A band parade at the hall has now become traditional over the last number of years and is held on the third Wednesday in June each year.

L.O.L. No.1158 KNOCKNANIN

The first mention of warrant No.1158 appears in Marcus Synnot's report to the Select Committee reporting to the House of Commons for enquiring into the state of Ireland so as to develop the true nature of the Orange Institution in 1834.

The 1856 register informs us that 1158 was meeting at Tullinageer (Co. Monaghan) but still within the Newtownhamilton District under the mastership of William Thompson and that the warrant had been renewed on the 10 July 1829.

Another 1158 warrant was also operating at this time at Covranarva in the Killeshandra District of Co. Cavan under the mastership of Johnston Morton.

By 1875 the Newtownhamilton District's 1158 was under the mastership of John Hillis and there was now no mention of the Co. Cavan warrant.

Strangely enough the only place of meetings stated in all of the registers is at Tullingeer. This was in the register of 1856. Local knowledge recalls however that by the end of the 1800's the place of meeting was in David Hanna's barn, Knocknanin townland.

In 1905 the W.M. was still William Hunter of Formal Drumacrib and the Secretary was William Hanna of Drollagh. Both continued in office to 1909 according to the Co. Armagh Grand Lodge report of that year, with the

Lodge meeting on the first Monday of the month at Knocknanin, Presumably this was still in David Hanna's barn as the next year or two were rewarded with strenuous efforts by the Lodge to build a new hall on the eastern slopes of Mullyash mountain.

Honour was attributed to L.O.L. No.1150 in 1912 as the Newtownhamilton District held their 12th July celebrations at Mullyash as part of the celebrations regarding the opening of the new hall.

For five years no 12th of July celebrations were held during the Second World War until a large gathering met in Armagh on July 12 1945. Although the majority of Newtownhamilton District Lodges met in Newtownhamilton to celebrate their own 12th, Knocknanin, Anyart and Aughnagurgan attended Armagh.

However to ensure they arrived on time with their banners and band instruments these had to be smuggled across the border some days before hand in order to avoid delay on the 12th morning from the Free State customs. This practise had become customary for the Southern Lodges attending gatherings in the North from partition in 1921. For example, on the 12 July 1934, held in Armagh, the Co. Grand Master Lieut. Col. Sir William Allen D.S.O. give a special welcome to the Lodges attending from the Free State. As he knew even then, their band instruments and banners were in some cases smuggled over the border days before the meeting to ensure the Free State Customs would not find an excuse to hold them up.

Members of the Lodge who have held or hold higher office in the Orange Institution are Tom McBirney who has been District Secretary and is currently Deputy District Master. Geoffrey Glenny who was District Chaplain form 1993 to 1997 and Willy McNeice who served as District Treasurer from 1979 to 1998.

The Lodge holds an annual service in July each year rotating between McKelveys Grove and Garmanys Grove Presbyterian Churches.

In the early half of this century the Lodge had its own Flute Band which was later replaced by pipes and in 1973 accordions were obtained to form a new accordion band which is still going strong.

An earlier newspaper report of the opening of the Hall in 1912 referred to the Lodge being colloquially known as 'McNeeces'. That can equally be said today except with the spelling having changed to McNeice as indeed a large number of the brethren and a larger number in the band are from the McNeice families.

L.O.L. No.1162 CARRICKAWILKIN SILVER STAR

For a period this warrant also operated in the Carnagh area, also sitting in Argues' barn.

Its earliest mention in the 1856 register records it operating at Ballintemple in the Newtownhamilton District under the mastership of John Smith and that it had been renewed on the 24 November 1829. By 1875 it was under the mastership of John McClenaghan, still in the Newtownhamilton district, but its place of sitting was not stated.

This is when it came to the Carnagh area as William James Smith lived in Drumnahaville, Derrynoose. The next record is from the 1905 Armagh Guardian newspaper of July 21, 1905 when it was reported the Lodge attended the 12th celebrations in Newtownhamilton, still under the mastership of William James Smith.

The next record in the 1913 Co. Armagh Record Book must be questioned as 1162 was stated to be meeting at Carnagh under the mastership of William Burke of Ballintemple with Alex McKee as Secretary and the Lodge then had 11 members. However neither of these are Carnagh names and although there is no record of the renewal of the warrant in Grand Lodge's registers around this period, it must be assumed that the warrant had again returned to the Ballintemple area. According to the Armagh Guardian the Lodge attended the 12th July celebrations at Keady this year (1913) with the W.M. William Burke.

At most Carnagh's second Lodge No.1162 operated for no more than 11 years from 1902 to 1913.

The next report on L.O.L. No.1162 is at the 12th July celebrations in Newtownhamilton in 1918 when the Lodge attended with Joseph Cooke as their W.M.. In 1920 it was stated to be the Newtownhamilton L.O.L. with J. Cooke, Newtownhamilton W.M. and another J. Cooke Newtownhamilton, Secretary.

By 1924 Rev. R. B. White had been elected W.M. of Newtownhamilton L.O.L. No.1162 and was assisted by John Cooke as secretary.

Bro. Rev. R. B. White B.A. was still W.M. in 1930 when the Lodge attended the 12th July celebrations in Markethill.

With no returns being entered in the Newtownhamilton District register from 1933 it must now be assumed that the Newtownhamilton L.O.L. No.1162 had ceased working around this time.

The warrant next begins its workings at Carrickawilken in 1946 under the mastership of Bro. David Dickson with William J. Adams of Tullyglush, Darkley, secretary.

As mentioned earlier in the history of warrant 363, this had ceased to work at Carrickawilken in 1940 and following the period of the Second World War, William Adams stirred the enthusiasm and began working the Lodge again under warrant No.1162.

Although their place of sitting has now moved to Darkley Orange Hall they are still known today as Carrickawilken Silver Star.

The place of meeting was in the original Carrickawilken School located at the end of the Mountainy Road (now Clea Road) just as it crossed the border into Co. Monaghan. The building was originally built as a school under the management of McKelvey's Grove Presbyterian Church but it may also have been intended for other church use as the Ulster Scots Gaelic derivation of Carrickawilken is thought to be Kirk-nu-Welkan – church without a roof. This may hold some truth as indeed there is no townland of Carrickawilken.

The building continued to be used as a school some time up to the beginning of the First World War. But when it was actually first used as an Orange Hall by 363 is unsure. Certainly by 1925 when the 363 warrant was working under George Silvey, the old school house was in use by the Lodge. The old school was still used for an occasional Sunday service up to the 1930's.

By 1961 the Lodge now consisted of 12 brethren who dug deep to commission a new banner. This banner depicted the late Bro. George Silvey on the front with King William III on the back. Their previous banner had been bought from Tullyvallen L.O.L. No.630 in 1946 and repainted.

With the onset of the troubles in the early 70's the hall received a number of attacks and as the Army were involved in closing the cross border roads by building strong barricades or in some cases using explosives to crater the roads, inevitably the hall suffered further damage.

As the barriers were being by passed by new roads built by the locals and reblasted by the Army, eventually the hall was blown up by the I.R.A. in 1972 and later the stones were carried to fill in some of the craters to create a by-pass around the barrier.

The members continued to meet in Keady Church of Ireland Hall for a time, but as Darkley Hall was standing idle enquiries were made and eventually 1162 purchased it from the District and have used it for their meetings since April 1988.

MARKETHILL DISTRICT L.O.L. No.10

This District Lodge has fourteen Warrant numbers, two of which are dormant Warrants - L.O.L. No.167 and 510. Of the remaining twelve Lodges, each has their own Orange Hall. It is a widespread District area, stretching from Tullyhappy (near Bessbrook) to Redrock (close to Armagh) and from Belleek (deep in South Armagh) to Mullabrack (in safer territory).

The District has a proud history, stretching back to the formation of the first Orange Lodges, following the Battle of the Diamond in 1795. Lodges were formed in most townlands at the time, and the areas around Markethill were no exception. The first Minute Book of the Grand Orange Lodge of Ireland is dated 1798, the basis for Grand Lodge having been established in 1797. Lodges had come together to form Districts, with James Sloan of Loughgall the titular head of the movement.

On 12th July, 1796, an Orange parade was held in the Earl of Gosford's Estate and no doubt, brethren and Lodges from Markethill were present. It is estimated that there would have been approximately ninety Lodges at this time in Ulster, mostly in the Armagh, Tyrone and Down areas. Early meetings were secret, and the original oath taken by candidates was:-

> *'I....... do solemnly swear that I will, to the utmost of my power, support and defend the King and his heirs as long as he or they support the Protestant ascendancy.'*

Sometime before the formation of the Ulster Grand Lodge in 1797, the Orangemen had established an inner circle or higher order. At first, this was called the Orange Marksmen, soon becoming the Purplemen, and hence the Lodges had two Orders - the Orange and the Purple. Later, so-called Black Lodges came into existence as a further inner circle of Orangeism, but these were, in the early years, against the rules of the Orange Order and membership in them was forbidden.

Research has unearthed the minutes of a meeting of Markethill District L.O.L. No.10, held on 2nd September, 1816. Resolutions were passed, appointing Bro. Joseph Mathers of Maytone as Worshipful District Master, Bro. John McGowan of Mountnorris as Deputy District Master, and Bro. Daniel Mason as Secretary. It was further resolved that these three brethren together with Bro. David Edwards and Bro. Alexander Douglas would:-

> *"represent this District Lodge at the meeting of Co. Armagh Grand Orange Lodge, to be held on the first Monday in November, in Armagh."*

By 1836, there were twenty-three Lodges working in the District area including Divernagh L.O.L. No.99; Mullurg L.O.L. No.132; Loughgilly

L.O.L. No.619A; Mullaghmore L.O.L. No.743; Keadybeg L.O.L. No.958; Brackley L.O.L. No.1181; and Lisnalee L.O.L. No.1242. Of these Warrant numbers, only L.O.L. No.132 (now Kilcluney) remains within the District today. By 1856, a Bro. Wm. Singleton of Mullabrack, was Worshipful District Master.

In the latter half of the 19th Century, Warrant numbers moved from District to District, as Lodges endeavoured to obtain lower numbers. The situation was further compounded by the fact that Co. Armagh and Co. Down Grand Lodges continued to issue new Warrants, after the dissolution of Grand Lodge.

By 1905, sixteen Lodges were noted as working in Markethill District. In these early years of the 20th century, membership fluctuated between three-hundred and four hundred brethren. Lodges had difficulty in meeting during the years of the First World War, as many brethren had enlisted in H.M. Forces.

It is interesting to note that by 1914, Royal Arch Purple Chapters were being established. At least four Lodges in the District had associated Royal Arch Purple Chapters, at this time.

The 1926 Co. Armagh Grand Lodge Directory indicated that L.O.L. No.619, meeting at Bolton, Loughgilly, had three members, and L.O.L. No.620, meeting at Lurgaross had one member! By 1928, L.O.L. No.619 and Markethill L.O.L. No.743 had become dormant. Kilclooney L.O.L. No.936 had surrendered their Warrant and taken out a lower No. - L.O.L. No.132, which had gone dormant some time previously. Therefore by 1930, the District Lodge comprised fourteen Lodges, namely those of today.

It has not proved possible to ascertain when the practice of holding an annual Church service was established. Certainly, it was held for many years on the last Sunday in July; at the District meeting in April, 1968, it was decided to bring this date forward to the Sunday prior to the '12th.'

For a variety of reasons, details are scant of the activities of the District Lodge in the early years of this century; minute books for example, have either been lost or destroyed. However, detailed information is available from 1939.

During the Second World War, the military used Markethill Orange Hall, and no '12th' parades or services were held during the war years. On '12th' July, 1945, the District held a parade in Markethill, meeting at the Fair Green at 2.00 p.m. In October of that year, at the District meeting, the District Secretary was asked to write to relatives of Orange brethren who had been killed during the War.

A new District bannerette was purchased in 1949 - it cost £46.00 and was dedicated at the Square on the '12th' morning 1950. During 1953/54, there were considerable discussions on a request from seven Bessbrook brethren for leave to form a Lodge, taking the dormant Warrant, No.167; the District gave permission, provided the Warrant remained in this District. The matter was settled when the Bessbrook brethren resolved their differences.

During 1959, the Orange Hall was transferred from District ownership to that of Lattery L.O.L. No.222. In 1960, the District Master, Worshipful Brother William J. Black, J.P., was awarded the O.B.E.

It is interesting to note that at this time the District had five Clerical Chaplains - Canon Rev. W. G. Kerr, Rev. A. McCurdy, Rev. R. Mcllveen, Rev. R. L. Hutchinson and Rev. H. J. W. Moore. The County '12th' demonstration was held in Markethill in 1959, the field being Brother G. Allen's, on Newry Road.

In 1962, it was agreed to purchase a new District bannerette - a levy of 9d. per member was fixed. The bannerette was unfurled by Brother J. Wallace at the District meeting on 17th April, 1963; it was dedicated by Brother Rev. F. A. Noel. The election of officers in October of that year was carried out by Brother Rev. Noel and Brother Rev. J. Rankin. These two local Ministers gave a series of lectures on the principles of the Protestant faith, to the brethren, during 1966.

In April, 1968, the District Master, Worshipful Brother S. Revels, J.P., was awarded the M.B.E. in the Queen's Birthday Honours List. The '12th' was again held in the town in 1969, Burney's field on the Keady Road, being used; at the request of the District, the County agreed that there would be no political speeches.

The District was shocked to learn of the murder of five brethren in Tullyvallen Orange Hall, Newtownhamilton, in September, 1975; in January, 1976, in the Kingsmills massacre, Tullyhappy L.O.L. No.59 lost their Worshipful Master, Brother R. Freeburn and Kilcluney L.O.L. No.132 lost Brother R. Walker.

In 1980, the County '12th' demonstration was again held in Markethill, the venue again being Burney's field, Keady Road - it was very successful. Three District Lodges - Markethill, Newtownhamilton and Bessbrook- combined on Sunday, 23rd October, 1983, to hold a special service in the Upper Presbyterian Church to commemorate the birth of Martin Luther.

At the October District meeting 1983, the District Treasurer, Brother K. Rainey, was given permission to look into the possibility of purchasing an

Arch, for erection in Main Street. During the ensuing months, funds were collected and the Arch was made by Brothers R. and O. Haire. The official opening took place on Saturday, 7th July, 1984, by Brother. J. Nicholson, M.P. and dedicated by Brother Rev. E. D. Smyth.

During 1984, the County Junior Grand Lodge asked the District to consider forming a Junior Lodge. After deliberation, it was decided to proceed. There had been a Junior Lodge in Kilbracks prior to the Second World War, and Junior Grand Lodge gave approval to re-issue the existing Warrant. Kilbracks Bible and Crown Defenders J.L.O.L. No.75 came into being and the inaugural meeting was held on 17th February, 1986, the Superintendent being Brother B. Marshall.

Following the signing of the iniquitous Anglo-Irish Agreement in November 1985, the District was well represented at the massive rally at Belfast City Hall on 23rd November, 1985. Other rallies etc. held in subsequent years were also well supported by the Markethill brethren.

In January, 1986, it was decided to erect a Memorial Stone in the Square to those brethren who had been murdered during the present troubles. A Committee was formed under Brother G. Cochrane, District Lecturer, and the stone was unveiled on 5th September, 1986, by the Grand Master, Right Worshipful Brother Rev. Martin Smyth, M.P. In the years since, the District revived a former custom of forming a circle in the Square each '12th' morning and holding a short religious service.

In 1988, the District purchased a new District bannerette and two Union Flags; the bannerette was the first of its kind in Co. Armagh, depicting the fourteen Warrant numbers of Lodges in the District. The bannerette was unfurled by the late Brother H. McCusker, M.P. in July of that year.

The District lost one of its stalwarts in November, 1988, when the Deputy District Master, Brother S. Cromwell died. He was a committed Orangeman, and in his memory the Arch was re-dedicated in July, 1989, and now bears an appropriate plaque.

In Tercentenary year, Markethill District was perhaps one of the most active in organising various events. The highlight was undoubtedly the 'Gosford Orange Festival,' held during the week preceding the '12th.' During the year, the District formed a fraternal friendship or 'twinning' with Ballynafeigh District L.O.L. No.10, Belfast.

In the past 30 years of I.R.A. terrorist activity starting in 1969 there have been 10 Orangemen of the District murdered.

Bro. R. Freeburn, Tullyhappy L.O.L. No.59,
Kingsmill Massacre, 5th January,1976

Bro. R. Walker, Kilcluney L.O.L. No.132,
Kingsmill Massacre 1976

Bro. R. Lockhart, Belleek L.O.L. No.528,
R.U.C. Constable, murdered by a landmine explosion at Millvale Road, Bessbrook in 1979

Bro. M Robinson, Lattery L.O.L. No.222,
murdered on 27th April 1981

Bro. T. Cochrane, Lurgaross L.O.L. No.620,
U.D.R. Sergeant, abducted and murdered, October 1982

Bro. C. Spence, Mullabrack L.O.L. No.1406,
R.U.C. Reserve, blown up by a car-bomb 10th November 1982

Bro. S. Corkey, Lurgaross L.O.L. No.620,
R.U.C. Reserve, shot dead at security barrier in Markethill on 16th November 1982.

Bro. M. Marshall, Redrock L.O.L. No.788,
R.U.C., blown up in a car ambush in Belleek 20th October 1989.

Bro. D. Sterritt, Ballylane L.O.L. No.479,
R.U.C. Constable, blown up by a landmine on the Killylea Road, Armagh. 24th July 1990

Bro. R. Crozier, Redrock L.O.L. No.788,
U.D.R. blown up in a bomb attack in May 1991 at the Glenanne U.D.R. Centre.

There have been 4 Orangemen of the District wounded.

In addition 12 relatives of Orangemen have been intimidated and 4 relatives of Orangemen have been murdered. Other Orangemen have had to move house to safer areas because of their work in the security forces.

Orange Halls have been attacked many times in what amounts to a concerted attack on the local Protestant community.

1969 Belleek Orange Hall was damaged by an arson attack.

1970 and 1971 Belleek Hall was damaged by bomb attacks.

1971 at Tullyhappy an attempt was made to burn the Orange hall.

1974 Belleek Orange Hall was partly destroyed by a bomb – it was speedily re-built.

1992 an attempt was made to burn Lurgaross Orange Hall.

1995 Belleek Orange Hall was completely destroyed in fire and a new hall built.

1995 Mountnorris Orange Hall was completely destroyed in an arson attack – it was also totally re-built to modern standards.

Also in the District an attempt was made to burn Cladymore Church Hall and also Kingsmill Presbyterian Church Hall.

In Glenanne, the U.D.R. Centre was destroyed by lorry bomb and 3 U.D.R. men were killed.

Markethill Town Centre has been wrecked by car bombs numerous times, the latest during the so-called ceasefire.

Bunting and flags has been removed from Markethill and surrounding villages numerous times. Flags have been removed from Orange Halls in the District, even Mullabrack Hall in a supposedly safe area.

DISTRICT MASTERS OF MARKETHILL DISTRICT No.10

1902-1913	DAVID SPENCE	L.O.L. 346
1914-1917	REV. J. H. LUCAS	L.O.L. 936
1918-1933	W. JOHN SCARR	L.O.L. 346
1918-1934	W. J. BLACK	L.O.L. 788
1963-1969	S. REVELS	L.O.L. 59
1970-1972	W. ELLIOTT	L.O.L. 346
1973-1983	ERNEST STERRITT	L.O.L. 479
1984-1985	J. AGNEW	L.O.L. 132
1985-1997	DAVID McCULLOUGH	L.O.L. 222
1997-	ROBERT HAMILTON	L.O.L. 528

THE PRIVATE LODGES OF MARKETHILL DISTRICT

TULLYHAPPY TEMPERANCE L.O.L. No.59

The warrant of this Lodge was first issued on 1st May, 1819. The Register of Warrants dated 1825/29 shows the Lodge to be working in Markethill District with the Worshipful Master being Samuel Vint. The 1855 Register advises that the Lodge is actually meeting in Kilcarron in Markethill District.

Minute Books are available from September, 1919 and it is noted that in the early days, meetings of the Lodge were held in a barn at Keadybeg, Mountnorris. Around this time, a suggestion was mooted that the Lodge should transfer from Markethill District to Bessbrook District, that village being a lot closer. There were protracted discussions with the District Lodge, following the vote being taken to transfer; these went on until 1936, when it was agreed to remain in Markethill District.

A new banner was unfurled on Saturday, 2nd July, 1930, and in August, 1934, it was decided to build a new Orange Hall, the old one being beyond repair. The Hall was named the W. & D. Cairns Memorial Orange Hall and was opened on Saturday, 16th October, 1937.

At one time, the Lodge had a Pipe Band, but during the 1940's the Lodge was led by their Flute Band, which unfortunately was not going well. At 12th parades and Church services, the Lodge used Mullaghglass and Ballygorman Bands.

In 1947, a Ladies' Lodge was formed at Tullyhappy, their warrant number being W.L.O.L. No.189.

During early 1953, it was decided to form a new accordion band, to be called Tullyhappy Coronation. The new band instruments were dedicated on Friday, 22nd June, 1953

The Lodge decided to purchase a new banner in 1959. The unfurling ceremony took place on the first Friday in June of 1960, Sir Norman Stronge doing the honours.

With the advent of the present troubles, the Lodge did not escape being affected. The Hall was burnt in 1971, and on 5th January, 1976, Bro. Robert Freeburn, along with ten workmates, was murdered by terrorists at Kingsmills, as they returned home from work in Glenanne factory. He was Worshipful Master of the Lodge and Chairman of the Band. A plaque was dedicated in the Hall, to his memory, on 5th May, 1978, by Rev. A. E. Crawford, Bessbrook.

On 16th May, 1980, new band uniforms were dedicated by the Grand Master, Most Worshipful Bro. Rev. Martin Smyth. The band lost a stalwart member, through the death at the beginning of 1985 of Bro. Erastus McCammon; he had been Drum Major for many years.

KILBRACKS BIBLE AND CROWN DEFENDERS L.O.L. No.119

Kilbracks L.O.L. No.119 is possibly one of the few Lodges within the District which has records available dating back to the year 1800. This Warrant number is included in the 1798 minute book of Grand Lodge. Lodge records show L.O.L. No.119 to be working in Markethill with sixty-three members, with the Worshipful Master, Brother Robert Aughaltree and the Deputy Master Brother James Cleeland.

The minute books from the years around 1834, show the Lodge to be meeting in a house in the townland of Lattery.

The Lodge over the years had many by-laws made, and detailed below are those implemented for the '12th' July, 1841:-

1) Member not attending '12th' before 11.30 a.m. to be fined 6d.
2) Member getting drunk to be fined one shilling.
3) Member quarrelling in Lodge room on '12th' to be expelled for one year.
4) Visiting member on the '12th' would pay two shillings 6d., for his exchange, with a line or a certificate.

The 1856 Minute Book records the Lodge meeting at a house in Corhammock, with Brother Benjamin Parr, W.M. and Brother David Scarr, D.M.. By 1876, the Lodge had moved to Kilbracks, with Brother William Agnew W.M. and Brother James Hutton, D.M..

For the '12th' July, 1885 the following liquid refreshments were ordered:- 1 gallon whiskey - sixteen shillings; 2 bottles sherry wine - four shillings; 1/2 pint of malt - one shilling and two pence.

In the late 1920's the Lodge decided to build a new Orange Hall; this was officially opened on the last Saturday in June, 1930.

A new Lodge banner was purchased in 1939 and around this time the Lodge had its own flute band.

The Anderson and Marshall families have always had a long association with the Lodge. Indeed Brother Edward Marshall was W.M. for twenty-three years. In 1972 a new banner was unfurled by Mrs. Jane Marshall, the Worshipful Master's wife, and dedicated by Brother Rev. Dr. Scott of Ahorey Presbyterian Church.

On occasions in past years, the Lodge has carried Lambeg Drums at '12th' parades, and more recently, the Kilbracks Bible and Crown Defenders Junior L.O.L. No.75 has accompanied the Lodge on parade; the Junior Lodge is under the jurisdiction of the District Lodge.

KILCLUNEY TEMPERANCE VOLUNTEERS L.O.L. No.132

This is the largest Lodge in Markethill District. The Lodge, under Warrant No.936, was founded by the Rector of the Abbey Church, Cladymilltown Road, Kilcluney Townland - Rev. Hutchings; the title was "Kilclooney Temperance Volunteers". It was in the 1920's that the Warrant No.936 was surrendered in order to obtain a lower one No.132, which had belonged to another Lodge in Markethill District, and which had gone dormant some time previously. Before this in 1798, No.132 had been meeting in the Maze District of Co. Down.

Meetings in the early days were held in the Abbey Church Hall, the present Orange Hall being built in the early 1930's. The foundation stones came from the Worshipful Master at the time, Bro. Thomas Johnston of Carricklane, and were drawn by horse and cart. The new Hall was opened on the third Saturday in June, 1934.

The Lodge has had four banners during this Century. A blue banner was obtained in the early 1900's and this is still in the Lodge possession. A second banner was purchased in 1928, a third during the years after the Second World War, and the present one in 1969.

A member of the Lodge, Bro. Bob Walker, was among those murdered in the Kingsmills Massacre, in January 1976, when Republican terrorists ambushed a bus carrying workers home from Glenanne Factory; a memorial tablet was subsequently erected in the Orange Hall.

The Lodge has its own band, Kilcluney Volunteers Flute Band, which has won many trophies at band parades, etc. The band has also been a fertile recruiting base for the Lodge, and this was evident in the 1980's, leading to the Lodge reaching its current numerical strength.

GLENANNE CROWN PRINCE L.O.L. No.133

In 1874 an Orange Warrant was issued to Bro. Joseph Maxwell Worshipful Master L.O.L. No.133 under which he could hold Orange Lodge meetings at Glenanne.

In those days meetings were held in the barn at the home of Andrew Patterson, their meeting place therefore became known locally as "Pattersons Barn", incidentally the building is still in use by the Patterson family. The building now used as an Orange Hall was constructed in 1859 for use as a school with dwelling house attached, on ground which at that time was part of the Gosford Estate.

The minute for June 19th, 1919, states that a new banner would be unfurled for '12th'- July demonstration, no other details are given.

In the year 1921 the Lodge decided to purchase the property from the trustees of Gosford Estate.

In lighter vein - in December 1926 the Lodge decided to purchase small collarettes for use in the Lodge room; the reason given was that members always arrived for meetings minus their regalia - why this temporary lapse of memory should occur amongst so many once every month was never discovered.

Another banner was again unfurled on July 12th, 1949 and a new bannerette on 30th May, 1959 to celebrate the centenary of the Orange Hall.

The present banner was unfurled on the morning of July 12th, 1978.

In November 1988 a fire destroyed the residence attached to the hall and badly damaged the hall kitchen. After some deliberation it was decided to clear the site of the burned building and erect a new hall. No time was lost in getting this project under way, and the new hall was officially opened on Easter Monday, 1st April, 1991.

"JOSHUA'S GUIDING STAR" L.O.L. No.167

A Lodge has not met under this Warrant number for approximately fifty-eight years; however, whilst the Warrant is dormant, the number remains within the possession of the District Lodge. This Lodge is the only one in the District which has had a distinctive title, not connected with the townland or area of origin or meeting.

It is known that the Lodge met at Drumlack near Mullabrack, and was sometimes called 'Dobbin's Lodge'.

In the first minute book of the Grand Orange Lodge of Ireland dated March 1798, Warrant No.167 is listed but no information is given. The Register of Warrants of 1825/1829 states that a Warrant was renewed on 2nd February 1829 to a Lodge in Richhill District with John Smyth, Worshipful Master.

However, by order of Grand Lodge the Warrant was transferred to the jurisdiction of Tandragee District with John Smyth remaining as Worshipful Master. This happened on 19th November, 1830.

The papers relative to the Parliamentary Select Committee of 1834 confirm that the Warrant was operating to Tandragee District.

The 1856 Register actually states that this Warrant was originally in Loughgall District and that on 7th May 1834 a duplicate to the Tandragee Warrant was again issued to Richhill District.

However by the year 1856 there was only one Warrant No.167 working and it was now in Markethill District, meeting at Drumlack, with the Worshipful Master being William A. Spence.

The actual Warrant held by the District Lodge, was issued to Brother John Robert Wallace, Worshipful Master, on 5th July, 1897. At this time, the Lodge had twenty-two members, and Brother Wallace was Worshipful Master until 1903, when Brother Robert James Wallace took over.

The Lodge was accompanied by Lambeg Drums and a Fifer during these years. The roll book records payments to a drummer of one shilling, and to a fifer of two shillings and six pence, in 1900.

L.O.L. No.167 ceased working in 1933, and with it a piece of history died too.

LATTERY PURPLE HEROES L.O.L. No.222

This warrant was operating in the year 1798. It was held by the Armagh Regiment, the Worshipful Master being a Sergeant McDowell and the Lodge had a membership of 107.

In 1823 the warrant was renewed to Markethill District, the Worshipful Master being Robert Black.

The Register of 1856 shows that the Lodge was meeting at Lattery less than two miles from Markethill, the Worshipful Master being Matthew Black.

A new banner was purchased on 22nd June 1907 from William Bridgett of Great Victoria Street, Belfast at a cost of £ 17-7s-0d. (Incidentally, Bro. Bridgett was a native of the Markethill area).

Lattery Lodge moved around quite a lot. From its original place of meeting at Lattery it moved to the town of Markethill, holding its meeting for a period in the District Hall, then moving to Kilcluney Orange Hall during the war years of 1939 to 1945, moving again to the late Bro. John Clarke's rooms at Main Street, Markethill. During this period the Worshipful Master was the late Bro. Robert Millar who was a leading figure in Markethill Royal Black District Chapter No.3, also County Grand Treasurer of County Armagh Grand Black Chapter. He was also a member of Tandragee Rural District Council, a Justice of the Peace and a very staunch Presbyterian, worshipping regularly at the local Church.

The late Bro. Millar passed on during 1943 and in his will he bequeathed to the Lodge a dwelling at Mallagh's Terrace for use as an Orange Hall.

This was used for a few years then sold off, the Lodge moving back to the District Hall at Main Street. In 1961 the District Lodge proposed disposing of their Hall and Lattery Lodge purchased the same on the provision that the District hold their quarterly meetings in the said premises.

The present banner depicting the Landing of William at Carrickfergus and on the reverse side the Martyrdom of Latimer and Ridley, was purchased in June 1958.

The Lodge has had the services of Markethill Pipe Band since the late 1930's. Previously 222 was accompanied by Lambeg Drums and indeed on several occasions a fifer was employed.

MOUNTNORRIS TRUE BLUES L.O.L. No.346

The warrant now held by the above Lodge firstly belonged to a Lodge in the 3rd Battalion Bredalbane Regiment with seventy members, and the Worshipful Master was Robert Whitten. By 1825/29 the warrant was working in Manor Cunningham, Co. Donegal, where it remained until 1888 when it is noted that no return was made to Grand Lodge that year. It was re-issued on Ist June 1892 to Bro. James Beattie for a Lodge in Markethill District. Mountnorris obtained the warrant on 11th June, 1906; issued to Bro. William John Scarr.

Unfortunately records of L.O.L. No.346 only go back to August 1933, when Bro. Hugh Collins was Worshipful Master and Bro. James Wallace Deputy Master. The deeds of the Hall were obtained in 1933 and the land on which the Hall is built was given by Bro. William John Scarr of Killycarron, Loughgilly, Co. Armagh.

A Junior Lodge was formed on 21st April, 1936.

The Senior Lodge was accompanied by the Brigade Band from Armagh on 12th July, 1935 who were paid £5.15.0 for their services. The Hall was used for dancing classes run by Bros. A. McMullen, G. Quinn and J. Black during 1940 and also the Coronation celebrations in the village of Mountnorris in 1953.

As no '12th' demonstrations were held during the war years the Lodge met each 12th and held a social evening.

The decision to purchase a new banner was made at a Lodge meeting on Friday, 4th January, 1946 and each Lodge member gave £1 towards the cost. Sister D. McNabb M.P. unfurled the new banner on 11th June 1949. Mountnorris Flute Band started up again in April, 1946, and accompanied the Lodge on 12th July 1946 to the demonstration in Markethill. Bro. Isaac Chambers from Loughgilly led the band and a Mr. Fred Denny from Poyntzpass taught. He cycled to each practice night regardless of the weather and a whip round was made to pay him which sometimes only amounted to 1/6 or 2 shillings. The venue in 1946 was Gosford Demesne and Tandragee District also paraded; Markethill District went to Tandragee on 12th July, 1947.

While the present Primary School in Mountnorris was being built the Orange Hall was used as classrooms by the Co. Armagh Education Committee.

At present the John Hunter Memorial Accordion Band accompany the Lodge each 12th July and use the hall on practice nights. It acquired this name in memory of the late Bro. John Hunter who was a tireless worker in the Lodge for many years.

On 22nd June 1990, a special evening was held in Mountnorris to celebrate the Centenary of the Hall being built and the Tercentenary of the Order. The guest speaker was Rt. Worshipful Bro. N. Hood, Co. Grand Master. A silver birch tree was also planted in the grounds of the Hall, and a Plaque unveiled to mark the occasion, by Worshipful Bro. Hood.

Wor. Bro. Spiers Black, Deputy District Master, is a member of this Lodge.

BALLYLANE TRUE BLUES L.O.L. No.479

Warrant No.479 is noted in the first minute book of Grand Lodge, but no information is given. In the Register of Warrants dated 1825/29 it is noted that the Lodge is meeting in the Castledawson District of Co. Londonderry. The Rev. J. Graham reported on 30th January 1854 that the Lodge was Dormant and L.O.L. No.510 in Markethill District supposedly surrendered their warrant to obtain a lower number.

A new banner purchased from A. M. Purce of Randalstown, was unfurled by Bro. William Cordner on 12th July, 1927. During 1928-29 repairs were carried out to the Orange Hall, money to do same being raised by means of socials and a heavy subscription.

During the early 1930's, the Lodge was led by Markethill Pipe Band. From 12th July 1934, and subsequent years, the Lodge was led by fife and drum. During those years, the Lodge held a party or social evening each 5th November; then, as now, the catering was in the hands of the Anderson family.

During the war, the Lodge met each '12th' evening, and had dinner together. In 1940, a request was received from a Captain Whiteside for use of the Hall for the Local Defence Volunteer force; the rental agreed was £l. Meetings were infrequent during the war years, and attendance was poor.

1950 saw an extension and repairs carried out to the Orange Hall.

On 1st August 1958, it was agreed to purchase a new banner depicting "The Secret of England's Greatness" and "King William III".

The first drumming match, to be held by the Lodge, was in 1971, and organised by Bro.. Ernest Sterritt; proceeds amounted to £20.

On the 12th July, 1988, the Lodge carried Lambeg Drums again, after a break of some 13 years.

In June 1989, the Lodge presented the Chaplain, Bro. Rev. William Bingham, with an inscribed Bible, following his licensing by the Presbyterian Church. Bro. Bingham is Grand Chaplain of the County Grand Lodge and has taken a leading role in attempting to resolve the Drumcree stand-off, even addressing the Labour Party Conference to explain the Order's case.

In 1990, the Lodge was devastated by the murder, outside Armagh, of Bro. David Sterritt, an R.U.C. member. Bro. Sterritt was an enthusiastic and committed Orangeman and the members feel his loss deeply. This brief account of the Lodge history is dedicated to his memory.

Wor. Bro. Roger Gardiner, District Secretary and Deputy County Grand Secretary, is a member of this Lodge.

KILMACUGH TRUE BLUES L.O.L. No.510

This Lodge is now dormant. The Warrant is noted as working in 1798 but no information is given in the Grand Lodge Register of Warrants. In the Register of 1825/1829 L.O.L. No.510 is noted as meeting at Charlemont but on 2nd September 1829 a duplicate Warrant number 510 is issued to James Gray for a Lodge in Markethill District. Much of the Lodge history was lost in a fire in Brother Thomas John Trew's house on 26th August.

In the early years of this century, the Lodge members met in their own Orange Hall; however, some time after the Second World War the decision was taken to close the Hall, and for a period of time thereafter, meetings were held in Markethill Orange Hall. Today the Lodge banner and box are held in Ballylane Orange Hall.

In the 1920s, the Lodge carried three Lambeg Drums and on some occasions, would have enlisted the services of a fifer. The drums depicted/or were called: "Cromwell of Dunbar," "The Queen," and "Shaker of the Nation."

A new banner was unfurled in Markethill in 1928 - this depicted "Latimer and Ridley". This banner was the Lodge's one and only.

The Lodge was known as "Trew's Lodge" down the years; a glance at the Lodge Worshipful Masters will provide evidence as to why. In recent years, one of the Lodge stalwarts was the late Brother Joseph Kelly. He was a member of the District Committee and had a wealth of Orange stories. Whilst he was Worshipful Master for twenty-eight years from 1959 to his death in 1987, he could not come anywhere near what must be a unique record in local Orangeism, in that Brother Thomas J. Trew was Worshipful Master for fifty years from 1908 to 1958!

BELLEEK BIBLE AND CROWN DEFENDERS L.O.L. No.528

For the history of the Warrant number, prior to 1892, Grand Lodge records indicate it to be working in Dublin in 1825/29. The original Lodge Warrant was No.620; this was later surrendered for the present one No.528. The 1856 Register confirms that No.528 is working in Belleek with John Mitchell the Worshipful Master.

Lodge records are available from 1892, when the Worshipful Master was Bro. Wm. G. McKnight; dues were 3d per month. In 1894, each member paid 1 shilling to seal and repair the Lodge room. In 1900, the Lodge purchased a Union Flag to be put on the spire of Belleek Parish Church; the member who erected the flag received a pint of whiskey

During the meeting in August 1918, each member was levied 5 shillings for the purchase of a new flag; it is not clear what type of flag, but it is assumed that it would have been a Lodge flag, the forerunner of the banners of today. During the war years, the Lodge held quarterly meetings only.

A banner was purchased in late 1918, and it was decided that the name of the Lodge should be "Belleek Arch Purple Marksmen." In June 1919, it was decided to hold an anniversary Church Service on the second Sunday of June each year.

At this time, plans were laid for the building of a new hall for the Lodge, a Mr. Aiken having given a site in August 1919. The hall was opened on 6th November, 1926, and the keys of the old premises were to be handed to the Clergy of Ballymoyer Parish Church.

In January 1924, it was decided to form a flute band, the services of a band teacher were obtained, and the band was formed on 5th May, 1924.

A new banner was purchased from Robinson's of Portadown on 3rd November, 1952, and it was decided to change the Lodge title to "Belleek Bible and Crown Defenders". The Banner was unfurled on 27th June, 1953.

In that same year, it was proposed to change the band from flute to pipe, but after further deliberation, it was decided to form an accordion band. The first accordions were bought in November 1954, costing £35 each.

During the troubles, the hall has been attacked three times by Republican terrorists. On 4th August 1970, structural damage was caused to the front gable wall by a bomb. The second attack on 7th December, 1971, caused more widespread damage. Repairs were carried out on both occasions and Brethren guarded the Hall to allow meetings to proceed. Before the Hall could be re-opened, the I.R.A. struck again in 1974, causing major structural damage. Meetings were held in Glenanne Orange Hall after that, and in November 1977, it was decided to build a new Hall. Eventually, the cost was considered too high, and the decision was taken to repair the existing property. The Hall, complete with extension, was re-opened in June 1980, by Most Worshipful Bro. Rev. Martin Smyth, Grand Master.

One of the Lodge members, Bro. Robert Lockhart, a Police Reservist, was murdered on 17th April 1979, by the I.R.A..

On 18th April 1988, members decided to form a bond of friendship with "Sons and Daughters of William" L.O.L. No.64, Perth, Western Australia and in 1990, the Lodge was visited by Bro. Bob Hunter, of that Lodge.

Wor. Bro. Robert Hamilton, District Master, is a member of this Lodge.

LURGAROSS ORANGE HEROES L.O.L. No.620

The Lodge started life on the 15th September, 1828 and held the number L.O.L. 1237. The Warrant, (which is still in the possession of a Lodge member), was issued to Thomas McKinney of Ballylane, and the Lodge was known as "Ballylane Orange Heroes. "Again as there are no documents one must rely on stories and nostalgic reminisces passed down from father to son, but by all accounts Thomas McKinney seemed to have been somewhat of a character. He enforced a bye-law for example that all Lodge members must wear a pair of buff coloured moleskin trousers, and he led the Lodge to demonstrations on horseback. The Lodge apparently sat at his house, and until recent times the compass and square enhanced the look of the garden gate.

In 1873 the Lodge took out a new number and warrant which was a common practice at the time. The new Lodge number was L.O.L. No.620 which had been previously held by Belleek, also of Markethill District, and who had acquired their new number 528. The new warrant was issued on 2nd December, 1873 and was signed by the then County Grand Master, Rt. Wor. Bro. William Verner. (It may be of interest to note that although the Grand Lodge had dissolved itself after the Cumberland Plot, certain counties namely Armagh and Down continued to issue warrants and this is the reason there are so many duplicate numbers; L.O.L. No.620 had a duplicate number in Saintfield, Co. Down).

For some reason in the early years of 620 the Lodge did not seem to have a home of its own and enjoyed the hospitality of various halls and houses for their meetings. They met for some time in Mountnorris Orange Hall, Lemmon's house and other (probably members) homes in the Glenanne area. The last of these being Sydney Russell's barn at Loughgilly before the move to the new hall at Lurgaross in 1936. During the nomadic years the Lodge acquired the rather 'tongue-in-cheek' title of "The Hounds," an obvious reference to the number of times the Lodge had been hounded from one meeting place to another. However, in 1936 under the guidance of the then Worshipful Master Bob Bell the new hall was opened and the Lodge's wandering days had ended.

The Lodge seemed to have run many socials and dances in the post war years, and would appear to have become somewhat of a social centre for the area. It would have been about this time that the hall was affectionately known as "Tin Town," a reference to the corrugated iron construction of the hall at the time. An annual picnic seems also to have been a favourite event. This was held in June or July to various fields and venues, and would appear to have been a very popular outing for both young and old.

Lurgaross was always known as a drumming Lodge and no-one can remember having a band to lead them on the '12th'. However, for a few years just after the war the services of two pipers were used. This was a common practice for Lodges at the time. Again Lambeg drums have made an appearance leading the Lodge on the '12th' since 1985 after an absence of about 20 years.

In 1986 due mainly to necessity, the Lodge undertook an extensive renovation of the hall. The work took about three years and was completed in 1989. The hall is now a more comfortable and secure building than the old tin structure but many of the original details have been left and the hall has not lost any of its character.

The Lodge has not been spared the torment of terrorism, and in late 1982 had two of its members murdered by the I.R.A.. The first was Bro. Tommy Cochrane, a Part-time Sergeant in the U.D.R., who was abducted on 22nd October and found shot dead in South Armagh on 27th October. A memorial banner to his memory was unfurled in 1983 and depicts his portrait and the U.D.R. crest. This banner was donated by a Lodge member. On 16th November 1982 whilst performing duty at the security barriers in Newry Street, Markethill, Bro. Snowden Corkey, a member of the R.U.C. Reserve, was shot dead along with another colleague. Both these Brethren are remembered on a memorial plaque in the hall, which was unveiled on 10th June 1989 by the wives of Tommy and Snowden.

REDROCK PURPLE STAR HEROES L.O.L. No.788

This Warrant was first issued to a Lodge in County Monaghan in 1818, but was re-issued to a Lodge in Markethill District on 29th September, 1823, with John Milligan of Cavanagrove, Worshipful Master. The early meetings of the Lodge were held in John Milligan's house and the Lodge assumed the title Cavanagrove L.O.L. The Lodge today still works under a Warrant dated 1st May, 1849, and issued to William Morgan. The Lodge then held its meetings at Morgan's house, where the Warrant was hidden up the chimney in the "parlour" as soot and smoke marks can still be seen on it.

In July 1924, a new Banner was unfurled costing thirty-two pounds fifteen shillings. Other Banners were purchased in 1949 and the present one in 1961, at a cost of ninety-nine pounds.

No definite date can be given when the Orange Hall was built, but it seems probable that this was during the 1880s, on pursual of old maps. The Hall was widened and new floors fitted, and re-opened on lst July, 1933. Again, the Hall was extended with new kitchen and toilet block, and re-opened by Sister Dinah McNabb M.P. during August 1955.

As well as having a fifer in the past, the Lodge had Lambeg Drums to accompany them on the '12th'. At the Demonstration in Armagh in 1924 the Lodge was accompanied by no less than six Lambegs; such was the vibration from these drums while they were paraded through Scotch Street that it caused jewellery in a shop window to fall off their stands and some were damaged. The owner vowed that while he lived he would never allow the "Rock" Drums back into Armagh. This seems to have happened for the Lodge purchased Flutes and Drums with a view to start a Band, however, six years later the Band had ceased and Lambegs again accompanied the Lodge unto 1946 when the Band was again revived. At present the Lodge still have in their possession three Lambegs. The Band, Redrock Purple Heroes Flute, accompany the Lodge and attend many Band Parades.

Tragically, the Lodge lost one of its young members, Bro. Michael F. L. Marshall (R.U.C.), murdered by terrorists on 20th October, 1989. A memorial was unveiled and dedicated to Michael's memory in the Hall on 21st June, 1990.

ENAGH NEW LIGHTS L.O.L. No.814

It is not known where or when this Lodge was formed, but only that it is one of the oldest Lodges in Markethill District. The Warrant is referred to in the 1825 Register when the Worshipful Master was given as Samuel Hawthorne; a subsequent register gives the Worshipful Master as John McCune in 1856. The Lodge met in Glassdrumman and W. J. Scarr was Worshipful Master from 1875 to 1907. This Brother who lived in the Killycarn area was a long serving Worshipful District Master of Markethill.

Like most Lodges in the nineteenth century, L.O.L. No.814 would have had a nomadic existence with meetings being held usually in the home of the Worshipful Master. This meant moving when another Worshipful Master was appointed. Around the turn of the century, the Crozier and Stevenson families from the Seagahan and Corran areas respectively, were active. Mr. William Stevenson was a spectacular sight on horseback in front of the Lodge on anniversaries in the early 1900s. About this time, the Lodge met in the barn of Mr. David Graham near the Flo Bog.

Mr. Gordon Gray of Enagh Cottage was the Worshipful Master in 1912 and the present Orange Hall was built on the site formerly owned by William

Gilmore about this time. Stones were raised in the local quarry and the building was erected by voluntary labour. In 1921 a banner which is still to the fore and may have been the first one for this Lodge, was supplied by William Bridgett of Belfast. This bore a painting of King William III crossing the Boyne and a scene from the 36th Ulster Division's plight at the Battle of the Somme on 1st July, 1916. The title Enagh True Blues was inscribed on the banner although the formal title is Enagh New Lights. It is believed that the original title could have derived from a liberal group within the Presbyterian Church in the mid-eighteenth century known as the New Light Movement. Their doctrine was Unitarian with the divine worship of God and led to the forming of the Non-Subscribing Presbyterian denomination. The stigma attached to the New Lights title was the reason why it was not portrayed and True Blues chosen probably because of the popularity of another local Lodge of that title.

In the 1920s, a flute band was assembled and members were resplendent in blue bush hats. In 1938, an accordion band was inaugurated by purchasing twelve secondhand accordions from Matchetts of Belfast. Prominent Lodge members during this era were Robert George Deens, Andrew Heaney Clarke (the renowned poet), George Graham, David Graham, William John Wilson and James McMullen. In 1952 the band and Lodge attended the opening of the new Orange Hall at the Diamond. The practice of visiting each District in turn for the County '12th' demonstration was started then.

A new banner was purchased in 1961 and again this was a silk purple centre with orange surrounds. The Enagh True Blues title was adhered to and "Markethill District" was added to the inscription but the Somme scene was exchanged for a theological depiction.

The band has been re-equipped and today boasts a membership of almost forty under the capable leadership of Mr. Crozier Graham.

MULLABRACK "HEARTS OF STEEL TEMPERANCE" L.O.L. No.1406

Mullabrack Orange Lodge meets in its own Orange Hall built in 1931, beside the main Markethill/Portadown Road, approximately 1.5 miles from the town of Markethill. Traditionally, it has always been one of the largest Lodges in the District and it draws most of its membership from around the Mullabrack area itself.

The Lodge Warrant was first issued in 1798, three years after the Battle of the Diamond in 1795, and was itself the year of the United Irishmen rebellion. The fact that the Lodge Warrant was issued in the same year as this rebellion should be seen as no coincidence as the Warrant was issued to Brother John McMullen of an "Armagh Regiment". Whilst the name of the Regiment is not given, it most probably was one of the local militias or yeomanry units raised in Co. Armagh to counter the rebellion that year. This view is given more credence by the fact that the Warrant was a "travelling" one, which allowed the Lodge to meet in whatever location or venue in which its members found themselves. So, if the "Armagh Regiment" was posted out of the Co. Armagh area, the Warrant went with it, thus allowing the Lodge to meet.

The title of the Lodge "Hearts of Steel" also gives an indication as to its origins. In the latter part of the 18th century, Ulster and particularly Co. Armagh was in the grip of an ongoing land war between both Roman Catholic and Protestant farmers. Both groups, due to the small acreage of land available to a dense rural population, often came to blows (and much worse) in arguments over who owned the land. Gangs were formed with the Catholic "Defenders" being the largest and best organised. Their counterparts on the Protestant side were the "Peep o' Day Boys" and the "Hearts of Steel", many of whom (and obviously so in the case of L.O.L. No.1406) were later to be submerged into the newly formed Orange Order.

The first mention of the Warrant of L.O.L. No. 1406 "coming home" to Mullabrack seems to have been around 1856, when it was renewed by a Brother William Singleton, who was also Worshipful District Master of Markethill. Since then, the Lodge has formed an integral part of the life of the Mullabrack area, and has had close connections with the local Church of Ireland parish, St. John's, where the Lodge holds its annual Church service on the first Sunday in July. That connection was re-emphasised when a portrait of the Parish Church was included on the new Lodge banner, unfurled in July 1989.

The Lodge had always a history of being a "drumming" Lodge. Since the end of World War II, the drums have been replaced by a flute band which was associated with the Lodge until its demise in the mid-1950s, and more recently by the Mullabrack Accordion Band, formed in 1984.

A final point of note was the unfurling of a new banner on 12th July 1989. The banner, as indicated previously, bears a portrait of St. John's Parish Church on one side and the late Brother Charles Spence, who was murdered by the enemies of Ulster in November, 1982, on the other side. This banner now serves as a sombre reminder to us all of the supreme sacrifice which has been made by so many for the old cause.

BESSBROOK DISTRICT L.O.L. No.11

Bessbrook District L.O.L. - the smallest of the County Armagh Orange districts - was formed about 1880 with warrant No.11 that formerly belonged to Markethill District L.O.L. No.10.

Seven Lodge warrants -77, 294, 303, 740, 927 ,959, and 1330 - have operated in the history of Bessbrook District and today four remain active - 77, 303, 927, and 959. Warrant 294, belonging to the now defunct Bessbrook Volunteers' Lodge, is now dormant but is still in the possession of Bessbrook District.

On April 21, 1888, warrant 1330 was taken out by brethren from the Craigmore area of Bessbrook and the Lodge existed under that number, with a small membership, until January 14, 1903, when it assumed warrant 740. By 1906, the Craigmore Lodge No.740 ceased to exist, the warrant being handed in and members joining other Lodges or a new Bessbrook Lodge -Star of Hope Temperance No.927, which had just been formed.

Until the late 1950s, Bessbrook District had five active Lodges, this being reduced to four when the Volunteer Lodge (formerly the May town Lodge) disbanded in 1960. Warrants 740 and 1330 are still in operation - 740 in Sandy Row District in Belfast with the Ulsterville Lodge and 1330 in Mourne District by an Annalong Lodge.

Bro. John McElroy was District Master in 1882 and others who followed him in this office were Bro. Samuel McKnight, Robert Moorehead, and John Cartmill.

Total membership in the early years of Bessbrook ranged from a peak of 195 in 1896 to 134 in 1906. Over the past 50 years membership has varied from 179 in 1983 to 152 in 1959.

The property of Bessbrook Spinning Company from its opening until 1968, the Town Hall was used as a sporting, cultural, and social venue and the life of Bessbrook has always transcended around it. Built of the best Mourne granite, the Hall is a spacious complex with an assembly hall reaching to a seated capacity of 600, large adjacent rooms, and modern kitchen facilities.

Down the years the hall has been the venue for inter-provincial badminton matches; top snooker and billiard exhibitions and varied entertainment presentations.

In 1968 when Bessbrook Spinning Company closed its factory in the village the Town Hall, affectionately known as The Institute, was sold to Bessbrook

District L.O.L. No.11 and a commitment was given by the four local Lodges to continue to use the building as a community meeting place for the people of Bessbrook.

Gambling and the consumption of alcohol is strictly prohibited under the deeds of the building, in keeping with the Quaker traditions of the Richardson family who built the Hall.

For the past 24 years the Orangemen of Bessbrook have sought to maintain the Hall traditions and several years ago when they embarked on an ambitious renovation scheme had the generous support of their brethren across Northern Ireland.

In addition to the four Orange Lodges, there is a Royal Black Preceptory, an Apprentice Boys of Derry Branch and three bands – Bessbrook Crimson Arrow Pipe Band, Divernagh Accordion, and Bessbrook True Blues Flute Band.

Bessbrook District L.O.L. No.11 owns two Orange Halls - Bessbrook and Divernagh, as well as Bessbrook Town Hall and the old Bessbrook Masonic Hall, which is now converted into two private houses.

The Armagh Guardian of July 14th 1939 contains the following article on the County Demonstration in Bessbrook:-

MAGNIFICENT ARMAGH TWELFTH RALLY

THOUSANDS UPON THOUSANDS AT BESSBROOK

OLD PLEDGE RENEWED

WHY THE SOUTH WANTS ULSTER

There was a splendid turn-out of County Armagh Orangemen for the Twelfth of July demonstration this year.

Fine weather, though dull, favoured the large crowds. The brethren of Armagh went to Bessbrook this year and there was a splendid gathering from all the Districts, the keynote of the speeches being the old determination to keep Ulster within the British Empire so that in peace the people could work for the prosperity of their country.

Sir William Allen, in the course of his address, said they thanked God they did not live in Southern Ireland, whose dictator had renounced all allegiance to our King, where the people were burdened by excessive tariffs and the cost of living was soaring every year, and whose parliamentarians were quarrelling over excessive expenditure and an enormous burden of debt, bringing that country to the verge of bankruptcy.

Two members of Bessbrook District have been murdered
in the recent "Troubles"

Worshipful Brother Joseph Leemon
and Brother James McWhirter
were shot dead by the Provisional I.R.A.
in the Kingsmills Massacre of Protestants
ordered off a workers' bus on 5th January 1976.

THE PRIVATE LODGES OF BESSBROOK DISTRICT

DIVERNAGH ANCIENT HEROES L.O.L. No.77

Warrant No.77 is listed in the 1798 minute book of the Grand Orange Lodge of Ireland, but no information is given. In the 1829 Register of Warrants it is listed as operating in Aughadowey District, Co. Londonderry.

It was then renewed to Markethill District on October 15, 1834. In 1856 the Worshipful Master was Bro. J. Allen and the Lodge was meeting at Diverna, Portnorris, Markethill District.

Bro. Samuel Barrow was Worshipful Master in 1888 and the Lodge was then operating under Bessbrook District. There is a duplicate warrant number 77 in Rasharkin District, Co. Antrim.

Divernagh Ancient Heroes L.O.L. No.77 is the only Lodge in Bessbrook District sitting in its own Orange Hall, about two miles from Bessbrook village. Lord Craigavon opened Divernagh Hall in 1935 and after an I.R.A. bomb explosion in 1973, a modern new hall was built in 1975. There was an attempt to burn the Hall in 1997.

Today the Lodge has its own Accordion Band and continues to provide the District with some of its leading officers. — District Masters from L.O.L. No.77 include Wor. Bros. John Cartmill, Nesbitt McIlroy, C. R. Morrow, Winston McCormick and the present District Master Gerald Cartmill.

Every Twelfth morning L.O.L. No.77 and its band walk the two-mile journey into Bessbrook to meet up with the village Lodges.

BESSBROOK L.O.L. No.294

No.294 -Warrant No.294 is listed in 1798 but no information is given. In 1829 the Lodge is listed as working in Markethill District with Bro. Thomas McIlroy as Worshipful Master.

The 1834 Register advises that the Lodge is meeting at Crankey in Markethill District. By 1856 the Lodge was actually meeting in the town of Markethill with Bro. James Linsay as Worshipful Master. Bro. Samuel McCombe was Worshipful Master in 1875 and remained so in 1888 when the Lodge was then working under Bessbrook District.

In Bessbrook District, L.O.L. No.294 was known as the May town Lodge, but later it was associated with the Doctor's Hill-Craigmore area of Bessbrook. A large proportion of 294 members served in the 1914-18 war, particularly at the Somme. A number were killed and injured, thus the changing of the name to Bessbrook Volunteers Lodge. A decline in members led to its folding up in 1960.

BESSBROOK BRITANNIA TEMPERANCE L.O.L. No.303

Warrant No.303 is listed in 1798 but no information is given.

In 1829 we note that Bro. James Sleeth was Worshipful Master and the Lodge was in Markethill District. In 1834 the Lodge was meeting at Tullyhappy in Markethill District with Bro. James McKenley as Worshipful Master. Bro. James Ewart was Worshipful Master in 1856 and the Lodge was still meeting at Tullyhappy. Bro. Richard Bittles was Worshipful Master in 1875 and remained so in 1888 when the Lodge was then in Bessbrook District.

The Lodge, known as Bessbrook Britannia, has been a temperance number for many years and is closely associated with the Moorehead family, whose ancestor Bro. Robert Moorehead was a District Master. Today, the Lodge is the smallest in Bessbrook District.

There is a strong Lambeg drumming tradition in this Lodge. Wor. Bro. James McCommack, Deputy District Master, is a member of this Lodge.

BESSBROOK STAR OF HOPE TEMPERANCE L.O.L. No.927

In 1798 this was a marching warrant with the Worcester Militia but then became dormant.

In 1888 it was operating in Portadown district with Bro. James Edwards as Worshipful Master. The first reference to Bessbrook District occurs in 1906 when Bro. John Stewart was Worshipful Master for this Lodge meeting in Bessbrook.

A portrait on the Lodge banner is of Derramore House, Bessbrook, where the Act of Union was drafted in 1800. This Banner was unfurled in May, 1982 by the late Bro. Harold McCusker, the Co. Armagh M.P. He negotiated on behalf of the Lodge with the National Trust to gain permission for Derramore House to be portrayed on the Banner.

Bessbrook True Blues Flute Band lead the Lodge on Twelfth parades.

BESSBROOK PURPLE STAR L.O.L. No.959

This Lodge originally met under Warrant No.976 in Markethill District (1829). In 1856 the Worshipful Master was Bro. Arthur Threw and the Lodge was meeting at Kilmacue in Markethill District. Bro. John Walker was Worshipful Master in 1875 and remained so in 1888 when the Lodge was operating in Bessbrook District.

Known as "The Star", Bessbrook Purple Star L.O.L. No.959 has been the largest of the Bessbrook Lodges for most of the past 100-odd years.

The Lodge's banner is dedicated to the memory of two members - Lodge chaplain Bro. Joseph Lemmon and James McWhirter, who were murdered by the I.R.A. in the Kingsmill massacre of January 5, 1976.

The last 959 banner was unfurled in 1962 when Bro. Rev. Canon A. S. O'Connor was a member during his period as Rector of Bessbrook.

The 959 secretary for the past 39 years has been Bro. William Kennedy, the Bessbrook District Secretary since 1967. Former District Masters from the Lodge include the late Bros. Thomas Martin, William D. King, J.P., William Kernaghan, James Little and Danny Kennedy.

The Lodge, headed every Twelfth by Bessbrook Crimson Arrow Pipe Band, had a strong Lambeg drumming tradition in past years.

Bro. Danny Kennedy is a member of the Northern Ireland Assembly for Newry and Armagh.

THE PARADES CONTROVERSY

The I.R.A. announced a ceasefire in August 1993. There was in place a pan-Nationalist Front consisting of Sinn Fein/ I.R.A., the S.D.L.P., the Clinton Presidency in USA, and the Eire Government. Republicans wanted to pressurise the British Government into negotiating a United Ireland. They realised that Unionists were confused and feared a sell-out. They had already secured from the Secretary of State a statement that Britain had:-

> *"No selfish economic or strategic interest in Northern Ireland."*

The tactic of street agitation appealed to the Republican leadership because, at little cost to themselves, it would:

1/ Keep "the Boys" busy now they were on ceasefire

2/ Keep the pressure on for more concessions

3/ Provoke the Unionists and Protestants into confrontation with the police and army

4/ Enable Republicans to accuse the Protestants of wishing to break the peace and so bring international dis-approval upon their heads.

Early in 1995 Gerry Adams called for a wave of protests in support of "Parity of Esteem":-

> *"If the British refused to listen to reasoned and reasonable argument, then let them listen to the sound of marching feet and angry voices."*

The chosen method was to form so-called Residents' Groups, but in fact merely fronts for Sinn Fein, which would challenge parades of the Loyal Orders in areas where nationalists had a local majority and could claim that the parading Protestants were going where they were not wanted; were bigots and fascists and not prepared to give parity of esteem to the Catholic residents.

Adams told the Sinn Fein Conference in November 1997:-

> *"Ask any activist in the North, did Drumcree happen by accident and they will tell you no.*
>
> *Three years of work on the Lower Ormeau Road, Portadown and parts of Fermanagh and Newry, Armagh and in Bellaghy and up in Derry. Three years of work went into creating that situation and fair play to those people who put the work in. They are the type of scene changes that we have to focus on and develop and exploit."*

On Sunday 9th July 1995 the first Stand-off known as Drumcree 1 started when the Orangemen of Portadown District emerged from the church to find their return route to Carleton St. Orange Hall blocked by the R.U.C. This followed a period of agitation by the Garvaghy Road Residents Association who had threatened a counter-march and a sit-down protest.

The District Master, Harold Gracey appealed for support from Orangemen from all over Ulster and with the help of the County Grand Master, Rt. Wor. Bro. Norman Allen, and the other County Officers, a massive rally took place on the Monday night in a large field behind the church. The rally was one of the largest ever seen in the County and had to be started an hour late to allow the crowds to arrive safely.

The following Resolution was passed at the Rally. It has become known as the "Drumcree Resolution"

Resolution passed at Drumcree, Portadown, on July 10th:-

> *"We the Orangemen assembled at Drumcree, loyal subjects of her Majesty Queen Elizabeth, do hereby resolve that we will maintain and defend our civil and religious liberty.*
>
> *We will not accept a ghetto system. As free-born Britons we demand equal treatment with every other British citizen.*
>
> *We repudiate the slander of those who accuse us of triumphalism and intimidation in the expression of our cultural and religious identity.*
>
> *We totally condemn the tyrannous and unnecessary interference with the peaceful procession returning from a Protestant place of worship on the Sabbath Day.*
>
> *We re-assert that the Queen's highway belongs to all law-abiding citizens. No faction, under any pretence whatever, can claim it as their own exclusive territory.*
>
> *We call upon the police to uphold this fundamental principle. That is their duty to the citizens of this land"*

While Drumcree 1 ended with the parade being allowed down the Road amid scenes of policemen removing protesters who had sat down on the highway, there followed four more stand-offs, and the imposition of a Parades Commission by the Labour Government, with a requirement for 28 days notice for any parade - no matter how uncontroversial and traditional. It has seemed to the Orangemen of County Armagh that they are mere pawns who can be sacrificed in a much larger political game of appeasing the I.R.A. at all costs so as the ceasefire and the Peace Process can be maintained.

In 1997 the County Grand Master and County Grand Chaplain wrote to each household in the Garvaghy Road area to explain the Order's position in advance of the parade as follows:-

County Armagh Grand Orange Lodge

June 1997

Dear Resident

We are writing to all the residents of the Garvaghy Road area to explain our position about the annual walk by members of Portadown District Orangemen from the service of worship at Drumcree Parish Church in July.

This is a sincere and genuine attempt to deal with the many misconceptions concerning the walk and there are a number of points we would like to make for your information:

1. *The service on the first Sunday in July is partly to remember those who died at the Battle of the Somme in 1916. We pay tribute to all those of both communities who died for the cause of peace and justice.*
2. *The Orange Order is traditionally a parading organisation. We see our parade as an outward witness to our sincere belief in the Reformed Faith. For that reason, we see attacks on our parades as both a denial of civil liberties and an attack on our religion. For us, this is as distressing as the disgraceful protest - which we unreservedly condemn - outside Harryville chapel.*
3. *In the interests of harmony, mutual respect and reconciliation the Orange Order has acknowledged objections raised by the Nationalist community and has already implemented the following principles for the Drumcree Church parade:*
    a. *The number of parades in the area has been reduced from ten to one in the past ten years.*
    b. *Only members of Portadown District parade.*
    c. *No bands take part which could be perceived as antagonistic to our Nationalist neighbours. Accordion bands lead the parade playing hymn music that is common to both traditions.*

d. The Orangemen walk four abreast so that the walk will pass anyone given point in less than five minutes.

e. The Order marshals and disciplines its own members to ensure there will be no confrontation on our part. If this was reciprocated, then there would only be a need for a minimal police presence.

f. The right to walk peacefully and in a dignified manner and the right to protest in a peaceful and dignified manner should not be denied to anyone.

It is the sincere hope of the Orange Order that the vast majority of the people of Portadown will work together in a new spirit of tolerance to defeat extremists who want confrontation this Summer. As a matter of principle, we cannot be involved in talks with convicted terrorists because of what they have inflicted on our community. But we do want to listen to all those within the community who want to promote harmony and mutual respect among the people of Portadown and would welcome constructive comments which should be sent to the following address:

Co. Armagh Grand Orange Lodge
c/o House of Orange
65 Dublin Road
Belfast
BT2 7HE

We sincerely hope that this letter will go some way towards building up inter-community confidence and respect so that we can look forward not only to a peaceful Summer but to a more peaceful and tolerant era for all the People of our land.

Yours faithfully

Denis Watson — COUNTY GRAND MASTER

William Bingham — COUNTY GRAND CHAPLAIN

Also, following the result of the General Election in 1997, when a New Labour Government took power, the County Grand Master wrote to the new Prime Minister, Mr Tony Blair:-

COUNTY ARMAGH GRAND ORANGE LODGE
HOUSE OF ORANGE 65 DUBLIN ROAD
BELFAST BT2 7HE — 17th June 1997

Dear Prime Minister,

On behalf of County Armagh Grand Orange Lodge we would like to congratulate you on becoming prime minister. We assure you of our support and co-operation as you try to bring peace to Northern Ireland. It is the deepest desire of our hearts to avoid a repetition of the terrible scenes of violence and intolerance that occurred as a result of the ban on the parade at Drumcree last summer. It is only in the interests of Sinn Fein/I.R.A. and other extremists to have another summer of bloody conflict.

For the last year we have worked night and day to try to bring about a peaceful solution to the dispute over our annual traditional walk from morning prayer at Drumcree church down the Garvaghy Road. Orangemen feel strongly that the right to walk in a peaceful and dignified manner from church should not be denied anyone - whether it be our Catholic neighbours in Harryville or our brethren in Portadown, but they accept also that such freedoms bring responsibilities.

For many months now we have been engaged in discussions with local residents, with senior politicians in the United Kingdom and the Irish Republic, with clergy, police officials, diplomats and the business community. We have also had a lengthy process of consultation within the Orange Order itself. Drumcree is a very emotional issue for us, especially since we have given up nine of our ten annual Portadown parades. Having secured agreement from our brethren we wrote to all the residents of the area offering what we believe to be a fair and sensible basis for agreement, which could promote harmony and mutual respect within the community.

Our proposals were:

1. *The walk from morning prayer will be by people from the local community only. No one outside of Portadown District will be permitted to participate.*
2. *No bands which could be perceived by our nationalist neighbours to be antagonistic will take part. Accordion bands will play hymn tunes only which are common to both traditions.*
3. *The Orangemen will walk four deep so that the parade will pass any one given point in less than five minutes.*
4. *The Order will marshall and discipline its own members to ensure there will be no confrontation on our part. If this can be reciprocated then there would be need only for a minimal police presence.*

Further to this, as an Order we gave assurances that there would be no triumphalism, and that in keeping with our belief in civil and religious liberty, we acknowledge that the cultural and religious heritage of both traditions in Portadown should be afforded equal respect.

We are sad that the response from the spokesmen of the Garvaghy Road Residents' Coalition was negative.

We have no ground left to give. If the parade is banned, the moderate Orange national and local leadership will be discredited and our influence destroyed.

It is the sincere hope of the Orange Order that the vast majority of the people in Portadown will work together for real peace in a new spirit of tolerance. We certainly will do our best to build up confidence and respect within the community as a whole, so that we can look forward not only to a peaceful summer but to a more peaceful and tolerant future.

May we assure you that the Secretary of State will have our full cooperation and prayers over the next few weeks in her praiseworthy efforts to defuse the terrible sectarian tension, which has been made so much worse by the murder of two of our local community policemen.

Yours sincerely,

Denis Watson
COUNTY GRAND MASTER

William Bingham
COUNTY GRAND CHAPLAIN

Harold Gracey
PORTADOWN DISTRICT MASTER

THE ANNUAL DRUMCREE CHURCH PARADE BY PORTADOWN DISTRICT

Drumcree is one of two 'mother' churches in Portadown - the other being Seagoe Parish Church.

The annual Orange service at Drumcree Parish Church is the oldest Orange service in Ireland.

The first service was held in 1807.

The Garvaghy Road is the shortest and most direct route between Drumcree Parish Church and Carleton Street Orange Hall.

The Garvaghy Road was originally bounded by farmland and was only developed for housing in the late 1960s and early 1970s.

The housing was originally mixed but intimidation and ethnic cleansing forced almost all Protestant families to leave the area.

In 1985 the R.U.C. conducted a demographic survey of the Garvaghy Road and approved it as a route for the Orange Parades. The main reason given was that few houses faced directly onto the Garvaghy Road.

It was also the main arterial route from that part of the town into Portadown town centre. The geography and demography of the area has not changed significantly from that time.

The parade takes less than 10 minutes to pass a given point.

Since 1985 the Loyal Orders have re-routed ten parades away from the Obins Street / Garvaghy Road area. The Drumcree parade is the only one left that passes along the Garvaghy Road.

Bands are only allowed to play Hymn tunes. Many of these tunes are common to both communities.

Bands refrain from playing whilst passing St. John's Chapel on the outward journey to Drumcree Parish Church.

In 1995 and 1996 as an act of good faith the bands did not play at all along the Garvaghy Road.

Stewards are appointed to ensure individuals on parade do not respond to provocation. In the long history of the parade the Orange Order has never been involved in any form of indiscipline during a parade along the Garvaghy Road.

Only local Orangemen, a small number of County officers and the local Member of Parliament, take part in the parade.

The parade is led by members of the Portadown Ex-Servicemen's Lodge and only their Standard and the District Bannerette are carried in the parade.

There are approximately 900 houses along the disputed 600 metre stretch of the Garvaghy Road.

Only 66 houses face directly onto the Garvaghy and Drumcree Roads.

Less than 10 houses (less than 1%) have addresses actually on the Garvaghy Road

75% of the houses are between 100 to 600 metres away from the Garvaghy Road.

It is impossible to see the Garvaghy Road from the vast majority of the houses along it.

It was statistics similar to these compiled in 1985 and 1986 that enabled the R.U.C. to approve the Garvaghy Road as a main route to the Orange Hall in Portadown.

The facts of the estates in the area are as follows:

Churchill Park
Contains approximately 200 houses, only 5 of which face directly onto the Garvaghy Road.

The Beeches
Contains approximately 100 houses, only 5 of which face directly onto the Garvaghy Road.

Garvaghy Park

Contains approximately 100 houses, only 10 of which face directly onto the Garvaghy Road.

Ballyoran Park

Contains approximately 500 houses, only 46 of which face directly onto the Garvaghy and Drumcree Roads.

Even in the serious situation of tension at the stand-off there were many examples of Ulster humour as the following example of a poster produced anonymously in 1997 shows:

DRUMCREE HOLIDAYS '97

* SPECIAL 4/5 DAY SUMMER BREAKS *

NEW Thrills -Ride on the Big Orange Digger

Inflatable Dolls: Paisley £7 ; Trimble £5
(The Paisley Doll is Bigger and holds more Hot Air)

RUBBER BULLET SOUVENIRS
(Available ONLY after the 4th day!)

Hear Rev. McCrea sing ; "The Men Behind the Wire"

VINTAGE CAR RALLY
* ALL NEWLY BURNT OUT CARS *

The Sky at Night
See Portadown skyline lit up with spontaneous Bonfires

Siege Medals Still Available Please state Year : ('95. '96, '97)

Let your friends abroad see you on TV !
Camera crews from Canada, Australia & the USA
will be in attendance

* Special this Year *
* Spirit of Drumcree *
in standard and litre size bottles
(Bottles Non-Returnable)

Ireland's largest Outdoor Holiday Camp

A SELECTION OF QUOTES ON DRUMCREE

"Near it is not through it"

- (The National Secretary of the A.O.H. 15th August 1995.)

"Let them march in peace."

- (The Times, 11th July 1996)

"It was an unfortunate decision in the first place and I will say that the background and history of this has been given scant attention."

- (Sir John Hermon, Former Chief Constable)

"You have to work hard to be offended by a parade on the wide Garvaghy Road, for only the gable end of the catholic estates back on to it."

- (Ruth Dudley Edwards in the Daily Mirror, 12th July 1996)

"This is no case of mob rule but of overwhelming popular resistance to what was rightly regarded as a stupid and unjust political decision."

- (Bradford's View, Newsletter, 15th July 1996)

"If a parade is peaceful, well marshalled and not provocative, the fact that others don't like it is not a reason for it to be banned because of a third party threat of violence."

- (Robert McCartney M.P.)

"I suppose I do not really care. What's the point of all this fuss, it only takes 15 minutes?"

- (Garvaghy Road Resident quoted in the Irish News July 1996)

"Orangemen should be allowed to march Garvaghy Road, YES 52,393 NO 11,296

- (Belfast Telegraph Telephone Poll, January 1997)

"Throughout these years Portadown Orangemen have always endeavoured to accommodate their Roman Catholic neighbours. We have never sought to intimidate and we have certainly never set out to be triumphalist."

- (Harold Gracey, 5th February 1997)

"The real difficulty for Mr. Trimble and the Orange leaders in Portadown is that they are being asked to talk and even negotiate with an organisation influenced by extreme republicans who so far have shown an unwillingness to be reasonable over an orderly Sunday Church parade which takes just 15 minutes to pass along the Garvaghy Road."

- (Morning View, News Letter, 24th February 1997)

"It will spell disaster for Portadown. The republican movement is making ghettoes because that's the environment they flourish in."

- (Councillor Mervyn Carrick, NewsLetter, 1997)

"Some commentators argue that the Orange Order, in the manner of it's protest at Drumcree, weakened one of the binding forces of the Union by putting the rule of the law in question. The response of the pro-union majority is that the laws themselves must conform to the principles of democracy. If a constitutional majority is deprived of politically accountable government, if it's administration is carried out in secret, if there are reasons to believe that decisions affecting it's ancient liberties and customs are taken at the behest of a foreign government, hostile to it's interests, the question then is raised as to whether the rule of law is being exercised in accordance with the accepted principles of democratic government. In November 1985, a quarter of a million Unionists staged a protest against the Anglo-Irish Agreement. The British political establishment ignored them. But I.R.A. bombs at Brighton, the Baltic Exchange and Docklands all paid handsome dividends for nationalists. Recent events have confirmed that both governments were pursuing a political agenda for which the ceasefire peace was merely a cover."

- *(Robert McCartney M.P., Sunday Telegraph, 21 July 1996)*

"Nationalist identity has never been more officially respected than now, so it seems perverse that internecine squabbles over the Twelfth are growing more bloodily divisive. Why is it that nationalists now object so strongly to expressions of Protestant identity which, in harder times, they largely tolerated? The truth is that the change in nationalist perception of the Orange Order, a change which has led directly to this week's unseemly and potentially explosive stand-off, has been engineered by the I.R.A./Sinn Fein as part of their strategy of driving Ulster protestants into a corner."

- *(Eilis O'Hanlon, The Times 11th July 1996)*

"We know what the Irish government wanted. They wanted to see violence. They wanted to see soldiers shooting Orangemen. They wanted blood. They wanted the blood of Unionists."

- *(David Trimble M.P., The Sunday Tribune, July 1996)*

THE GRAND LODGE RESPONSE TO THE IDEA OF A PARADES COMMISSION

The Grand Lodge of Ireland has published its response to the Government inquiry known as the "North Committee" which recommended the setting-up of the Parades Commission.

"In every democratic society the state has a responsibility to protect certain fundamental rights including freedom of religious belief, free speech, the right of free association, the right to live in peace and the right of cultural expression.

In many countries these rights are enshrined in either the constitution of the country or a Bill of Rights.

The right of free association and right of assembly underpin the right to parade.

The Loyal Orange Institution was formed in September 1795 and some ten months later on 12th July 1796, it held its first Boyne Commemoration Parade.

Parades therefore are very much part of the Orange tradition and heritage as two hundred years ago the founding fathers decided that parades were an appropriate medium to witness for their faith and to celebrate their cultural heritage. However the concept of parades by the community that gave birth to the Orange Institution was well established long before 1796 and it is a matter of historical record that parades were a feature of that community for many years prior to the formation of the Orange Institution. The Protestant community in Northern Ireland is not in any way unique in that aspect. People the world over love to parade.

In recent years the question of Orange Parades has provoked much discussion and debate. Much of the debate has been ill-informed as to the purpose and nature of Orange Parades. We have witnessed much media attention and ill-informed comment.

There are a number of inherent factors behind the organising of Orange Parades.

They are a witness for our faith and this is evidenced by parades to and from public worship.

Orange Parades are commemorative. Various events in the history of the people are commemorated by parades that take different forms. These range from the solemn remembrance of the Fallen at the Somme to the cultural extravaganza that is the 12th of July commemoration of the Glorious Revolution secured at the Battle of the Boyne. Those who glibly dismiss the Boyne Commemorations would do well to think of the benefits that flowed from the Glorious Revolution, benefits which enrich all our citizens irrespective of religion or politics.

The Parades are wonderful displays of pageantry. The colours of the collarette or sash, the uniforms of the bands and the beautiful paintings on the banners combine to make an Orange Parade a picturesque kaleidoscope.

The Flags and banners are full of religious, cultural, socio-economic and political symbolism depicting biblical scenes, famous people, landmarks or events in history, and in themselves they portray the rich cultural heritage of our people in picture form.

Orange Parades generally follow routes which have been used for many years. Parade routes are not picked to cause offence but by and large follow the main arterial roads along which successive generations of Orangemen have peacefully paraded.

The Grand Orange Lodge of Ireland Education Committee in its publication "The Order on Parade" provides the Institution's thoughts on its Parades.

As previously stated the right to parade is a basic legal right and is recognised as such throughout the democratic world.

In the United States of America the Constitution guarantees the rights of free expression and peaceful assembly.

The Federal Congress has its powers on these issues restricted in that:-

"Congress shall make no law — abridging the freedom of speech — or the right of the people peaceably to assemble" .

In the Republic of Ireland the Constitution likewise guarantees the right to peaceful assembly. Interestingly in the Republic under the "Offences against the State Act 1939" it is unlawful to hold a public meeting or procession in support of an unlawful organisation.

The Belgian Constitution includes the following provision in Article 26 "Belgians have the right to gather peaceably and without arms",

The Constitution of the Republic of Italy has a provision at Article 17 which reads as follows "Citizens are entitled to hold meetings peaceably and unarmed. No previous notice is required for meetings in places to which the public has access. For meetings in public thoroughfares previous notice must be communicated to the authorities who may forbid them only for well established reasons of security or public safety".

The basic law for the Federal Republic of Germany (1994) contains the following provision in Article 8 II. "All Germans have the right to assemble peacefully and unarmed without prior notification or permission", In the case of outdoor assemblies this is pursuant to law.

The Constitution of the Republic of South Africa (1996) contains a Bill of Rights. Article 17 states "Everyone has the right, peacefully and unarmed to assemble, to demonstrate, to picket and to present petitions". Article 18 states "Everyone has the right to freedom of association".

Article 36 deals with the limitation of rights and states as follows. "The rights in the Bill of Rights may be limited only in terms of law of general application to the extent that the limitation is reasonable and justifiable in an open and democratic society based on human dignity, equality and freedom.

The European Convention on Human Rights was signed in November 1950 and came into force in September 1953. It has been ratified by the United Kingdom.

Article II of Section I of the Convention guarantees freedom of peaceful assembly and association.:-

> *"No restrictions shall be placed on the exercise of these rights other than such as are prescribed by law and are necessary in a democratic society in the interests of national security or public safety, for the prevention of disorder or crime, for the protection of health or morals or for the protection of the rights and freedoms of others".*

The United Nations International Covenant on Civil and Political Rights expresses similar views in Article 21:-

> *"The right of peaceful assembly shall be recognised. No restrictions may be placed on the exercise of this right other than those imposed in conformity with law and which are necessary in a democratic society in the interests of national security or public safety, public order, the protection of public health or morals or the protection of the rights and freedoms of others".*

The concept of placing restrictions on the right of free assembly in the interests of public order is obviously directed at those whose intention is to parade to create disorder.

It is further noted that Courts in the various countries have generally upheld the right to parade.

In the Northern Ireland context and since the inception of the 1987 Order the following have found in favour of the right to parade.

Her Majesty's Court of Appeal in Northern Ireland.
In the Matter of an Application by Connor Murphy for Judicial Review.

In the High Court of Justice in Northern Ireland. Queens Bench Division.
In the Matter of an Application by Patricia Breen for Judicial Review

August In the High Court of Justice in Northern Ireland. Queens Bench Division.
In the Matter of an Application by Jennifer Armstrong for Judicial Review

In the High Court of Justice in Northern Ireland. Queens Bench Division.
In the Matter of an Application by Matthew Murphy for Judicial Review.

Case law in England endorses the principle that a lawful parade should be guaranteed a right of passage:

viz. Beatty V Gillbanks 1892 and Regina V Clarke 1963

The Supreme Court in the United States of America has frequently upheld the right of free expression and free assembly. Indeed both Federal Courts and the Supreme Court have protected the rights of free expression and peaceful assembly against any attempt to have them, banned or altered in some measure by those who are opposed to the views expressed or the principles of the organisation involved. The suggestion that parades be interfered with because they may cause offence has been totally rejected. On occasions the police have protected the marchers from a hostile crowd. An example of this policy involving an Orange Parade occurred in New York in 1871.

However the most famous case in America is the Skokie case when a group of Fascists was allowed to parade through a mainly Jewish area despite bitter opposition.

These are basic examples and the use of such illustrations obviously does not imply recognition that Orange Parades are in some way offensive.

This is obviously the interpretation that some so called "residents groups" would wish to portray.

The question of "OFFENCE" is an interesting one. If some of those people who live in the vicinity of the "North-West 200" are offended by the noise and inconvenience of the Annual Race, should the Race then be cancelled?

Despite the terminology they employ the known history and political affiliation of some of the leaders of these groups convinces us that they have no interest in "parity of esteem" or recognition of others traditions and heritage. Careful attention to the utterances of the majority of the spokespersons for such groups will show why this is so. They are clearly of the opinion that the way to appreciate a different tradition or culture is to remove it. As Eilis O'Hanlon put it in The Times on Thursday, 11th July 1996: "Republicans have now embarked on a crusade to suppress all the symbols of a Protestant state whose days, they believe, are numbered."

In a statement of July 1995 the Grand Orange Lodge of Ireland stated:

> *"The way to improve community relations cannot be achieved through a repression of a legitimate expression of culture, In this context it is correct to allow all traditional routes, and all the more so, if these involved the use of a main thoroughfare",*

It is a matter of deepest regret that the threat of violence by residents living along or near a route has prompted the Royal Ulster Constabulary to take action against those seeking to remain within the law.

In the August 1992 Application for Judicial Review Counsel for Mrs. Armstrong said that the "restraint" shown by the residents could not last much longer. Surely it is curious to use the threat of a calculated breach of the law while seeking the protection of the law?

The principle of consent is a major stumbling-block, The questions which arise in the minds of the law-abiding Protestants are –

> *"What consent was sought for the Anglo-Irish Agreement?", "Who gave consent for 'La Mon', 'Enniskillen, or Canary Wharf?"*

The theory of "consent" as portrayed by the "residents groups" is an extremely dangerous concept. Not only is it contrary to the principles of free expression and peaceful assembly which are vital in a democracy it has far reaching and very dangerous implications outwith the issue of parades. Pushed to its logical conclusion it could lead to a Bosnian style of cantonisation.

The point that "residents groups" basically tend to ignore is that Orange Parades are generally along main arterial routes and through commercial areas. They do not go through housing estates or streets leading off the main roads. Residents groups have also been willing to use illegal and intimidatory methods. Tactics used include the flying and waving of the Eire Tricolour, the illegal blocking of the Queen's highway, the brandishing of hurley sticks, the arranging of local all night festivals at extremely short notice and a spurious prayer vigil.

They also chose to ignore the fact that Orange Parades are organised locally by members of the Orange Institution living in the general area. When an attempt is made by "residents" to prevent a peaceful parade it therefore follows that it is not just an attack on the legitimate traditions and culture of a people and a denial of basic civil liberties but it is an offence against local people within the community. In our judgement it is also a breach of the Public Order N.I. Order 1987 for which no one has been charged or made amenable before the Courts.

It is a regrettable fact that the authorities in so many instances have chosen to take action against the legal parade rather than the illegal activities of those opposing parades and our perception is that the influence of the Maryfield Secretariat has not been helpful.

Action taken against law abiding people is contrary to the basic principles of human rights, but unfortunately it has been a feature which parade organisers have had to cope with over the past few years.

There is a widely held perception that this is politically motivated to "keep Sinn Fein/I.R.A. happy" and that it is deemed to be more expedient to take action against the ordinary law abiding citizen and curtail his or her civil liberties than to stand up to the source of threatened violence.

In essence this has resulted in the Public Order (N.I. Order) becoming a law breakers charter.

There is evidence to suggest that promises have been made to "ad hoc" groups concerning the future of legal parades.

A side issue, though nevertheless, important is the authorities failure to act impartially in so far as they have failed to press charges against those involved in illegally blocking lawful parades, as opposed to their attitude to those involved in protest after a parade has been blocked.

Obviously in any democratic society one must recognise all legitimate political aspirations. However, in the climate of Ulster, those Nationalists who demand that their aspirations be recognised must also recognise in their turn that the right to process peaceably is a basic civil liberty and which is accepted as such across the democratic world. Specifically they must recognise that their neighbours' aspirations are at least as valid as their own and they therefore must be prepared to tolerate the expression of those aspirations.

As an organisation we are aware of our rights and responsibilities whilst on parade. That is why we seldom introduce new routes. We organise our own Marshals or Stewards for parades and there are countless parades when the need for a police presence is minimal.

Indeed it is a matter of record that there have been very successful legal parades at which there was no police presence at all. Our members are aware of the standards they are expected to meet on parade and will be subject to internal discipline if they fail to meet these. This applies equally to bands who are engaged for Orange Parades but whose members are not necessarily members of the Orange Institution. A code of conduct must be signed before a band is engaged.

Ultimately the police are the only people equipped to make a reasoned judgement on parades. No other body would be more acceptable and indeed another body could probably be less acceptable.

The police however must be given clear and unambiguous guidelines and these should also be made clear to the general public.

Those organising parades should be responsible for the provision of marshals or stewards and take precautions to ensure the good conduct of the participants. The police however, are ultimately responsible for ensuring that good behaviour in general is maintained and this should remain so. The police are also responsible for ensuring the free flow of traffic or necessary diversions.

Problems can be posed by parades which are politically motivated especially when the organisation concerned has not been engaged in processing along the route before. In such circumstances questions of acceptability and public order should be of greater importance than in respect of long established processions and should only be permitted when it has been determined that the proposed event has not been deliberately designed to provoke resentment or disorder.

If allowed such processions would need to fulfil very strict conditions. Flags, banners, or placards carried should not be such as to cause offence and as far as possible should be restricted to arterial routes and/or commercial districts. Disorder and misbehaviour by persons participating should necessitate further careful consideration by the police as to whether the procession could be repeated. So far as possible they should not pass through residential areas unless the overwhelming majority of the inhabitants are known to support those processing.

No new parade or demonstration should be permitted at a time or place where it is intended to or may in fact, clash with a traditional event.

The basic principle should be that law abiding citizens should be allowed to parade on their normal routes and not be diverted from them simply because a body of persons threaten violence.

When assessing whether a procession should be allowed on future occasions it should be the behaviour of those processing that is taken into account and this is of particular importance in the case of new routes and/or new bodies holding demonstrations and parades. Strictly speaking anything outwith this should be irrelevant.

When there is a measure of acceptance that in a free society men and women can protest, demonstrate and/or parade in a peaceful fashion and receive police protection while so doing then much of the problem would vanish.

If our desire is to live in a multi-cultural society with mutual respect and toleration then we must uphold the basic rights of free expression and free assembly.

It is our opinion that the R.U.C. have incorrectly interpreted Section 4 of the Public Order (N.I.) Order and we would query the role of the Anglo Irish Secretariat in influencing this interpretation. As a result peaceful activity has been prevented by the threat of violence from another group. Down that road lies anarchy.

The motto of the Orange Institution is "Civil and Religious Liberty". Our concern is for all law abiding citizens. We are on the side of tolerance and are upholders of peace. To surrender basic rights would not make for peace but would in the long run result in greater disorder.

Drumcree has also inspired attempts at poetry such as this anonymous effort in 1995 shown opposite:-

THE SIEGE OF DRUMCREE

It was a quiet Sunday
As brethren left for prayer
But one thousand R.U.C. men
Were waiting for them there

Freddie Hall, he had the choice
That day in Portadown
He told his men, go to Drumcree
And face the Orange down

They won't protest to us he said
We've done this all before
What Freddie didn't realise
The Prods could take no more.

Harold Gracey said We're here
And here we're going to stay
We have the legal right to walk
Down any Queen's highway.

So go back to Garvaghy
And clear the road for us
We'll walk with pride and dignity
And we won't make a fuss

But Police put on their riot gear
Preparing for a fight
And the siege of Drumcree Churchyard
Began that Sunday night

They came from every County
As word was passed around
The countryside a sea of Orange
Prepared to stand their ground

The support for loyal Portadown
It really was immense
Food and drink came pouring in
Some even pitched their tents

As the siege approached its second night
The Police Chiefs they all knew
The only way to keep the peace
Was let the parade pass through

So on the Tuesday morning
The 11th of July
The Orange walked Garvaghy Road
With heads and colours high

No more calls for compromise
Or trying to appease
The Protestants of Ulster
Have got up off their knees.

The Millennium Service

ORANGE CREDIT UNIONS IN COUNTY ARMAGH

In 1976 the County Grand Lodge asked Bro. Harold McCusker to research the possibility of starting Credit Unions. The members of the County Lodge were very conscious of the benefits which the Irish League of Credit unions had brought to the Roman Catholic community.

The main problem for Orange Brethren and their families was the close connection of many Irish League credit unions with local Parishes in the Roman Catholic Church, the presence of many Priests on their Boards of Management, usually as Chairmen, and the fact that all their surplus funds were invested in Dublin.

Bro. McCusker reluctantly reported in 1978 that he could see no way to start up independent credit unions at that time. The County Grand Lodge, however did not give up entirely on this project and when Rt. Wor. Bro. Norman Hood became County Grand Master he was made aware that a group of Orangemen in the Sandy Row area of Belfast had discovered a way to start British Credit Unions in Northern Ireland. Representatives from Belfast were invited to a meeting in Armagh Orange Hall in 1989.

On the 2nd May 1989 fifteen Orangemen attended the meeting in Armagh to discuss forming a Credit Union. Bro. Richard Copeland and his wife Gladys and Bro. Alfie Hennessy, all from Belfast spoke to the meeting about the workings of Credit Unions and how they were affiliated to the National Federation based in Bradford, England. They also explained that the first Credit Unions had been set-up in Germany by a Lutheran Pastor in the 19th century to encourage small farmers to stay on the land in a time of hardship and famine. After a lot of discussion it was decided that if a decision was not taken then and there then it would never get off the ground. The fifteen present agreed to form the first committee, the name Orchard Credit union was chosen as it recalled the Orchard

County. The grand total of £54 was collected to open a bank account and the officers elected that night were:

Chairman: Wor. Bro. Norman Allen, Deputy County Grand Master

Secretary: Bro. Richard Whitten, L.O.L. No.102

Treasurer: Bro. David McKee, L.O.L. No.108

It was agreed to open in Armagh Orange Hall on Friday nights to collect money and welcome new members. The first members had to also learn and study the Rules of Credit Unions and the 1985 Credit Union Order. It was decided to arrange a caravan in the demonstration field on the Twelfth at Keady in 1989 to publicise the credit union.

On 28th February 1990 seventeen members forming the first committee passed an oral examination conducted by the Registrar of Companies and from 1st March the credit union was empowered to give loans to members. Guests present at this exam were four members of the Northern Ireland Regional committee from Belfast, eight members from Lisbellaw Savings group and two members from Pomeroy Savings group. The question session chaired by the Registrar lasted over one hour. After examining the Treasurer's books and all the relevant forms the Registrar stated that the Orchard Credit Union would be allowed to become a limited company. Wor. Bro. Norman Allen concluded the meeting by thanking all those who had learnt the rules over many Saturday nights and the Copelands for their help and advice.

The first loan was taken out in March 1990. At that time the maximum loan was £2500 and a member could borrow 2.5 times his savings. Norman Allen retired as chairman in March 1991 and the Late William Burden became chairman. In May 1991 Wor Bro. Robert Orr, the first auditor of the credit union was murdered by terrorists in Armagh, and also in that month two small rooms were knocked into one and a proper counter installed to facilitate the steady growth in members. In April 1992 a computer system was installed, which was a further measure of growth. As membership rose, so branch offices, meeting on Friday nights were opened, staffed by volunteers, whose only enumeration was an annual Christmas Dinner. Soon there were offices at Cloncore Orange Hall, Keady Orange Hall, Tandragee District Hall and Markethill Orange Hall. Markethill grew so much in terms of membership that a computer was installed there linked by secure land-line to the main computer in Armagh.

By 1993 there were 699 members, with £418,000 in savings and £374,000 in loans. By November 1993 an important milestone was reached when the Orchard credit union had loaned it's first £1 million in total. The decision was taken with the Hall Management Committee to rent a much larger room, formerly used as a play-school and the modern office was constructed to a very high standard. The following article appeared in the Ulster Gazette for the week beginning 10th April 1995:

"The Orchard Credit Union celebrated an important milestone in its history on Saturday 8 April 1995 with the official opening of it's new suite of offices in the Armagh Orange Hall. Since the formation of the Orchard Credit Union in May 1989, under the auspices of the "National Federation of Credit Unions in Great Britain", rapid progress has been made. The office is open six days a week, and is fully computerised.

The Committee had been aware for some time that it was beginning to outgrow the small office that it had been using in the Orange Hall. When a large room became available the committee decided to create a new office suite. This was done by creating a public area, a three teller counter, an interview room where members can make inquiries in private, and a board room. This new office has the advantage of having separate access to the Orange Hall, so that members on Credit Union business do not get mixed up in any other function going on in the Hall.

The official opening was performed by Mrs. Gladys Copeland, National Treasurer of the N.F.C.U. As a long standing member of the Main Board of the National Federation, Gladys was able to speak from her own experience about the effort required by tellers and committee members, which is mostly on a voluntary basis, to make a Credit Union a success.

Other guests included Mr. J. Junkin, and Mr. A. Hennessy, members of the main Board of the National Federation of Credit Unions, Rev. Tom Taylor (former Rector of Tynan), who performed the dedication of the new office, and Mr. Norman Allen, the first Chairman of the Orchard Credit Union –and the present County Grand Master of the Orange Institution in County Armagh in this the bi-centenary year of the founding of the Orange Order

Also present were members from N.F.C.U. Credit Unions, namely Slemish (Ballymena), South Fermanagh (Lisnaskea), Lagan Valley (Ballinderry, Co. Antrim), Clifton St. (Belfast), Shaftesbury (Belfast), Kilrea (Co. Londonderry), Benburb & Killyman (Co. Tyrone), and Frontier (Newry). As well as the neighbouring Credit Unions in Co Armagh, - Star which operates in Gibsons Hill Orange Hall, Lurgan, and Carleton operating from Carleton St. Orange Hall Portadown.

All members and guests were able to view the office suite and computer system before retiring for a Supper Dance in the adjoining Orange Hall. The meal being provided by Orr's Corner. And music supplied by the County Boys.

During the function presentations were made to Mrs. Copeland to mark the official opening of the new offices, and to Mr. William Burden, the Treasurer of the Orchard Credit Union, as a token for the work he carried out in supervising the re-construction of the office suite.

To mark the official opening the committee held a special members draw for a Compact Disc Stereo system. This draw was won by Mrs. Lily Allen, Loughgall.

The committee would like to thank all the contractors who worked on the new office. Thanks are also due to the Armagh Orange Hall Management Committee for their support for the Credit Union. This support has been evident from the very first collection nights which took place around a small table in one of the committee rooms."

The hope of the County Grand Lodge and the first committee of the credit union was that it could cover the whole County, but the Registrar made clear at the outset that in view of the maximum membership now limited to 5000, he ruled out Portadown and Lurgan Districts. As a result Orchard covers and serves the Districts of Armagh, Killylea, Keady, Newtownhamilton, Loughgall, Markethill, Richhill and Tandragee. Members of Bessbrook District are encouraged to join Frontier Credit Union which meets in Newry Orange Hall.

Portadown District started their own Credit Union in 1993, initially called Bann Savings group. It soon changed it's name to Carleton Credit Union and took over the former caretaker's house next-door to Carleton Street Orange Hall. The first chairman was Wor. Bro. Eric Patterson of Derryhale.

The members of Bleary Orange Lodge expressed an interest in also forming a Credit Union for the Lurgan area and the Late William Burden taught them the rules. They formed Star Credit Union also in 1993 and it meets in Gibson's Hill Orange Hall on Friday Nights.

Orchard Credit Union is one of the most successful of the British credit unions in Northern Ireland. It has now passed it's tenth anniversary and has £2 million in savings from 2,500 members and the same amount in loans. It now has five part-time paid staff, including a Manager. The present Chairperson is Mrs. Mary Marshall of Markethill. Loans are now granted up to eight times savings to a maximum loan of £10,000 per member.

However first loans are limited to a maximum of £3000 and second loans to £6000. This is to establish a member's ability to repay on a regular basis before a large amount is loaned.

Asked to comment in a Belfast Telegraph article on Orange Credit Unions, Bro. George Patton, the Executive Officer, stated:

> *"In a sense, setting up Credit Unions was a natural extension of our role in the community – trying to help others."*

The credit union ideal of mutual assistance is also a central ideal in Orangeism. A Brother who saves with the Credit union has the assurance that he will be helping another Brother who has need of a loan. Since the Bicentenary we are all conscious of the religious, cultural and political dimensions of Orangeism. Now Orange Credit Unions are adding another dimension of financial security so that our people may go forward with confidence. The success of the Orange Credit Unions in County Armagh also gives the lie to those people who maintained that the Protestant people had no need of such a facility since they were so well-off. Could it also point the way forward for the Orange Institution as a whole in providing services to it's members?

Anyone who wishes to join the Orange Credit unions in County Armagh should telephone Armagh 028 3752 4506 weekdays 11am – 3.30pm and Friday nights 6pm – 8pm or write to: The Orchard Credit Union, The Orange Hall, Mall East, Armagh.

Juniors on Parade - en route to Bangor

BIBLIOGRAPHY

FOR FURTHER READING

The Editor has found the following publications useful in the preparation of The Millennium Book:-

The Ulster Crisis: *A. T. Q. Stewart.*

A History of Ulster: *Jonathan Bardon.*

For God and the King,
the Story of the Blackers of Carrickblacker: *James Kane.*

The Second World War: *Winston Churchill.*

Ulster Unionism: *Patrick Buckland.*

Orangeism in Portadown District: *W. H. Wolsey.*

The Orange Citadel: A History of Orangeism in Portadown District.

The Formation of the Orange Order:
The Wallace and Blacker Papers, G.O.L.I. Education Committee.

Phrases Make History Here:
A Century of Irish Political Quotations: *Conor O'Cleary.*

Steadfast For Faith and Freedom, 200 Years of Orangeism: *G.O.L.I..*

A Celebration 1690-1990 The Orange Institution: *G.O.L.I..*

The Order on Parade: Whitten and Montgomery: *G.O.L.I..*

The Diamond in it's Historical Setting: Cecil Kilpatrick: *G.O.L.I..*

Stand-Off! Drumcree 1995 and 1996: *Gordon Lucy.*

The Faithful Tribe:
An Intimate Portrait of the Loyal Institutions: *Ruth Dudley Edwards.*

The Standard Orange Songbook: *County Grand Lodge of Armagh, 1893.*

Portadown District Information Pack 1996

Presbyterians and Orangeism 1795-1995: *Finlay Holmes.*

The Twelfth Souvenir Booklets:
Portadown 1982 and 1993; Markethill 1991; Richhill 1994; Loughgall 1995; Tandragee 1996; Armagh 1997; Lurgan 1998; Killylea 1999.

Statistical Survey of the County of Armagh: *Sir Charles Coote, 1804.*

A Tour in Ireland: *Arthur Young, 1780.*

Harvest Home, A selection from the writings of T. G. F. Patterson relating to County Armagh: *Armagh County Museum 1974.*

Murder Without Sin, The Rebellion of 1798: *G.O.L.I..*

Making Sense of Northern Ireland, an Orange Perspective:
Rev. William Bingham B.A., B.D. (From a talk to a New Dialogue Labour Party Fringe Meeting at Brighton, September 1997). Published by G.O.L.I..

ABBREVIATIONS USED IN THIS BOOK

G.O.L.I.	*Grand Orange Lodge of Ireland*
Bro.	*Brother*
Rt. Wor. Bro.	*Right Worshipful Brother*
W.M.	*Worshipful Master*
W.D.M.	*Worshipful District Master*
D.G.M.I.	*Deputy Grand Master of Ireland*
C.G.M.	*County Grand Master*
D.C.G.M.	*Deputy County Grand Master*
A.O.H.	*Ancient Order of Hibernians*
R.U.C.	*Royal Ulster Constabulary*
L.O.L.	*Loyal Orange Lodge*
M.P.	*Member of Parliament*
N.F.C.U.	*National Federation of Credit Unions*

COLOUR PLATE SECTION

Banner of Co. Armagh Grand Orange Lodge

The County Grand Lodge Officers 2000

Front Row:- Isaac Walker - Inside Tyler, Rev. William Bingham - Grand Chaplain, Joseph Campbell - D.G.M., Denis Watson - C.G.M., Stephen McLoughlin - Grand Secretary, James Copeland - Grand Treasurer, Roger Gardiner - Deputy Grand Secretary

[illegible] Norman Allen - Past C.G.M., Sidney McIldoon - Grand Lecturer,

District Masters 2000

Front Row:- Harold Gracey No.1, Matthew Clarke No.2, Denis Watson, Thomas Forbes No.3, Richard Whitten No.4
Back Row:- George Proctor No.5, John Crozier No.6, William Lee No.7, Cecil Kinnear No.8, James Copeland No.9, Robert Hamilton No.10, Gerald Cartmill No.11

L.O.L. No.102 — A typical Country Lodge

Junior Parade, St. Marks Church, Armagh

Millennium Church Parade, Armagh

Presentation of Millennium County Armagh Bible to the Grand Master, 26th March 2000

Banner of L.O.L. No.13

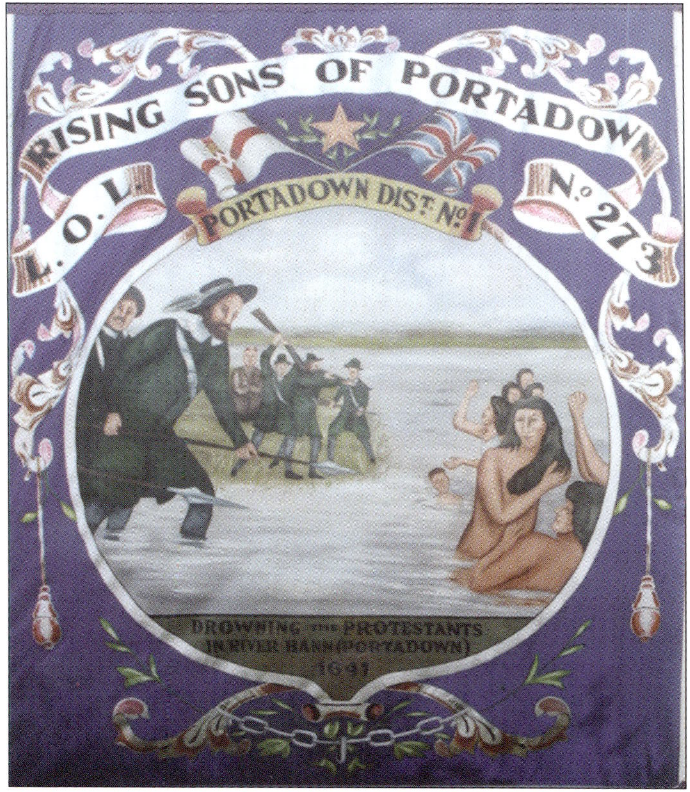

Banner of L.O.L. No.273

The Tea Ladies - where would we be without them